A Theology of Suffering and Difficulty: Corporate and Personal Aspects

Michael E. Lewis

PUBLISHERS
Eugene, Oregon

A THEOLOGY OF SUFFERING AND DIFFICULTY
Corporate and Personal Aspects

Copyright © 2006 Michael E. Lewis. All rights reserved. Except for brief quotations in critical publications or reviews, no part of this book may be reproduced in any manner without prior written permission from the publisher. Write: Permissions, Wipf & Stock, 199 W. 8th Ave., Eugene, OR 97401.

ISBN10: 1-59752-993-1
ISBN13: 978-1-59752-993-8

Typset by the author with the LaTeX documentation system.

Scripture quotations taken from the New American Standard Bible[R], Copyright © 1960, 1962, 1963, 1968, 1971, 1972, 1973, 1975, 1977, 1995 by The Lockman Foundation Used by permission. (www.Lockman.org)

To my brothers and sisters in Christ.

Contents

	Preface	ix
1	**Introduction**	**1**
1.1	The Possibility	3
1.2	The Necessity	3
1.3	The Real Tragedy	8
1.4	The Causes and the Cure	14
2	**The Sovereignty of God**	**17**
2.1	The Decrees	18
2.1.1	The Basis of the Decrees	19
2.1.2	The End of the Decrees	20
2.1.3	The Decrees in Brief	22
2.2	God's Sovereign Rule	23
2.2.1	Preservation	24
2.2.2	Providence	25
2.2.3	A Clarification	27
2.3	A Picture of God's Rule	33
2.4	Application	34
2.5	A Final Note: Job and the Sovereignty of God	36
3	**Proper Desires and Values**	**41**
3.1	The Case for New Desires and Values	43
3.1.1	Christ and the Scope of God's Gifts	43
3.1.2	The Glory of Christ	49

		3.1.3 The Glory of the Kingdom	50

4 The Kingdom of God: Introduction   51
    4.1 The Kingdom: Now but Not Yet 52
    4.2 The Nature of the Kingdom 54
         4.2.1 What the Kingdom is Not 54
         4.2.2 What the Kingdom is 56
    4.3 The Relationship to Trials 63

5 The Kingdom: The Sabbath and Jubilee   65
    5.1 The Sabbath 67
         5.1.1 Creation 67
         5.1.2 Manna 68
    5.2 The Sabbath Year and the Jubilee 71
         5.2.1 Agrarian Economies 74
         5.2.2 Economic Impact 76

6 The Kingdom: Sabbath & Jubilee Theology   83
    6.1 Motivation 83
    6.2 Something Else to be Learned 84
    6.3 Comprehensive Salvation 85
    6.4 Liberation 88
    6.5 Forgiveness 100
    6.6 Generosity and Compassion 103
         6.6.1 Compassion 104
         6.6.2 Generosity 105
    6.7 Economics: New Testament Emphasis 106
         6.7.1 Fallow Land 106
         6.7.2 Debt Release 112
         6.7.3 Contentment: Having Enough 114
         6.7.4 The New Testament 117
    6.8 The Impact on Kingdom Understanding 119

CONTENTS

7 The Kingdom: Further Foundations — **123**
- 7.1 The Love of God: Agape 123
  - 7.1.1 The Teachings 125
  - 7.1.2 Christ: Love Explained 130
  - 7.1.3 Suffering Love: Nonviolence 132
  - 7.1.4 Rejection of Reciprocity 138
- 7.2 A New Way: No Barriers, No Divisions 143
- 7.3 Servanthood 144
- 7.4 Conclusion 146

8 The Nature and Purpose of Trials — **151**
- 8.1 The Nature of Trials 153
  - 8.1.1 Characteristics of Trials 153
  - 8.1.2 Two Primary Types 154
- 8.2 The Purpose of Trials 163
  - 8.2.1 General Considerations 163
  - 8.2.2 A Father's Discipline 170
  - 8.2.3 Specific Reasons 174

9 The Nature of Maturity — **179**
- 9.1 The Imperative 179
- 9.2 The Nature of Christ 180

10 Weakness and Strength — **187**
- 10.1 The Necessity of God's Power 191
- 10.2 God's Predisposition to Use the Weak 197
- 10.3 The Spirit of God, Weakness and Power 207
  - 10.3.1 The Spirit of God 208
  - 10.3.2 The Divine Presence and Fire 209
  - 10.3.3 Pentecost, Fire and The Spirit 212
- 10.4 Weakness and Trials 216

11 The Role of Loss — 221
11.1 Philippians 3 — 221
11.2 Loss in the Life of the Christian — 226
11.3 The Discipline of Trials — 229

12 Our Hope in Christ — 233
12.1 Our Previous Condition — 234
12.2 Our Present Inheritance — 235
12.2.1 Our Standing With God — 235
12.2.2 God's Provision — 243
12.2.3 The Restoration of Relationships — 244
12.3 Our Future Hope — 252

13 Our Response — 257
13.1 Patiently Enduring — 259
13.1.1 Advice from James — 261
13.1.2 The Armor of God — 264
13.2 Building the Kingdom of God — 266
13.3 A Final Thought — 268
Bibliography — 269

Preface

I first thought of writing a book on suffering and difficulty in 1993, during the start of a long and difficult trial. Going into it I had a premonition that things were going to get much more difficult and remain so for a long time. I figured I had better understand what God had to say about trials if I were going to remain faithful. (The premonition was correct.) With that thought I began to study God's word and found that there was much written regarding trials. I seriously doubt that I would have remained in the faith if I had not taken the time to discover what God's word had to say about trials.

Once again I find myself in the midst of another very difficult trial and have had to carefully reaffirm God's teachings on trials. In a way, I have written this book as a personal review and to challenge myself to do God's will in this new trial. Writing this book has had a profoundly positive effect on me.

As I look at my life from a worldly perspective, one not centered on God, I can't make much sense of quite a lot of it. My health and life outside the home have been very difficult. When seen from a Biblical perspective, God's perspective, my life makes perfect sense. Fortunately, my burden is limited and my home life has been very good, as I have a wonderful wife and two teenagers that love God.

I know that there are many who have had far more difficult lives, but despite my failure to always respond properly and not having suffered as much as I might, it is my hope to set out God's teachings on trials, for I see so much confusion and so little hope in many around me.

I do not claim to have any special insight or new truths on the subject, nor is my knowledge on the subject complete. I am certain that there are many who understand this whole topic far better than I. But even given my miserable failures to live up to what God wants, I feel compelled to write. And by writing I am more confronted and convicted by my failure and more drawn to God and what he values. My only contribution may be that I may have succeeded, in some measure, in integrating in one place, some of what is taught in the Bible on this subject and given a new perspective. The reader will judge the extent of my success or failure.

The following quote sums up my misgivings as well as the need to write despite being painfully aware of my inadequacy.

> I realize that in communicating the truth to follow that I am condemning myself as an unprofitable servant. But shall the truth of God be forever suppressed because of the failure of God's people? Is it not true that the message is always greater than the messenger? Is it not proper that God be true and every man a liar?[1]

The end to which the whole cosmos is directed is the glory of God. In a Christian's life this is most fully accomplished as God conforms us to the image of his Son and builds his Church. It is in light of this truth that we must understand trials. Hence, God's plan and purpose in our trials is to glorify himself, and he accomplishes this as he conforms us to the image of Christ and builds his Church. Trials are, perhaps, the most powerful method God has to transform us and build his Kingdom. Isn't one who

---

[1] MacDonald, *True Discipleship*

is conformed to the image of Christ best able to glorify God and a fit citizen for the Kingdom of God? We see then that the life of Christ and his teachings in the Gospels are central to what God is doing in our lives. The life of Christ is normative for the Christian. It is a way of life we are to imitate. "Be imitators of me, just as I also am of Christ." (1 Cor 11:1)

In this body we will not reach perfection, but God wants us, commands us, and empowers us to move in that direction. Even now God is conforming us to the image of his Son. We are to be like Christ. But what does this mean? We often just restate the imperative without examining the life of Christ. It is impossible to develop it here in the preface, but Christ was nonviolent, rejected earthly power, focused entirely on God and his will, loved as no other human has, or ever will love, completely selfless, had no concern for his reputation, was found among the weak and the outcasts of society, given to taking care of the needy, willing to go to any lengths to obey God, even dying on a cross to bring us into God's kingdom. Have you ever considered how lovely Christ is? How desirable it is to know him? It is into his likeness that we are being transformed. Just imagine it!

God is also glorified as his people live lives worthy of their calling, resulting in the proper functioning and expansion of his Kingdom. Our trials take place among our brothers and sisters in Christ, the Body of Christ, in the midst of the world, and are not only designed for our personal spiritual growth. Trials not only refine us and make us fit citizens of the Kingdom, but they also provide essential material for the Church to operate in one of its most fundamental modes: the demonstration of love among Christian brothers and sisters. It is in this demonstration of love within the Body of Christ that God is glorified — My Father is glorified by this, that you bear much fruit — and the Church witnesses to the world — by this will all men know that your are my disciples, if you have love for one another.

The ultimate goal of this book is not simply to deepen our understanding or help us respond properly to God in our trials. To be sure, I hope to achieve these, but my ultimate goal is to use this understanding to free us from our confusion and rebellion in trials so that we may more properly focus on glorifying God, build his Church and do his will. We must refuse to be turned inward, absorbed with our problems, and give our lives, time, money and resources freely to others and, thereby, to God. It isn't about us. It is about God, doing his will and loving our neighbor.

Michael E. Lewis, October 19, 2005

Chapter 1

Introduction

It is my intention to present a theology of suffering and difficultly. This might, at first, seem somewhat strange, after all, suffering and difficulty[1] are common to all and occur often. Although they are common, they are seldom understood in their proper theological context. The result is an improper understanding of and response to trials.

The approach used here is two pronged. We will look at trials from both personal and corporate perspectives. The personal perspective considers the relationship of the sufferer to their trial and their responsibility to God. The second perspective is corporate and sees trials as they relate to the Body of Christ, the Church. For reasons to be discussed later, I will, from now on, usually use the Kingdom of God when referring to the Church[2]. We will see

---

[1] I will often refer to suffering and difficulties as trials and frequently interchange these terms.

[2] I do not intend to equate the Body of Christ and the Kingdom of God, for they are not the same. However, the Kingdom of God, even if it has not come in its fullness, is in a real sense breaking out even now. Fairly often, I have, in part, chosen to use the term Kingdom of God rather than the Body of Christ or the Church since the Kingdom seems to entail a wider scope, something I want to capture. Namely, life in Christ, life among the brethren,

that the personal and corporate aspects of trials are tightly bound and cannot be separated. This approach is unusual, but it captures essential teachings in God's word and will shed considerable light on the current weakness of the Church.

I am writing for a Christian audience. I assume that the reader has a real relationship with God based solely on the work of Christ. Not only this, but I further assume that this person has made Christ King of their life and is a functioning member of the Body of Christ. This is not to say that the non-Christian will derive no benefit from reading this book. On the contrary, I hope that the non-Christian will find the message so attractive that they will be drawn to Christ.

This book will, in all likelihood, drive some away. God's Kingdom is an inverted kingdom in comparison to the kingdoms of this world, operating on very different principles; peace rather than violence, love rather than hate, weakness rather than strength, poverty rather than riches, loss rather than gain. Many will find it unattractive as they cling to the wisdom of the world.

Despite the radical nature of what you will find here, I sincerely hope that you will prayerfully consider what is said before giving up. I have only used what God has already taught in His Word.[3] I have added nothing to it, nothing original is found here and many others already understand what follows. However, God's Word presents a radically different picture of suffering and difficulty compared to what many of us believe and what we have

---

a distinct life among the kingdoms of the world and, finally, the notion of a body of ethics that governs the kingdom. Therefore, given these qualification and those to come, I hope that my use of the Kingdom will be acceptable.

[3] Many Biblical quotations, some quite long, are intentionally used to clearly demonstrate the Biblical context. I believe that there is great power in seeing the Biblical text along with the discussion, especially in those cases where the principle being taught appears so contrary to conventional wisdom. On such matters I prefer to bring out God's word and let it speak for itself.

been taught.

As a disclaimer I want to make it clear that I am not attempting to give an answer to the problem of evil and pain in the world. Much has been written on this and I do not want to repeat it here. My focus, rather, is the context, purpose and the proper response to trials for the Christian. As we will see, the Bible has much to say, and all of it positive.

1.1 The Possibility

Some may say that it is not possible to find a theology of trials; there just isn't much said about it. This, however, is not the case, not by any measure. The Bible is literally full of trials and it contains a clear, consistent teaching on them as to the reasons why they come, what God is doing in them and what our response to them should be. Contrary to the opinion of most, very little about our trials are mysterious and unknowable and we certainly have no reason whatever to ask why a trial has come. We should never, never, never ask why; we are told why in the clearest language.

1.2 The Necessity

The necessity of a theology of trials arises from their importance, their ubiquity, and the great and many misunderstandings surrounding them. The end to which all of creation is directed is the glory of God, and in a Christian's life this is largely accomplished by God conforming us to the image of Christ and by the building up and proper functioning of the Kingdom of God. Trials must be understood in this larger context. Trials are important then, in light of the above, because they are the most effective means that God uses to bring about maturity, maturity of the kind that is seen in the life and character of Christ. It is to the image of Christ that we are being conformed. (Rom 8:29) This maturity and the witness of a proper response to trials bring glory to God, which is, after all, the point of it all. Given the frequency at which trials appear, it would be a tragedy to live so much of our life in confusion and miss what God is doing. I fear that the vast majority of Christians are unable to make sense out of much of their lives and live in quiet desperation.

It is also necessary to understand our trials within the context of the Body of Christ, or as I will often refer to it, the Kingdom of God. I use the term Kingdom of God because I want us to think in terms of a larger scope, one involving our relationships to one another and the relationship of God's Kingdom to the rest of the world. When looked at from a corporate point of view we find several important principles.

First, we see that trials refine us and make us fit citizens for the Kingdom of God. Second, they provide an occasion for those in the Kingdom to demonstrate God's care and love for other Christians in the Kingdom. The one in the trial sees God's love worked out in the actions of their brothers and sisters. In this way we see that trials provide much of the basis for essential Kingdom activity. Third, as our love for one another is demonstrated in the community of believers, the world sees that we are Christ's disciples and they are attracted to the message of Christ. Our most profound witness to the unsaved world is the love we express toward one another, often in the context of trials, within the community of believers. And in this way, those outside the Kingdom are drawn into the Kingdom and in this way it is extended. Our love is our greatest witness.

In most of Evangelical Christianity, the understanding of our corporate life in the Body of Christ has atrophied or become anemic, if not lost altogether. Considerable time is spent in chapters four through seven to address this shortcoming.

The last reason we need a theology of trials is, in many ways,

1.2 The Necessity

the principal reason why this book was written. The level of confusion surrounding our understanding of trials is deep and disturbing, robbing us of most of our Christian witness, joy in life, and, most troubling, resulting in a failure to glorify God.

To begin to get an idea of our poverty just listen to our public and private prayers. Inevitably, when praying about trials, we ask that the trial be lifted. It doesn't matter what it is; "God, just deliver us from it. Please send in the cavalry." We seldom, if ever, pray that God would first use it to his glory and that he would accomplish, both in us and in those about us, what he wants. We act as if the greatest miracle is for God to restore our health, or get a good job, or whatever[4], when the real miracle is what God is doing in the trial, namely conforming us to the image of his Son, building his Kingdom and glorifying himself. Isn't it more amazing for someone to count it all joy when a trial comes and embrace it, expectantly waiting to see what greater knowledge of God will come, how they will be further conformed to the image of Christ and how God might be glorified? This response is an amazing sight to see in our own life and an encouragement when seen in the lives of others. It is what God teaches in his Word and what he expects from us. This may be at odds with what you currently believe, but why should this surprise you seeing that you live in the inverted Kingdom.

In the New Testament, instances are few in which we find someone praying for the removal of a trial. One is found in 2 Corinthians 12 where Paul prays to have his physical trial lifted. Interestingly it is never lifted and Paul gratefully accepts it, even

---

[4]American Christians are particularly vulnerable to this. We live in an amazingly wealthy country and suffer little to no persecution. We expect things to go well. Add to this the particularly virulent and deviant strains of Christianity that teach that God's blessing on you should, no must, be visible with wealth and success in abundance and you get terribly confused and misguided thinking.

glories in it. The vast majority of the time the Bible tells us to gratefully and joyfully accept our trials knowing what is actually being accomplished. And it treats them as common, something to be expected. It is illuminating to find that in countries where trials and persecution are commonplace the Christians are not focused on removing the trial. They are more interested in God's glory, being conformed to the image of Christ and building his Kingdom. Unlike many of us, they desire God himself more than the things that God gives. Would to God that we would have such desires.

It is not improper to pray for deliverance from a trial, but it is improper to focus on being delivered. God will lift the trial in his time. Why not focus on what God is doing in the trial and cooperate with him? This would be far more effective. Focusing on deliverance is a sure recipe for failure.

The question, "Why me?" also reveals our lack of knowledge and preoccupation with ourselves. Our view is entirely self-centered; we see the whole trial looking back on ourselves, mourning our loss, complaining of our pain. Given the fallen state of the world and the certainty of death, how can we even begin to ask such a question? With respect to death, we are told that we have wages coming, wages paid by our death, for the sins we have committed. The saved and unsaved alike are destined to this.[5] From this perspective alone we should more properly ask, "Why have things gone so well?" But if we then add to this basic knowledge of the fallenness of the world, the fact that God is glorifying himself, building his Kingdom, conforming us to the image of Christ and taking us to heretofore unknown knowledge of him, how can we even begin to ask "Why me?" Furthermore, it is not about 'me', it is rather all about God, his glory, his desires, his plan.

---

[5]It is the second death, the eternal lake of fire, that the Christian avoids, and instead enters eternity with God.

1.2 The Necessity

What an unseemly question for a Christian to ask. This is not to say that we are not part of his plan, we are, but it is first about God, not 'me'.

A common response to trials reveals further our lack of understanding, "God's ways are not our ways. We must trust." To be sure, all this is true but only when taken in the proper sense. God's ways are not our ways and we understand little about the infinite God, and we must trust him, but to give this, or something like it, as a complete response to someone enduring a life-shattering trial is unconscionable. We may not know exactly what caused the trial or what part in God's plan it plays, but what we do know with certainty is that God will glorify himself, build his Kingdom, conform us to the image of Christ and reveal himself to us as we obey. The common response, if only it is given, is more likely to result in confusion, or worse, rebellion. The reason it fails so badly is that it does not address the teleological question, "What is the purpose of this trial?" To this question we have a great deal to say. God has not kept it a secret. The answer is all through God's word; trials are full of purpose.

Compounding the problem is our misunderstanding of "the good." The extent to which the American understanding of "the good" has corrupted our reading of Romans 8:28 is astounding. We pour whatever is our current desire or want into "the good" and expect God to provide it. But what is "the good?" It is that which glorifies God, conforms us to the image of Christ and builds God's Kingdom. It is not about things material or otherwise. It does not exclude them, but things are peripheral (1 Cor 4:16–18) and only important as they relate to the good.[6] For us, what is good is that which moves us closer to God and builds his Kingdom. Certainly being conformed to the image of Christ is good since it both glorifies God and brings us closer to him. Whatever,

---

[6] "The good" is understood as that which glorifies God.

accomplishes this is *very* good, and what seems to do it best are trials. Have you ever grown more in Christ than in your trials? If you are honest, your answer will be no. And building God's Kingdom is *very* good for by it we have a foretaste of life in heaven among loving brothers and sisters and we bear witness of God's love to the world.

1.3 The Real Tragedy

The real tragedy in a trial is learning nothing from it, or rebelling while in it, not the trial itself. For those who know what God is doing in trials and ought to know better, but still rebel, the tragedy is even greater. I remember a very difficult trial, lasting many years, during which, at least at first, and for much of the time, I largely responded properly. I was fully aware of God's plan and purpose in trials. Near the end I developed a very bad attitude. To sum it up, I knew what God's interests were, but I wasn't buying and wanted things fixed now. Graciously, God miraculously and abundantly, more than abundantly, delivered me from the trial. The day it happened I wept. I wept for a very long time. I was filled with shame, sorrow and regret. God had given me what I wanted but what had I lost? If I had responded properly, valued what God valued, patiently endured, joyfully accepted the trial, how much closer would I now be to God, how much more would I be like Christ and how much glory had I denied God. I had lost much by gaining what I wanted. I would have been better off losing what I had wanted in order to gain what was really valuable, that which could not be taken from me. This principle of lose to gain is all through the gospels, especially during a call to discipleship. There was a young martyr from the 1950's, Jim Elliot, who understood this well, for in his diary he had written, "He is no fool who gives up what he cannot keep, to gain what he cannot lose." I suspect that God knew that I was

1.3 The Real Tragedy

likely to break under the current trial and that we would get back to the lesson soon enough. Thankfully, God had not given up on me and has graciously provided more trials, some easy and short, some long and very hard, and I have and continue to learn much through them. I have so far to go; I don't always respond as I should, but I am making progress. I am confident that God will complete in me the work which he has begun.

Another tragedy, one on a much larger scale, is that the Church does not function properly; it fails to obey Christ, refusing to act as the Church by largely ignoring community and by implication does not function as it should. One of the primary activities within the Church is loving the brethren, for Christ himself has given us the command to love one another, even as he has loved us, and in this all men will know that we are his disciples. (John 13:34,35) How powerful would our witness to the world be if we were to love one another as Christ loved us? There is nothing more powerful we might do to effectively witness to the world. Forget about marketing, making your church seeker friendly, having theater or relevant music; just love one another as Christ commands.

But what does this love look like? How do we know if love is present? Love is demonstrated by caring for the brethren, brethren in need. The New Testament understands love and faith in terms of acts of love, often physical and material.

> But whoever has the world's goods, and sees his brother in need and closes his heart against him, how does the love of God abide in him? Little children, let us not love with word or with tongue, but in deed and truth.
>
> 1 John 3:17,18

> What use is it, my brethren, if someone says he has faith but he has no works? Can that faith save him? If a brother

> or sister is without clothing and in need of daily food, and one of you says to them, "Go in peace, be warmed and be filled," and yet you do not give them what is necessary for their body, what use is that? Even so faith, if it has no works, is dead, being by itself.
>
> Jas 2:14–17

Love and faith are demonstrated by taking care of the brethren. Why is this so important? Because "We know love by this, that He laid down His life for us; and we ought to lay down our lives for the brethren." (1 John 3:16). In the deepest love imaginable, Jesus took care of our most desperate need and in this he is our example.

Furthermore, it is by our love for one another that the world knows we are Christ's disciples and sees the love of God. (John 13:34,35) No other activity is mentioned by Christ that demonstrates to the world that we are his disciples. This is extremely important. Just how important it is is seen in Acts.

> And the congregation of those who believed were of one heart and soul; and not one of them claimed that anything belonging to him was his own, but all things were common property to them. *And with great power the apostles were giving testimony to the resurrection of the Lord Jesus, and abundant grace was upon them all. For there was not a needy person among them,* for all who were owners of land or houses would sell them and bring the proceeds of the sales and lay them at the apostles' feet, and they would be distributed to each as any had need. (Italics added)
>
> Acts 4:32-35

Notice, their witness was powerful because there were no needy found among them. This was love in action and it formed the ba-

1.3 The Real Tragedy

sis of a powerful witness.[7] Why was this witness so powerful? Because the world cannot build communities that operate on selfless love. A community where everyone considers the needs of the other more important than their own is miraculous. Only God among men can accomplish it. Communities operating in this way is what the Kingdom of God looks like.

The behavior of the early church is normative; the church today must do the same. It is what Christ and the Apostles commanded. We don't get a pass because we live in the 20th Century. Some will say that it cannot be done today. This is simply not true, for no real obstacles prevent us from living like the early church in both its commitment to physical assistance to fellow believers and in its commitment to peace and nonviolence. We simply refuse to obey.[8]

The church today does not see as a primary goal taking care of the needy within it. It rather sees "personal spiritual" activities as the proper activities in the life of a believer. These include personal salvation, Bible study, prayer and a devotional life. There is also a focus on the development of personal character with an emphasis on kindness, meekness and gentleness. The personal, rather than Christian community is emphasized. Community is

---

[7] How different the efforts of many today. We must first do a marketing survey, give them a good show with contemporary music and theater. We need to become "relevant" and meet their perceived needs. This strategy will bring them in, but it will utterly fail to make disciples of Christ and really impact the world beyond self-help and the provision of a social club. It is bankrupt in the extreme.

[8] One of the greatest obstacles is modern government that promises to take care of our needs from cradle to grave and protect us by its use of power and violence. In many ways it becomes an idol providing the things that only God can provide. For the Church, the results are devastating. What happens is that the Church no longer sees that it is responsible to take care of the needs of the Christians within it; after all, the government has programs for this. As we embrace the government's provision and refuse to take care of our own from our own means, our witness to the world is blunted or even eliminated.

not seen as an essential aspect of the Christian life. I am not arguing that personal spirituality should be eliminated at the expense of community. On the contrary, If we have not had a personal encounter with Christ where we have made him Lord and Savior of our life, the commitment to Christian community is not possible. But, if we are truly spiritual, having faith and love, we will be committed to living in a community where we take care of our Christian brethren.[9]

If Christ and the Apostles are to be taken at their word, there is *no more important activity for the Church than taking care of the needy within it. Taking care of needy brethren is the heart of faith and love! In these acts, faith and love are proven and the Church finds the basis for a powerful witness to the world.* Let us examine ourselves and make sure that we are practicing the first principles and then move out. God's desire for the kingdom of Israel was for there to be no poor (needy) within it.[10] This was never realized in Israel, but it was in the early Church. But it did not stop in Jerusalem, for the Church, for many hundreds of years, has continued, even beyond Constantine, in this manner.[11]

Is it any wonder then that the Christian church has little to no power to affect the societies in which she finds herself? If all we can say is that Christ offers personal salvation and a hope in heaven, then we say little more than what other religions say. Yes, what we say is true, real salvation is only found in Christ and we have a better apologetic argument, it makes more sense, *but do*

---

[9]When I speak of community I do not mean sectarianism or isolation. This is a community of believers that can exist in any social setting and cultural environment. It is in the the world, but not of it, loving those within it and loving those outside it. Sectarianism and isolation destroy our ability to witness to the world.

[10]Of course, new poor are always entering the community, the never go away, but as they enter they are to be taken care of.

[11]This practice may have lessened during and after Constantine, but it has never disappeared, and among many, continues today.

1.3 The Real Tragedy

we live differently, does it make a difference?[12] Do we really love one another, are we really one as Christ prayed that we be one, do we care for those we call brothers and sisters? To our great shame we largely do not, and yet we are surprised that the world marginalizes us and refuses to listen to us. Astonishing!

What changed the Roman world was the power of God demonstrated in Christians living out the truth and salvation of Christ's gospel. Today, however, to really buttress our claims, and really witness we pull out the big apologetic guns and demonstrate the depths of our knowledge and truthfulness of our claims.[13] God help us. We are doomed to irrelevance if we continue in this way. It is rather our lives that must be our greatest apologetic. The apologists of the early Church knew this well, pointing out that the proof that God exists and that he came in Christ is the way they lived, taking care of their needy and refusing violence as they were persecuted.

Notice that I am not talking about a social gospel. By that I mean that the gospel is understood only as care for the poor and needy, where the salvation Christ brings is minimized or ignored. This would be a gross misunderstanding of what Christ and the Apostles taught. In politically conservative circles, the minute a person starts to talk about the care of the poor and needy they are written off as a "liberal." Please do not do this. The care of the poor and the needy within the Church is not understood as "liberal," but is at the heart of the teachings of Christ and the Apostles. Not only this, but we can cast the care of the poor

---

[12]It is also true that many who claim to be Christians have a personal morality differing little, or not at all, from the society in which they live.

[13]I am not saying that apologetics of this type are not useful, they are. I have committed much of my life to this type of apologetic. However, we must not think for a moment that it is sufficient. The most convincing apologetic is our lives of obedience to God and the love we demonstrate to our brothers and sisters. This is the most powerful evidence of God among men.

and needy in even more dangerous language: social and economic justice. Now we are really sounding like liberals. But no, we are not. Listen to Christ's condemnation of the elites' exploitation of the poor, his acceptance of all regardless of social or economic status and James' condemnation of preferential treatment of one person over another. No, this is not a social gospel or a "liberal" diversion. As we care for the needy within the Church, ignore barriers, condemn exploitation, love indiscriminately, always forgive and refuse violence, we find our most powerful witness to the world.

Despite the failures of the past and the present, we must take up the task Christ sets before us: living in and building his Kingdom. If we do not, we will continue to fail, have little to no power in the world, and look little different than a social club or the current religion *de jour*. What we are currently doing constitutes an enormous tragedy. Is anyone weeping?

1.4 The Causes and the Cure

The causes of an improper understanding of and response to trials are due to several factors. In some cases it is a lack of knowledge of God's word that is not entirely the individual's fault. Perhaps they do not have God's Word or did not sit under someone who could teach it. More likely, it is a combination of very poor doctrine and a refusal to submit to God's plan for our life, which is, more properly called, rebellion.

If we are to understand trials properly we must understand the theological context. First, God is sovereign; he reigns over our lives as well as the universe and all that happens within it. If God decides to lift me up and give me wealth and recognition, or if he should decide to take my life and pour it onto the ground as a drink offering to himself as he has done with some of our brothers and sisters who have spent twenty-five, thirty years or more in

1.4 The Causes and the Cure

solitary confinement for identifying with Christ, then that is his business. It is his decision, not mine. We are to submit to God's plan for us, for he is our Sovereign. He leads, we follow. It is after all, all about God and all that is done by him is first done for his glory, as he sees fit. But loving us and dying for us is part of his plan and his glory.

Second, we do not value what God values. Our values are misplaced. We can have full knowledge of what God wants, and yet, if we do not value what he wants we will not be interested in seeking it and our response to trials will be poor. In some cases we may not value what he wants because we have not taken the time to find out or have not been exposed to it. But if a person knows what God wants and still does not value it, I strongly suspect that this person is not God's child.

God most highly values his glory and he values us and desires that we be conformed to the image of his Son. We must also most highly value God's glory as well, and our greatest good is knowing God. We come to know God by being obedient to his will and becoming more like Christ. Because of this we should value that which brings these things about.

We must also value God's Kingdom and endeavor to build it, to live as worthy citizens and do all we can to further it and strengthen its witness to the world.

To remedy this crisis of values we must refocus our hearts affections, find out what God values and work with him to obtain it. We must seek to glorify God by conforming to the image of his Son and building his Kingdom.

Third, we do not know what God has said regarding the nature and purpose of trials. Much has been said about the purpose of trials, glorifying God — being conformed to the image of Christ and building his Kingdom — but let us linger on the notion of being conformed to the likeness of Christ. As we are conformed to Christ's image we are better able to glorify God, obey him and thereby come to know more of Christ. But becoming conformed to the image of Christ is more than just proper knowledge and belief; it must result in concrete action, living as he lived; we are to have the character of Christ. Like Christ, we are to be committed to the Father, doing his will, building his Kingdom, committed to bringing God's love to others, not only in the verbal message of salvation, but salvation in the form of concrete examples of sacrificial love by caring and helping. As I develop the thesis we will see how Christ was committed to the principles of the Sabbath year and Jubilee, social and economic justice. We will examine his indiscriminate love and forgiveness, his kindness and gentleness, his inclusion of all, his compassion and care of the poor, outcast, sick, sinner, tax collector, his condemnation of the rulers and wealthy for their exploitation of the disadvantaged, his demand for social and economic justice, his example of and demand of servanthood, and that the reach of the Kingdom, now breaking into the world, and its practices are to be for all men at all times. To look at the life of Christ and seriously consider how he lived and what he taught is to understand what it means to be conformed to the image of Christ.

If we stop with only proper knowledge, proper belief and personal spirituality and do not move to loving action, we really know nothing of what it is to be Christ-like.

Chapter 2

The Sovereignty of God

Any theology must begin with God. To begin anywhere else is utter foolishness and to begin anywhere other than the Word of God is foolishness compounded. To begin to understand the purpose and meaning of our trials we must look long and hard at who God is and the nature of our relationship to him, for this is the most fundamental context in which we live. We must understand that "God alone is God" and God may do with us as he pleases.

To say "God alone is God" is to recognize that God is essential, and we are not. That something exists rather than nothing demands that there be a necessary being from which all else derives. God needs nothing, relies on nothing and is complete entirely within himself. He is self-sufficient and needs nothing outside himself. And yet he made the universe and mankind.

We, on the other hand, are not necessary beings, we could be or not be; the universe would not cease to exist if we did not exist. We occupy a completely subordinate position below God, a position not only subordinate but utterly dependent; our very existence requires God. God provides the air we breathe, the water we drink, the food we eat, the proper function of our bodies, our ability to use language, all of our cognitive capacities and logic itself. We could do nothing without his provision and sustaining power.

2.1 The Decrees

The decrees of God are his eternal purposes, which he has freely chosen, for his own glory, and ordained, either determinatively or permissively, all that comes to pass.[1] By this we must not understand that everything is predetermined, but that despite contingency, that is, man's free will, God's purposes are accomplished.

The decrees of God are his eternal purpose; God does not change them; they are set for eternity. God's decrees are based solely on God's wisdom and counsel, no one has instructed him. God's decrees are freely determined by God; nothing constrained God to decree as he did, nor was he under any obligation. However, his decrees are neither arbitrary nor capricious, the result of raw will, but rather are consistent with his character. The glory of God is the end of God's decrees. Some of God's decrees are determined while others are permitted, that is contingent[2]. Lastly, the scope of God's decrees extends to all events, past, present and future.

> That the events in the universe are neither a surprise nor a disappointment to God, nor the result of His caprice or arbitrary will, but the outworking of a definite purpose and plan of God, is the teaching of Scripture.[3]

Many passages could be mentioned,[4] but the passage from

---

[1] What follows in sections 2.1 to 2.2 relies heavily on Henry C. Thiessen's *Introductory Lectures in Systematic Theology*

[2] Thiessen, Henry C., *Introductory Lectures in Systematic Theology*, 148

[3] Thiessen, Henry C., *Introductory Lectures in Systematic Theology*, 148

[4] Eph 1:9,11; 3:11; called according to his purpose, Rom 8:28; worketh all

2.1 The Decrees

Isaiah is particularly instructive.

> The LORD of hosts has sworn saying, "Surely, just as I have intended so it has happened, and just as I have planned so it will stand," . . . This is the plan devised against the whole earth; and this is the hand that is stretched out against all the nations. For the LORD of hosts has planned, and who can frustrate it? And as for His stretched-out hand, who can turn it back?
>
> Isa 14:24,26,27

God has a plan and we are assured that he is working it out and nothing can stop it.

2.1.1 The Basis of the Decrees

The basis of God's decrees are God's wisdom and holiness, which are themselves consistent with his character — holy, perfect, loving, caring, just and righteous. Some have claimed that there is no set of divine values that determines God's will, rather that *whatever* God wills is right and proper. This cannot be the case for God is not simply "a will willing," but rather is internally self-consistent with his essence. It is not that his character stands apart from him forcing him to act in a particular manner. We are, rather, to understand him to act consistently with his character. God could not, by the exercise of his will, decree that murder or adultery is good and their opposite evil, for to do so would be inconsistent with his character. If it is by sheer will that something is made so by God, then it was not necessary for redemption to come by Christ's death and resurrection; some other method could just have easily been decreed. The incarnation, the substitutionary death and the resurrection were simply arbitrary, not

---

tings after the counsel of his will, Eph 1:11; eternal purpose, Eph 3:11; I Pet 1:20; Rev 13:8; Eph 1:4; II Tim 1:9; Titus 1:2

necessities.

That God wills in a manner consistent with his character must not be seen as an external constraint. It is simply God acting self-consistently. To do otherwise would be chaos. If God is anything he is consistent. He is the same yesterday, today, and tomorrow. He changes not.

God's decrees, all that happens on earth and heaven, are exactly what God has either determined to happen or permitted to happen. He is not surprised, disappointed and neither does he fret. Things happen just as he has decreed.

2.1.2 The End of the Decrees

The end of the decrees, the focus of all activity in heaven and earth, is the glory of God. We must understand, in a negative sense, that the ends to which all is directed is not first to our happiness or holiness. God, to be sure, is concerned with these, but these are not that to which creation is directed. It is a matter of emphasis. Our happiness and holiness are provided for as God glorifies himself, not because our happiness and holiness have an absolute priority over all else. The universe is not centered around man but more properly around God. Our focus then is the glory of God.

> We say, then, that the end of all things is the glory of God: and only as we also adopt this as our real goal in life are we living on the highest plane and in full harmony with the purposes of God.[5]

The heavens themselves glorify God, "The heavens declare the glory of God: ..." (Ps 19:1). In Isaiah 48:11 we have, "For mine own sake, for mine own sake, will I do it; for how should my name be profaned? and my glory will I not give to another." Paul tells

---

[5]Thiessen, Henry C., *Introductory Lectures in Systematic Theology*, 151

us, "Whether, then, you eat or drink or whatever you do, do all to the glory of God." (1 Cor 10:31) And the twenty-four elders in heaven cry out: "Worthy are You, our Lord and our God, to receive glory and honor and power; for You created all things, and because of Your will they existed, and were created." (Rev 4:11) Any preoccupation other than glorifying God is simply wrong.

God is the creator of all, omnipotent, omniscient, omnipresent; he is love, he is perfect in his very essence, he is holy, just, righteous; and, with unfathomable grace, the redeemer of mankind. In Christ his Son we have the summit of his self-revelation to man. For these reasons, and in ways that we cannot understand with finite minds, it is right and proper that the entire universe, and all the activity within it, should be directed to God's glory. It would be unseemly for it not to.

God Glorifying Himself: A Complementary View

As we just mentioned, God is glorified by virtue of who he is and by the creation itself; the creation shouts his glory. These truly bring glory to God, but other acts of God, acts benefiting us, bring glory to God. Most important among them is God's work of salvation. Who do we see in the book of Revelation on the throne, worthy of all honor, glory and blessing? It is not God in royal robes, but God as the Lamb that was slain, slain to bring salvation to his creation.

> *Worthy is the Lamb that was slain* to receive power and riches and wisdom and might and honor and glory and blessing. And every created thing which is in heaven and on the earth and under the earth and on the sea, and all things in them, I heard saying, To Him who sits on the throne, and to the Lamb, be blessing and honor and glory and dominion forever and ever. (Italics added)
>
> Rev 5:12,13

Now consider several passages from the first chapter of Ephesians.

> In love He predestined us to adoption as sons through Jesus Christ to Himself, . . . , to the praise of the glory of His grace, . . .
>
> Eph 1:5,6

Here we see a specific aspect of God's salvation, we have been adopted by God and are now his children, and by extension, fellow heirs with Christ. What a gift and blessing. In this is God glorified.

> In Him also we have obtained an inheritance, . . . , to the end that we who were the first to hope in Christ would be to the praise of His glory.
>
> Eph 1:11,12

Here we see that those who were the first to hope in Christ bring glory to God.

> In Him, you also, . . . — having also believed, you were sealed in Him with the Holy Spirit of promise, . . . to the praise of His glory.
>
> Eph 1:13

And here we see that God, sealing us in Christ with the Holy Spirit, brings glory to himself.

Clearly, God is not some stern master, far off in heaven, bringing glory to himself only in abstract ways. Rather, God delights in loving his creation and brings glory to himself by saving it and doing good to his children.

2.1.3 The Decrees in Brief

The most basic decree is the decree to create the material and spiritual universe and all they contain. The creation is a gift of God, for it is not necessary; God could have decided to do otherwise.

The decrees[6] in the moral and spiritual realm are:
- To Permit Sin: Sin entered the world through Adam's sin.
- To Overrule Sin for the Good: We see this in the life of Joseph, Paul, and in Christ's life. (We could mention many more.) Satan had sought to destroy by the cross, but Christ is victorious by it. God is ever redeeming evil for good.
- To Save from Sin: To this end God has provided the work of Christ. However, not all men are saved, but choose to remain in rebellion.
- To Reward His Servants and to Punish the Disobedient: Those that have been saved from sin are given a future and a hope: an eternal life with God, a new heart, and a resurrected body. The disobedient are given to eternal punishment.

2.2 God's Sovereign Rule

An excellent working definition of the sovereignty of God, given by Henry Thiessen, is that

> ... by the sovereignty of God we mean that as Creator of all things visible and invisible, God is the owner of all; that He, therefore, has an absolute right to rule over all (Matt 20:15; Rom 9:20,21); and that He actually exercises this authority in the universe (Eph. 1:11).[7]

Like God's decrees, his sovereign rule is exercised in wisdom, holiness and love and similarly, his rule is for his glory.

We find claims of God's sovereign rule in many passages; "Yours, O LORD, is the greatness and the power and the glory

---

[6]Thiessen, Henry C., *Introductory Lectures in Systematic Theology*, 153–160

[7]Thiessen, *Introductory Lectures in Systematic Theology*, 173

and the victory and the majesty, indeed everything that is in the heavens and the earth; Yours is the dominion, O LORD, and You exalt Yourself as head over all. " (1 Chr 29:11); "But our God is in the heavens; He does whatever He pleases." (Ps 115:3); All the inhabitants of the earth are accounted as nothing, But He does according to His will in the host of heaven and among the inhabitants of earth; and no one can ward off His hand or say to Him, 'What have You done?' " (Dan 4:35); ". . . who works all things after the counsel of His will, . . ." (Eph 1:11).

God rules absolutely and that by right; no one informs him as to his governance, but he rules with justice and love. We could ask for no better and fair Sovereign than this.

2.2.1 Preservation

Once again we turn to Thiessen for a working definition.

> By preservation we mean that God, by a continuous agency, maintains in existence all the things which He has made, together with all their properties and powers.[8]

The creation is neither self-existent nor self-sustaining; because of this, God, by a continuous and direct agency must preserve the creation, that is maintain in existence what he has created. We see mention of God's sustaining work in the following passages: "You alone are the LORD. You have made the heavens, the heaven of heavens with all their host, the earth and all that is on it, The seas and all that is in them. You give life to all of them ..." (Neh 9:6); "He is before all things, and in Him all things hold together." (Col 1:7); "And He is the radiance of His glory and the exact representation of His nature, and upholds all things by the word of His power ..."(Heb 1:3).

---

[8]Thiessen, *Introductory Lectures in Systematic Theology*, 174

2.2 God's Sovereign Rule

God is not only responsible for the creation, but also for its continued existence, and he does so willingly, free of any compulsion. He does so for his glory and for love of his creation.

2.2.2 Providence

God's sovereign control is also called providence.

> ... providence means that continuous activity of God whereby He makes all the events of the physical, mental, and moral phenomena work out His purposes; and this purpose is nothing short of the original design of God in creation.[9]

God exercises his sovereign control over the physical universe, the animal creation, the nations of the earth and over the lives of individuals. Absolutely nothing is outside of God's governance.

God is sovereign over man's birth and lot in life; neither are accidental. We find that "Your eyes have seen my unformed substance; and in Your book were all written the days that were ordained for me, when as yet there was not one of them." (Ps 139:16); "Before I formed you in the womb I knew you, and before you were born I consecrated you; I have appointed you a prophet to the nations." (Jer 1:5); "But when God, who had set me apart even from my mother's womb and called me through His grace, was pleased to reveal His Son in me so that I might preach Him among the Gentiles,..." (Gal 1:15,16).

God is sovereign over the fortunes of men; (Ps 75:6,7); "He has brought down rulers from their thrones, and has exalted those who were humble." (Luke 1:52); The LORD kills and makes alive; He brings down to Sheol and raises up. The LORD makes poor and rich; He brings low, He also exalts. He raises the poor from the dust, He lifts the needy from the ash heap to make them sit with nobles, and inherit a seat of honor;..." (1 Sam 2:6–8); "The LORD

---

[9]Thiessen, *Introductory Lectures in Systematic Theology*, pg. 177

said to him, Who has made man's mouth? Or who makes him mute or deaf, or seeing or blind? Is it not I, the LORD?"(Exod 4:11).

God is sovereign over the supply of the needs of his people; "And we know that God causes all things to work together for good to those who love God, to those who are called according to His purpose." (Rom 8:28); "And my God will supply all your needs according to His riches in glory in Christ Jesus." (Phil 4:19); "For from days of old they have not heard or perceived by ear, nor has the eye seen a God besides You, Who acts in behalf of the one who waits for Him. "(Isa 64:4).

And God is sovereign over the destinies of the saved and unsaved: "The steps of a man are established by the LORD, and He delights in his way. When he falls, he will not be hurled headlong, because the LORD is the One who holds his hand." (Ps 37:23,24).

God's sovereign rule has as one of its goals the happiness of his creatures and his goodness is given, among other things, to lead men to repentance (Rom 2:4). To his children Christ has given joy, and he works all things for good and he will withhold no good[10] things from us.

God also exercises his governance over the preparation of his people for their ultimate redemption, inheritance and life with him in heaven. This hits close to home, directly addressing our current study. As we will learn, God uses trials to refine us and conform us to the image of his Son. This is the work of preparation.

However, the world is not as God wants it. We pray for his Kingdom to come and his will to be done. He would have all to be saved but most are not.

---

[10]Recall that at a minimum the good is understood as what brings glory to God and draws us to him. It is not primarily things.

2.2.3 A Clarification

God is indeed the sovereign ruler of the universe, but he has sovereignly decreed that men and angels have free will. However, through the fall of the angelic host and the Fall of Man, and the subsequent enslavement to corruption of the physical universe[11] we have the kingdom of Satan and Kingdom of God in conflict. It is a real conflict, not a fiction. God has not lost control and the victory has never been in question, but God has permitted the rebellion along with its consequences[12]. The conflict that has, and now rages, is not acceptable to God, being the result of man's sin, and man is unable to rectify the situation. God, therefore, has provided the means to deliver his creation and man from the consequences of man's sin.

That the acts of men are contingent,[13] and, more often than not, violate God's will is found throughout the Bible. One of the most striking examples is found in the Lord's prayer. Here Christ, God the Son, tells us to pray that God's will be done. If God's will is done in all matters, then why pray that it be done? The only answer is that God's will is not always accomplished. Something more complex than a one-dimensional will is involved. Obviously, God's will has at least two aspects. In some cases God chooses to exercise an efficacious will where an outcome different than what he wanted is not possible. In other cases God chooses to exercise a permissive will where he permits men to do things not according to his desires. However, God is sovereignly directing all to his glory.

We find another instance of this in Matthew 23:37: "How often

---

[11] Romans 8:19-22

[12] A real dualism, permitted by God, a battle between good and evil temporarily exists.

[13] A contingent event is one that could have been otherwise. Multiple outcomes were possible. Men really do have free will and are morally responsible to God.

I wanted to gather your children together, the way a hen gathers her chicks under her wings, and you were unwilling." (See also Luke 13:34) Christ is grieving over the nation of Israel for their refusal to obey him; he would rather they had come to him and repented.

In 2 Peter 3:9 we find a similar thought: "The Lord is not slow about His promise, as some count slowness, but is patient toward you, not wishing for any to perish but for all to come to repentance." God does not wish any to perish, but most do. This is not a declaration of God's failure, but man's rebellion.

We see the same idea taught in the Old Testament. The following passages from Ezekiel are especially instructive.

> Do I have any pleasure in the death of the wicked, declares the Lord GOD, rather than that he should turn from his ways and live?
>
> Ezek 18:23

> Repent and turn away from all your transgressions, so that iniquity may not become a stumbling block to you. Cast away from you all your transgressions which you have committed and make yourselves a new heart and a new spirit! For why will you die, O house of Israel? For I have no pleasure in the death of anyone who dies, declares the Lord GOD. Therefore, repent and live.
>
> Ezek 18:30b–32

> Say to them, 'As I live!' declares the Lord GOD, 'I take no pleasure in the death of the wicked, but rather that the wicked turn from his way and live. Turn back, turn back from your evil ways! Why then will you die, O house of Israel?'
>
> Ezek 33:11

2.2 God's Sovereign Rule

Men make real choices and could choose to obey if they would. Why would God, through his prophets make such pleas if it were not possible for man to respond to God's call? These verses demonstrate that men often do not do God's will, and that men have real moral freedom.[14] As men exercise their moral freedom in rebellion against God's rule they commit acts of evil that God hates, but nevertheless permits. These acts often have far reaching consequences bringing trials to many.

Despite man's freedom, man's free acts are completely under God's rule.[15] Importantly he has decreed the nature and the limits of our freedom to act. Clearly, God permits great freedom for mankind to act, sometimes permitting sin to fully manifest itself. He limits it little or not at all. In other cases he takes direct action and prevents evil acts. In still other cases he puts limits on the extent to which evil can develop. In all cases God remains sovereign; evil acts occur only by God's permission.

An important question still remains, "In what sense does God overrule evil for good?" How is it that God works evil for good, and what are some examples of God working evil for good?

Before answering this question it would be wise to consider evil for a moment.[16]. It is important that we see evil in its proper light. David Bentley Hart, in *The Doors of the Sea*, says

> Christian thought, from the outset, denies that (in them-

---

[14] It is true that the Scriptures say that the unregenerate man does not understand God or his word and that none do good. However, it also teaches that we have a choice to make regarding Christ, do we accept him, or reject him. We make the decision, it is not made for us by God. If we agree that man as a consequence of his rebellion is unable to respond to God or do good, then we must accept (if we are unwilling to embrace Reformed theology) that the work of Christ extends a common grace to all to at least make a basic simple positive response to God.

[15] Thiessen, *Introductory Lectures in Systematic Theology*, 181–183

[16] Much of what follows in the next few paragraphs is form the book *The Doors of the Sea* by David Bentley Hart

> selves) suffering, death and evil have any ultimate value or spiritual meaning at all. It claims that they are cosmic contingencies, ontological shadows, intrinsically devoid of substance or purpose, however much God may – under conditions of a fallen order — make them the occasions for accomplishing his good ends.[17]

Understanding this is critical; death, suffering and evil, in themselves, have no ultimate value or meaning. But, God does use them to accomplish his ends.

Is evil a created thing? Evil is not a created thing; it is not a substance, it has no positive ontological status. But, what is the source of evil? Evil springs from the will; it comes from creatures who have been given moral freedom. But in this moral freedom, from which comes evil, we find the gift of God by which he makes possible the "union of free spiritual creatures with the God of love."[18]

But freedom is not only understood as a potentiality actualized when one chooses a particular course out of a number of possibilities. Freedom understood this way is a kind of confinement and subordination. The choices come to us from outside ourselves; we do not create them and the choices are mutually exclusive.

> Freedom, so understood, would consist in no more than a certain kind of largely vacuous and limited potentiality dependent upon other limited and limiting potentialities.[19]

A higher understanding of freedom is one where we are free to flourish as the kind of being that God intends us to be. When we choose poorly and refuse to become what God wants us to be

---

[17] Hart, *The Doors of the Sea*, 61
[18] Hart, *The Doors of the Sea*, 69
[19] Hart, *The Doors of the Sea*, 71

2.2 God's Sovereign Rule

we do not become more free, but rather, enslaved.[20]

It is in this higher understanding of freedom that we must understand God's freedom and his relationship to evil.[21] God is infinite actuality. Potentiality cannot be attributed to God, for to do so would mean that God could become something other than he now is. God does not possess freedom in the sense that he is able to choose one among many possibilities; to do so would be to limit himself; the choices would lie outside himself and, after choosing he could not pursue the other possibilities. This would be a limitation of God. God, however, is fully actualized and fully realizes himself, nothing limits what he is and in this he possesses absolute freedom.

For God to be capable of evil, or for it to be necessary for him to use it to accomplish his ends, would make God less than what he is, for he would need something outside himself, something that springs from the moral freedom he has given to his children. And further, if evil possess substance and does not spring from our moral freedom then God is the author of evil. But this cannot be.

Therefore, God, being free, has no part in evil. He did not create it and it is not necessary for him to employ it to accomplish his purposes. He does, however, permit evil as his creatures exercise their volition. But God is not defeated by evil, rather he redeems it, using it to accomplish his ends.

To emphasize, evil comes from the exercise of out will. Death, evil, and the resulting misery are our doing, not God's.[22] We see,

---

[20] Hart, *The Doors of the Sea*, 71

[21] This and the next two paragraphs borrow from Hart's, *The Doors of the Sea*, 71-75

[22] Given that God is omniscient we could ask why he created the universe in the first place given the sin, misery and death he knew would come? Is this love? Would it not have been better for him not to have bothered in the first place? I have not found a satisfactory answer to this question apart from

by their own free will, sinful men doing evil against other sinful men, bringing suffering to one another. We see that death has entered into the world by our sin, we all die, for death is what we have earned; we have to collect our wages.[23] We also see suffering come to us in the convulsions of the earth as it groans under the effects of our sin. We are responsible for what has happened to us. It was not done to us by some ogre of a God.

Given all this, God in his mercy has chosen to save his creation in the fullest sense, by the incarnation, death and resurrection of his Son. And as this salvation advances and develops through history he redeems our evil, using it to glorify himself, conform us to the image of His Son and build his Kingdom.

Even death has been defeated and is not dreaded, for we have been given the gift of eternal life. If we should die from evil done to us, we know that we are better off since we are absent from the body and present with the Lord (2 Cor 5:8) and at Christ's coming we will receive bodies incorruptible. We simply cannot lose as evil comes to us. God overrules it for good.

Not only does God overrule evil for us personally, but he uses it as occasions for his people to demonstrate his love and thereby show the love of God to the world.

I have only scratched the surface of God's victory over evil. It is not my intention to present a complete treatise on the subject of the problem of evil and God's victory over it, since the issue at hand is an understanding of trials from the perspective of a child of God. The Scriptures make it sufficiently clear that the trials

---

Christ. God has indeed shown us his love for us and his creation. God only did one hard thing and it was not creating the universe, nor is it sustaining the creation, it was rather redeeming his people and his creation from the sin of man. We look to the cross and know he loves.

[23] Thanks be to God that the power of death and the grave have been defeated because if we are redeemed our destiny is not corruption and punishment, but a glorified body and eternal life with God himself.

that come to us, by the contingency of evil, are fully redeemed by God.

God, by his power and wisdom, rules over all the acts of men, and with respect to trials, nothing comes to us except by his specific intervention or by his explicit permission. We are not at the mercy of the capricious acts of men or creation. The trials that come to us are controlled by God, and he can chose to give us few or many, easy ones or hard ones, it is all up to him; but he, by his wisdom and power, glorifies himself in them, conforms us to the image of his Son and builds his Kingdom.

If God chooses to bring many trials into your life be glad, for you have been given a great gift; we are stubborn and learn only with great difficulty. Remember, our stubbornness is a result of our own sin, but as God brings trials, he redeems us from our pathetic condition.

2.3 A Picture of God's Rule

Consider now a specific case of God's Sovereign rule, viewed from a specific perspective. The case considered is the Kingdom of God as it is now constituted from the perspective of those in the Kingdom.

The Kingdom of God "is now and is not yet"; it is not in its final form, but it does exist and has as its members the children of God. It is a kingdom in the world but not of the world. As King of this realm, God exercises sovereign rule in several ways. First, by ruling over all the affairs of men, and second, by virtue of his kingship he has laid down principles and commands for his subjects to obey.

The important point to see is that God's will is neither capricious nor simply an exercise of sheer power, but fully informed by his holiness, justice and love. God is, not surprisingly, consistent with his own character.

At the heart of the Kingdom are principles and commands for indiscriminate love and forgiveness, a refusal of violence and retaliation, subordination of ourselves and our interests to those of others, active caring for one another and social and economic justice.[24] Those who live this way in the Kingdom directly experience God's love and a foretaste of eternal life. Those who only see a stern God exercising an inscrutable will do not see God properly. All the principles and commands of the Kingdom are designed to glorify God, but as we practice them, and live in communities that practice them, we, the subjects of the Kingdom, derive tremendous benefit.

The end of all things is certainly to glorify God, but God in his wisdom and love chooses, as he is being glorified, to bless his creation. More than this, however, is happening, for God is glorified by blessing and *restoring* his creation.

2.4 Application

God's decrees and his sovereign rule have profound and immediate consequences for us. God rules over *our* lives individually, as well as the universe. And *our* lives, as well as all that is in the universe, are to be focused on glorifying God.

This all sounds well and good except when God decides to glorify himself by means and methods we find painful. We are not so inclined to embrace God's glorification if it means difficulty for us. "Couldn't he glorify himself without making my life so difficult?" "Isn't there a quicker and easier way to be conformed to Christ and know God more fully?" And then we argue with him, "If you did this or that it would be more efficient." Or worse, we know and understand all the good he brings in our trials, and we

---

[24]Notice that the Kingdom of God is completely lacking in legalistic requirements such as specific ways of dress, religious practices, etc. The Kingdom of God is focused on more important matters.

2.4 Application

still refuse to accept them. In any case, we refuse God's sovereign rule over our lives, and we attempt to usurp God's power and rule; it is the same act of rebellion as Satan's. We, the clay, demand God answer our question, "Why have you made me thus? and What are you doing?" What arrogance, what insubordination! How dare we approach God and make demands. God may do with us as he will. We make no claims upon our life. He is God and we are not.[25]

What is it to us if God should take our lives, doing nothing more than simply pouring them out on the ground as a drink offering. No great fanfare, no worldly success, no flash of glory, just a hard life full of disappointment, sorrow and loss, lived in obscurity. If God should do this he will not feel as if he failed you. This life is the one he has determined to be the one that glorifies him the most and is the greatest benefit to you, for trials are to be embraced and counted as joy because we know that they conform us to the image of Christ and deepen our relationship with God. And how could we benefit more than this? Isn't God's glory to be pursued at all costs and isn't it enough to know God? What more could we want or need?

Ah, but here's the rub, all this makes sense, even if it is hard to live out, only if we value what God values. We may know that it is God's glory that we must seek and we may know that trials bring us closer to God, but if we do not value these things we will not embrace our trials for they bring nothing of value. There is great danger here. If we respond in this manner, it may indicate that we are not numbered among God's children. If, after examining ourselves, we find this attitude, but still believe we are

---

[25] Do not forget what was said above; the world is not now as God intends. Things occur, not only by his direct intervention, but by his permission. Yet his sovereign rule extends even to these and he permits them to enter our lives and by his sovereign rule he redeems them, glorifies himself, builds his Kingdom and conforms us to the image of his Son.

his child, we must seek God's power to change. We cannot remain in this state of rebellion indefinitely.

Nothing surprises God, he is never disappointed, and he never frets. This knowledge should profoundly affect us, changing how we live and respond to whatever comes to us. We can be surprised because we do not have the knowledge that God possesses, but we should not be defeated and we must not fret. In the grand scheme of things, if we know that what comes will be redeemed by God to glorify himself and bring us into a deeper relationship with him, how then can our disappointment be final; we know that God is in control and has our best interests at heart so how can we worry; our King is on his throne. The illness may not be healed, the loss never replaced, the trial may be chronic, but we have God's love and presence and the knowledge that he is glorifying himself in the circumstances of our life. What more could we ask?

2.5 A Final Note: Job and the Sovereignty of God

The importance of the book of Job cannot be overestimated. It tells us that God is sovereign and may do with us as he will and it reveals to us some of the conflict in heaven between Satan and God, and finally, it shows that trials come to the very best of us.

The occasion of the story is a challenge Satan presents to God.

> The LORD said to Satan, "Have you considered My servant Job? For there is no one like him on the earth, a blameless and upright man, fearing God and turning away from evil." Then Satan answered the LORD, "Does Job fear God for nothing? Have You not made a hedge about him and his house and all that he has, on every side? You have blessed the work of his hands, and his possessions have increased in the land. But put forth Your hand now and touch all that he has; he will surely curse You to Your face."

2.5 A Final Note: Job and the Sovereignty of God

Job 1:8–11

What follows in the rest of the story is how this challenge develops on earth. It is important to see that at the center of the story is the conflict between God and Satan, something completely unknown to Job and those around him. However, it profoundly affects Job and his friends.

At the end of this first exchange Satan is permitted to trouble Job, but God limits Satan's activities; "Behold, all that he has is in your power, only do not put forth your hand on him." Job proceeds to lose all he has, and yet he does not sin against God, and speaks some of the most remarkable words found in the whole Bible.

> Then Job arose and tore his robe and shaved his head, and
> he fell to the ground and worshiped. He said,
> "Naked I came from my mother's womb,
> And naked I shall return there.
> The LORD gave and the LORD has taken away.
> Blessed be the name of the LORD."
> Through all this Job did not sin nor did he blame God.
> Job 1:20–22

Job understood several important concepts: God is truly sovereign and God is the owner of all things and gives and takes what we will.

Satan, however, is not done with Job and believes that God can still be defeated. He comes to God and demands more.

> Satan answered the LORD and said, "Skin for skin! Yes, all that a man has he will give for his life. However, put forth Your hand now, and touch his bone and his flesh; he will curse You to Your face."
> Job 2:4,5

God simply replies, "Behold, he is in your power, only spare his life," and Job promptly lost his health, was tormented with terrible boils, and sat down in sackcloth and ashes. Even his wife abandoned him saying, "Do you still hold fast your integrity? Curse God and die!" Job replied, "You speak as one of the foolish women speaks. Shall we indeed accept good from God and not accept adversity?" Job is not going to reject God; his commitment to God is deep and he understands more than those about him.

The news of the fall of such a great man travels quickly and several of his friends made their way to him. The record of their coming is moving.

> When they lifted up their eyes at a distance and did not recognize him, they raised their voices and wept. And each of them tore his robe and they threw dust over their heads toward the sky. Then they sat down on the ground with him for seven days and seven nights with no one speaking a word to him, for they saw that his pain was very great.
>
> Job 2:12,13

This is a scene of complete devastation; his friends did not even recognize him as he sat in his sackcloth and ashes with puss covering much of his body. And his physical and emotional pain must have been terrible to see, for they sat for seven days and nights and spoke not a single word.

The bulk of the story now begins. A discussion about why this has happened ensues with Job's *friends* insisting that he must have some secret sin and Job countering that he does not. As their discussion develops, Job desires to defend himself before God thinking that if he could only speak to God he could move him to relent and lift the suffering. In the end, neither Job nor his friends speak truthfully about God; no one understood what was going on.

2.5 A Final Note: Job and the Sovereignty of God

After a very lengthy discussion God steps in and he is not gentle. He only addresses Job.

> Then the LORD answered Job out of the whirlwind and said, "Who is this that darkens counsel by words without knowledge? Now gird up your loins like a man, and I will ask you, and you instruct Me!"
>
> Job 38:1–3

This is an extraordinary reply. Job has been devastated by God's permissive will. How could God be so harsh? It is because both Job and his friends have veered far off course attributing to God things that are not true. God's glory and sovereignty were being challenged.

God goes on for three chapters interrogating Job showing him that he knows nothing, has no power, pounding home that he cannot challenge God or question his acts. He is as nothing before God. To this, Job responds.

> Then Job answered the LORD and said, "Behold, I am insignificant; what can I reply to You? I lay my hand on my mouth. Once I have spoken, and I will not answer; even twice, and I will add nothing more."
>
> Job 40:3–5

It would seem that Job is beginning to understand God, but God is not done and continues to drive his point home. Job has not learned what he must.

After further interrogation, Job is ready to repent and completely surrenders.

> Then Job answered the LORD and said, I know that You can do all things, and that no purpose of Yours can be thwarted. Who is this that hides counsel without knowledge? Therefore I have declared that which I did not understand, things too wonderful for me, which I did not know.

> Hear, now, and I will speak; I will ask You, and You instruct me. I have heard of You by the hearing of the ear; but now my eye sees You; therefore I retract, and I repent in dust and ashes.
>
> Job 42:1–6

What is it that Job now understands, why does he no longer challenge God's actions? He understands that God is as far above him as the heavens are above the earth, that God is absolutely sovereign and may do as he desires. We have no basis to challenge any of his acts. In this way we must also see and understand God.

Chapter 3

Proper Desires and Values

It is not enough to simply see that God's purpose in trials is to glorify himself, conforming us to the image of Christ and building his Kingdom. We may know this, but if we do not desire and value what he is accomplishing, we will not embrace trials. This sounds almost trivial, but it seems that many do not understand this.

It is difficult to know what to put in this chapter, because to do so is to answer the question "What can be said to redirect a person's desires?" Facts alone are not up to the task. Desires and values are fundamental and built upon the basic leanings of a person's heart. It would seem that what we really need to do is change the person — an impossible task for man. But with God, all things are possible. So let us go forward trusting in God to do the work only he can do.

It may be that one does not desire what God is accomplishing in trials because they do not know that God is actually accomplishing something. It is almost inconceivable that a person could be exposed to the Bible and not understand the purpose of trials, but I am sure it does happen and probably in large numbers. This lack of knowledge is most likely due to a lack of Biblical teaching in our churches and a lack of time spent with the Bible and in prayer on a personal level. Couple this with a culture that embraces health, wealth, property and unlimited consumption and we have a recipe for extremely distorted thinking.

Some of this darkness is due to an unregenerate heart. Identifying with Christ seldom costs American Christians anything, therefore, there are many in our churches who know little or nothing of the saving work of Christ. They have grown up in a church or attached themselves to a church, but they have never encountered Christ despite believing the contrary. It is not surprising then that many do not embrace trials and do not work with God in them.

Those outside of Christ cannot be persuaded merely with words to embrace God's ends in trials and thereby embrace trials. The preaching of the cross is foolishness (I Cor 1:18) to them and neither can they understand it (I Cor 2:14). What is needed is a transformation, one only made possible by an encounter with Christ.

A refusal to embrace trials and the accomplishing of God's ends should cause us to seriously examine our commitment to Christ and ask further, "Is Christ really my Savior and Lord?" There is real danger in refusing to embrace our trials. The answer we give to this question will have a dramatic impact on how we live and our eternal destiny.

The other possibility is that we have lost sight of God's purpose in trials. I believe that this is quite common, especially among mature Christians. Trials have an overwhelming immediacy, they seem to scream at us for attention, demanding to be removed. In times like this it becomes very difficult to stay focused on God's plan; instead we become disillusioned, angry and worried. It is not possible to avoid these retreats into defeatism, but we can gain victory over them. What is needed is an active prayer life, devotion to God's Word in devotional reading and study, obedience to his commands, meditation on God, our future hope in Christ, an appreciation for what he has already done, a focus on the needs of others, reliance on the power of God, and a commitment to Christian fellowship. In other words, it takes a continuous, sustained effort and complete reliance on God, losing of ourselves in his love and in love for others.

3.1 The Case for New Desires and Values

3.1.1 Christ and the Scope of God's Gifts

Christ is to be desired because he is God, the creator.

> And He is the image of the invisible God, the firstborn of all creation. For by Him all things were created, both in the heavens and on earth, visible and invisible, whether thrones or dominions or rulers or authorities – all things have been created through Him and for Him. He is before all things, and in Him all things hold together. He is also head of the body, the church; and He is the beginning, the firstborn from the dead, so that He Himself will come to have first place in everything. For it was the Father's good pleasure for all the fullness to dwell in Him, and through Him to reconcile all things to Himself, having made peace through the blood of His cross; through Him, I say, whether things on earth or things in heaven.
>
> Col 1:15–20

Christ is not simply a great man or teacher. Christ is not a good man who died for us. Christ is the Second Person of the Trinity, God himself who came to earth, showed us how to live, became the propitiation for our sins on the cross, rose from the dead, ascended to the Father and brought in the Kingdom of God. But not only this, Christ *is* the creator and the creator has redeemed his creation at a staggering cost to himself.

But consider how he came and how he did what he did. Don't forget that what follows is about God incarnate.

> Have this attitude in yourselves which was also in Christ Jesus, who, although He existed in the form of God, did not regard equality with God a thing to be grasped, but emptied Himself, taking the form of a bond-servant, and being made in the likeness of men. Being found in appearance as a man, He humbled Himself by becoming obedient to the point of death, even death on a cross.
>
> Phil 2:5–8

God the Son did not require or insist on manifesting his effulgent glory or exercising all of his godly prerogatives; it was a tremendous emptying, a staggering "giving up." And while emptying himself he became the God-Man; while remaining God, he took on the likeness of a man, he became a man. But not any kind of man, but a bond-servant, a servant by choice to God the Father and to us as well; it was an enormous humbling. But he humbled himself further by becoming obedient to death, the death on the cross where he redeemed us and paid the penalty for our sin.

All this was by his choice; he could have chosen otherwise and called down six legions of angels, avoided the cross, and left us in our sin. But he is both just and loving, not willing that any should perish, finding a way to satisfy his justice and yet redeem us from our bondage to sin. So he emptied himself and went to the cross for the whole world, thinking nothing of himself.

And what has he done in his magnificent display of love and mercy? Much indeed. If we understood what it is that God has done for us in the cross and by letting us know him personally, we would be embarrassed to ask for anything else. We would be

3.1 The Case for New Desires and Values

content with just this. This might sound radical but isn't this what Paul is saying in Philippians 3? Actually Paul is even more radical. Listen carefully.

> But whatever things were gain to me, those things I have counted as loss for the sake of Christ. More than that, I count all things to be loss in view of the surpassing value of knowing Christ Jesus my Lord, for whom I have suffered the loss of all things, and count them but rubbish so that I may gain Christ, and may be found in Him, not having a righteousness of my own derived from the Law, but that which is through faith in Christ, the righteousness which comes from God on the basis of faith, that I may know Him and the power of His resurrection and the fellowship of His sufferings, being conformed to His death; in order that I may attain to the resurrection from the dead.
>
> Phil 3:7–11

Paul's focus is to know Christ and the power of his resurrection, nothing else really matters; things hold no value for him. But not only this, things that were gain to him, that which he valued, are now a loss, no not simply a loss, but rubbish, for they gave him an opportunity to trust in himself (Phil 3:1–6) and prevent him from knowing Christ. Is this how we see things? If we did, trials would not be so difficult.

Why would Paul see such value in knowing Christ and sharing in the power of his resurrection? Is it not true that Christ is so lovely it defies description. The real depths of it are experienced rather than spoken, but let us try to speak of it, and yet only scratch the surface.

The life of Christ is presented in the four Gospels and it breaks upon the world both as a tsunami and a wonderful transforming power. It hits destructively on the powers arrayed against God: spiritual powers, corrupt religion and the kingdoms of men. But it also comes as a wonderful transforming power conforming us to the image of Christ, delivering us from the kingdom of Satan and transferring us to the Kingdom of God.

We see his love, kindness and gentleness freely given to the poor, outcasts, sinners, tax collectors, prostitutes, the lowest of the low. He heals the sick, delivers from demons, feeds the multitudes. He confronts the religious leaders on behalf of the poor and outcasts and condemns them for their treachery and twisting of God's Law.

His life showed us how to live in the Kingdom that he was bringing into the world, demonstrating how to love, telling us that, in him, we could be one, and that we must be one.

By his work on the cross and his resurrection he did many things, things which only God in the flesh could do. (Read the passages that follow carefully. They are simply breathtaking when read together.) He broke the power of sin

> But thanks be to God that though you were slaves of sin, you became obedient from the heart to that form of teaching to which you were committed, and having been freed from sin, you became slaves of righteousness.
>
> Rom 6:17

He removed the power of death and the grave:

> Death is swallowed up in victory. O death, where is your victory? O death, where is your sting? The sting of death is sin, and the power of sin is the law; but thanks be to God, who gives us the victory through our Lord Jesus Christ.
>
> 1 Cor 15:54b–56

We are no longer condemned, but have peace with God.

> Therefore there is now no condemnation for those who are in Christ Jesus.
>
> Rom 8:1

3.1 The Case for New Desires and Values

> Therefore, having been justified by faith, we have peace with God through our Lord Jesus Christ, ...
>
> Rom 5:1

He reconciled us to God:

> And although you were formerly alienated and hostile in mind, engaged in evil deeds, yet He has now reconciled you in His fleshly body through death, in order to present you before Him holy and blameless and beyond reproach ...
>
> Col 1:21,22

He transferred us from the kingdom of darkness to the kingdom of light:

> For He rescued us from the domain of darkness, and transferred us to the kingdom of His beloved Son, in whom we have redemption, the forgiveness of sins.
>
> Col 1:13,14

He made us alive with him and forgave us all our transgressions:

> When you were dead in your transgressions and the uncircumcision of your flesh, He made you alive together with Him, having forgiven us all our transgressions, having canceled out the certificate of debt consisting of decrees against us, which was hostile to us; and He has taken it out of the way, having nailed it to the cross.
>
> Col 2:13,14

He triumphed over the rulers and powers:

> When He had disarmed the rulers and authorities, He made a public display of them, having triumphed over them through Him.
>
> Col 2:15

God now lives in us (Acts 1) and we are temples of God:

> Or do you not know that your body is a temple of the Holy Spirit who is in you, whom you have from God, and that you are not your own? For you have been bought with a price: therefore glorify God in your body.
>
> 1 Cor 6:19,20

We are children and heirs of God:

> Therefore you are no longer a slave, but a son; and if a son, then an heir through God.
>
> Gal 4:7

We are being conformed to the image of Christ:

> ... those whom He foreknew, He also predestined to become conformed to the image of His Son, so that He would be the firstborn among many brethren; ...
>
> Rom 8:29

We have a future and a hope.

> Do not let your heart be troubled; believe in God, believe also in Me. In My Fathers house are many dwelling places; if it were not so, I would have told you; for I go to prepare a place for you. If I go and prepare a place for you, I will come again and receive you to Myself, that where I am, there you may be also.
>
> John 14:1–3

I have let the Scripture speak for itself, for there is tremendous power in it and I have presented these passages with little comment. As we read them one after the other it is almost overwhelming. And we could go on, for I have not presented it all, failing to mention that Christ has opened the way to the Holy of

3.1 The Case for New Desires and Values

Hollies and we may now approach God with confidence (Heb 4:16, 10:19) and that God has saved us "so that in the ages to come he might show the surpassing riches of his grace in kindness toward us." (Eph 27) God has lavished his goodness on us; why would we not desire what he desires and accomplish his ends? How could we not, in love and gratitude, give all we have for him? If we understand what he has done no other response is reasonable. Not only so, any other response is evil.

3.1.2 The Glory of Christ

Above we looked at Christ's divine glory and the glory that is his in the cross, but there is much more. In the gospels we have recorded for us the life of Christ and in it we see a beauty and glory like no other.

Christ's compassion for the poor, sick, outcast, sinner, and the rest of what the world calls human debris, is like nothing ever seen on earth. His compassion, however, does not stop at feelings but moves to action — healing, forgiving, including, feeding, and confronting the powers on behalf of the weak — and ultimately it takes him to the cross.

Christ is so gentle, kind, patient and forgiving. Consider his patience with his disciples who, more often than not, failed to understand. Think of the gentleness, kindness and forgiveness that he extended to the prostitute who anointed his feet, to the woman with the hemorrhage, to the woman caught in adultery, to the Samaritan woman at the well, to the Roman centurion, to the rich young ruler, to the despised tax collector Zacheaus, to all the sick who came to him, to the whole world in his death on the cross. We could go on and look at many more passages and in all of them we would find Christ, God the Son living among men, demonstrating what it is to be found in his image, revealing a beauty and loveliness that only the God/Man could reveal. Why would we not want to conformed to this image?

3.1.3 The Glory of the Kingdom

We will spend much time on the Kingdom of God. We will see how the Old Testament principles were expanded by Christ for all men at all times. Christ taught a radical new kind of economics and was intensely interested in social and economic justice. We will see how Christ showed us how to live, exercising indiscriminate love and forgiveness, breaking down any and all barriers, refusing violence and retaliation. And in the example of his life he taught us what it is like to live in his Kingdom.

So few of us have seen the Kingdom properly function, but is there a more desirable place to live than in the Kingdom of God, his Church, his Body, a place where we consider the needs of others more important than our own, where we are united as one in love, where we care for one another to such an extent that there are no needy among us as happened in the early church? And if it so desirable, being a taste of life in heaven, why would we not do all we can, in God's power, to bring in the Kingdom?

Chapter 4

The Kingdom of God: Introduction

It might be surprising to see a chapter on the Kingdom of God in a book on the theological perspective of trials, but it is essential in the full development of the theological and social context in which trials take place. If we fail to understand the Kingdom of God in sufficient detail, and how trials are integrated into it, we will not understand our trials well at all. In particular, when we understand the Kingdom of God, and the importance of the Sabbath year and Jubilee principles to it, we find that we have much to say to those who can help others passing through trials, as well as, to the one in a trial.

Trials, except in rare occasions, do not take place in isolation, but in a community. As Christians, our primary community is the local body of believers, the local church, which is a part of the larger body of Christ, which itself contains the citizens of the Kingdom of God on earth. Any society has clear, even if not always written, rules that govern the social interactions between its citizens. Expectations, boundaries, requirements and the types of permissible relationships are communicated by the written and unwritten laws. In this regard, the Kingdom of God is not different from any other, but in its social and spiritual content it is the complete inversion of man made kingdoms. To understand this Kingdom we must look to Christ and the apostles as well as to a careful reading of the Mosaic Law. In what follows, we will see that the Kingdom relates in important ways to trials.

4.1 The Kingdom: Now but Not Yet

Christ came to teach us about, and bring in the Kingdom of God. The Kingdom of God was central to Christ.

> From that time Jesus began to preach and say, "Repent, for the kingdom of heaven is at hand."
>
> Jesus was going throughout all Galilee, teaching in their synagogues and proclaiming the gospel of the Kingdom, healing every kind of disease and every kind of sickness among the people.
>
> Matt 4:17, 23

> Jesus was going through all the cities and villages, teaching in their synagogues and proclaiming the gospel of the kingdom, and healing every kind of disease and every kind of sickness.
>
> Matt 9:35

> When day came, Jesus left and went to a secluded place; and the crowds were searching for Him, and came to Him and tried to keep Him from going away from them. But He said to them, "I must preach the kingdom of God to the other cities also, for I was sent for this purpose."
>
> Luke 4:42, 43

The Kingdom of God is at the center of Christ's ministry, and all he said and did must be understood in light of the Kingdom.

4.1 The Kingdom: Now but Not Yet

The Kingdom was not one of many things Christ was interested in, it encompassed everything he did.

As to our relationship to the Kingdom of God, the apostle Paul tells us that if we are Christ's we have been placed into his Kingdom.

> For He rescued us from the domain of darkness, and transferred us to the kingdom of His beloved Son, in whom we have redemption, the forgiveness of sins.
>
> Col 1:13, 14

Those who name the name of Christ are in the Kingdom now. However, on earth, the King of this Kingdom is not physically present. He has no army and his administrators do not exercise direct control of any institutions outside the Kingdom.[1] It is a separate Kingdom within the world. This state of affairs is quite different from that mentioned in Revelation.

> The kingdom of the world has become the kingdom of our Lord and of His Christ; and He will reign forever and ever.
>
> Rev 11:15

Obviously, God has not yet set up his temporal Kingdom on earth. Rule over this world and its nations has been given, by God, to Satan, the Prince of the power of the air.[2] Nevertheless, God's Kingdom has come; it is and is not yet. But a time is

---

[1] Christians in God's Kingdom may be in government, that is a kingdom of this world, but they do not exercise power within it in the name of the Kingdom of God. The kingdoms of this world cannot be incorporated into the Kingdom of God at this time. This is yet to come. The rule of the kingdoms of this world have been given, temporarily by God, over to the rule of Satan.

[2] Eph 2:2, Eph 6:12, John 12:31 — God has only given a limited rule of the world to Satan and will, at a time of his choosing, defeat Satan. God can and does override Satan as he sees fit. Satan rules only as God permits. Recall Satan before God when he seeks permission to destroy Job. (Job 1—2)

coming when God's Kingdom will come in all its fullness and God will reign on earth as absolute monarch.

At the moment, God's Kingdom is present in the world, but not in its fullest extent. It is not of the world but it is certainly in it. Obviously, this Kingdom is rather unusual and quite different from a normal kingdom. What then is the nature of this Kingdom that "is now" and "is not yet?" It is to this question we now turn.

4.2 The Nature of the Kingdom

4.2.1 What the Kingdom is Not

Before discussing what the Kingdom of God is we must first address what it is not, for misconceptions are pervasive. In Protestant Christianity, as distinct from Anabaptist Christianity, the Kingdom is most often spiritualized, thereby doing great violence to the Kingdom of God. Additionally, Christ's life on earth is often not seen as presenting a norm for Christian behavior. It is not taught that we must live as he lived.[3] It is frequently explained that since Jesus was God and we can't use his life as an example to live by, we must instead go to the epistles for direction. Contrary to these ideas stands the teachings of Christ, apostles and the early church, for the Kingdom was not merely spiritual and Christ's life does provide a normative example for Christians. As we look at Christ's life we see how to live now in the Kingdom.

Many claim that the Kingdom of God is only "spiritual." But what does it mean to say that the Kingdom of God is only a spiritual Kingdom? It means at least that the Kingdom is of the spiritual realm, the incorporeal[4] realm, and finds its relevance only in this realm. It has little to do with the corporeal[5] world. More

---

[3]Clearly we cannot emulate the divine aspects of his life, we are not God. I am only referring to his character.

[4]non-material or non-physical

[5]material or physical

4.2 The Nature of the Kingdom

often, this means that until the rule of God appears on the earth in its fullest sense, the Kingdom for the Christian is simply "spiritual" fellowship and having our eternal salvation secured by the work of Christ. In this interpretation Christ's life is seen primarily as a record of the incarnate God's activities upon earth leading up to the crucifixion and resurrection. The focus is entirely on these two events. The life of Christ is seen more as a history than a way of life to be copied by all Christians. This understanding of the Kingdom and the life of Christ may seem to be extreme, but it does appear to be held, to a greater or lesser degree, in some form, by most in the Protestant world. However, the Bible, the Apostles and the early church know of no such understanding of the Kingdom of God and the life of Christ.

An improper distinction between the spiritual and profane, the private and social, is often made when discussing the Kingdom of God. Even among those who believe that the Kingdom is more imminent than what was mentioned above, there is a sense that the spiritual — personal righteousness, personal ethics, devotional life, correct doctrine, and so on — is ethically distinct from and superior to the social aspects — peace, care for the poor, oppressed and sick, social justice, etc. — contrary to what is presented in James 2:14-17 and I John 3:16-18 where faith and love (the spiritual aspects) are demonstrated and proven by the provision of physical and material care for others. Faith and love simply cannot exist without a demonstration of physical and material care of others. Typically the focus is only on the private spiritual life and does not include the social life within the Church and the wider social life of the Church in the world. Once again, the Bible, the apostles and the early church know of no such separation or priority.

Another misconception is that, in its present form, the Kingdom of God has been fully realized. Many argue that the Kingdom of God is fully present today in the world and Christians are to strive for political and religious dominance to exercise their kingdom prerogatives. This is not only wrong, but has resulted in tremendous evils being visited on mankind down through the centuries.

The Kingdom of God is far more nuanced. It is not simply spiritual or already present or not present at all. Currently, the Kingdom is present both physically and spiritually, having "broken out" into the world, but not in its final glory.

These unfortunate misunderstandings arose, at least in part in Western Christianity, from the notion of a Kingdom of God with two parts, the spiritual and the secular, that came out of the Protestant Reformation of Luther and Calvin, which finds its roots in the Christian empire of Constantine and the Catholic Church. The one part is for the soul while the other is for the body. Much more could be said on this topic, but it exceeds the scope of what must be communicated here and the reader is directed to the bibliography for further information.[6]

4.2.2 What the Kingdom is

The Kingdom of God and the Church

The New Testament writers, when referring to the corporate body of believers today, use the term *ekklesia*, which, from an etymological perspective, describes any group of people called out to form an assembly (*ek* - out and *kaleo* call or summon).[7]

We find this word used in several ways in the New Testament: In Acts 9:31, when referring to the Christian churches; once in Acts 7:38 when referring to the assembly of Israel in the Old Tes-

---

[6]For an excellent discussion see *The Anatomy of a Hybrid* by Leonard Verduin.

[7]Most of the material for this section comes from *The Greatness of the Kingdom*, Alva J. McClain.

4.2 The Nature of the Kingdom

tament; once in Acts 19:32 when referring to a riotous mob in Ephesus; once in Acts 19:39 when referring to a lawful governmental assembly in Ephesus.[8]

The Old Testament assembly of Israel and the lawful assembly in Ephesus had at least one thing in common, the exercise of governing power. Therefore, governing is also an aspect of the Christian *ekklesia*, the church. The church must not be seen as simply a collection of individuals "doing their own thing." It is rather a corporate body, under the authority and care of Christ and his law. We will spend much time developing these ideas in the next few chapters.

The Kingdom of God, in its fullness is the physical reign of God on earth. God will set up a literal kingdom and rule from Jerusalem for one thousand years. It is the kingdom promised by God to the nation of Israel. In this kingdom there will be no war, all will be cared for, and there will be perfect justice. The earth has never seen anything like it.

It is the kingdom in its final sense that Christ offered to the nation of Israel in the early part of his ministry. The offer was genuine, but it was firmly rejected, thus delaying the coming of the Kingdom of God in its final glory. However, in the interim, we have not only the *ekklesia*, the church, but a breaking out of the future Kingdom of God.

What then is the relationship of the Church to the Kingdom of God, and what qualifications must we claim to legitimately use the term Kingdom of God to describe the people of God today given that the Kingdom of God is in abeyance, in the sense of its actual establishment on the earth?[9]

The Kingdom of God has a present *de jure*[10] existence.

---

[8] McClain, *The Greatness of the Kingdom*

[9] McClain, *The Greatness of the Kingdom*, 439

[10] As a matter of law. Latin for "by right." Something that is rightful, legitimate or just according to law or equity. The term describes a state of

> God is saving and preparing in the *ekklesia* the members of the royal family who are destined to rule with Christ in the future established kingdom; and, second, in the sense that, as those born into the royal family, we enter judicially into the Kingdom before its establishment, a divine action so remarkable that Paul speaks of it as a translation (Col. 1:13).[11]

We in the *ekklesia* also enjoy certain important blessings that are assigned to the Kingdom of God.

> It must be admitted also that the Church of the present age is enjoying many of the *spiritual* blessings which in the Old Testament were predicted in connection with the Messianic Kingdom of the future; e.g., pardon for sin (Isa 55:4-7), justification through faith by means of imputed righteousness (Jer 23:6), regeneration (Ezek 36:27-28), and the coming of the Holy Spirit upon men (Joel 2:27-28).[12]

Not only do these spiritual things come to us, but we also see that Christ has taught, lived and made possible a new way of life for those in his Kingdom. It is the glorious life of the Kingdom which we will discuss in depth in chapters to come. In this, God brings not only spiritual salvation, but physical as well.

In a very real sense, the Kingdom of God has broken out into the world. It is yet to come in all its glory, but we are, in a very real sense, in it (Col 1:13) and it is in the world. It is in this sense, and for this reason, that I use the Kingdom of God when referring to the people of God today.

---

affairs or a condition that exists based on a right under the law, rather than a de facto condition in which something exists in fact regardless of its right to exist. Definition taken from www.ncbuy.com/credit/glossary.html

[11]McClain, *The Greatness of the Kingdom*, 439

[12]McClain, *The Greatness of the Kingdom*, 439

4.2 The Nature of the Kingdom

Another reason I have used the Kingdom of God is that I fear that the word Church, through many years of misuse, has lost much of its impact on Christians. Most understand the Church to be only spiritual and a loose collection of individuals. Of course, it is nothing of the sort, but I am concerned that this misconception will be difficult to break through. By using the Kingdom of God, I want to capture the grandeur that is the Church in all its glory — a holy nation of royal priests, living in love and mutual submission, caring for one another, living under the law of Christ and obeying him as King.

Fleshing Out the Concept

At a minimum, a kingdom consists of a ruler and his subjects. For the Kingdom of God the king is God and the subjects are the children of God, those who have put their trust in Christ for their right standing before God. But a ruler and his subjects are not enough to define a kingdom. To complete a kingdom we need a full exposition of the social relationships within the kingdom and how the kingdom interacts with other kingdoms. Among these internal and external relationships we must specify loyalties, allegiances, requirements, obligations, expectations, policies, identity and so forth. After these are defined, along with the ruler and subjects, we have a complete kingdom.[13]

In the Kingdom of God it is God who rules and it is his commands that we obey. God has spoken to us in his Word, both written and living, and it to his Word that we go to understand what he demands of us. It is in God's Word that we come to understand the nature of the internal and external social relationships within the Kingdom. No subjective or private understanding is

---

[13] An excellent book on the Kingdom of God is *The Upside-Down Kingdom* by Donald Kraybill. Many of the ideas presented here are found in this wonderful book. Another excellent book is *Mere Discipleship* by Lee Camp.

permitted. The subjects of the Kingdom, as a corporate body, have an important role in determining what God is saying in his Word at a particular time and place. However, the Word is first to be understood, as much as possible, in the historical and cultural context of the original speaker and audience. Only then can the Church make a proper application.[14]

As subjects of the Kingdom of God, our allegiance is singular; we can have only one sovereign. It is a mistake to think that we obey two sovereigns each ruling over mutually exclusive realms, one over the spiritual realm and another over secular matters.[15] At Christ's resurrection, all powers were placed at his feet and he is sovereign over them all. Nothing is outside the scope of his rule. Furthermore, Christ has much to say about a Christian's conduct that will bring us into direct conflict with the kingdoms of this world. Christ demands our complete allegiance, we belong to a heavenly nation, as Peter puts it, and are pilgrims and strangers on this earth.[16] We are first subjects to the Kingdom of God by virtue of our choice to follow God and then God's mercy in placing us into his Kingdom. We are subjects of human kingdoms only by virtue of our location.[17] God does, however, permit us to interact with human kingdoms, in fact it is essential, but this

---

[14] This provides the basis for a commitment to excellence in Biblical scholarship at all levels. Unfortunately, this cannot always be done. It is gratifying, however, that the essential core of the gospel can be apprehended by the simple and uneducated. Biblical scholarship is most useful in avoiding errors and deepening our understanding of the gospel message, both of which are essential for growth.

[15] No distinction between sacred and secular is found in Biblical Christianity. The social and political context of the first century were such that the writers and hearers of New Testament could not have understood things in this manner. There is only one King and his authority extends to all realms.

[16] Heb 11:13, I Pet 2:11

[17] This is not to say that the human kingdom we find ourselves under is arbitrarily chosen for us. I only mean to indicate the relationship to this earthly kingdom.

4.2 The Nature of the Kingdom

interaction takes place under the primacy of the Kingdom of God. We are told to obey the laws of the human kingdom so long as they do not conflict with those of God's Kingdom.[18]

The Kingdom of God is not found in a particular place; it is not localized, but distributed throughout the world and is found wherever God's obedient people are found; people living in the world, but not of it, implementing God's will and way of life in both their personal lives and in their interactions with others both inside and outside the Kingdom.

It is also important to realize that God's Kingdom is in the world but not of it. An important implication, as Christ made clear to Pilate, is that God's Kingdom does not contend violently with the kingdoms of this world. (John 18:36) Those in God's Kingdom do not use force or violence to "make things right" or coerce others to believe a particular thing.[19] God's Kingdom is a voluntary association. Nor is the reforming of the kingdoms of this world a primary or central task of the Kingdom of God. Neither is the Kingdom of God interested in replacing the kingdoms of this world. Another consequence of being in but not of the world is that the Kingdom of God operates on entirely different principles than those of earthly kingdoms. We will see this as we study the nature of our relationships within the Kingdom of God.

The Kingdom of God is an image of life in heaven, how God wants all men in all places to live with one another. This, however, can only be done by the children of God and cannot be participated in by those who are not God's children. It is impossible to attempt to implement Kingdom relationships and principles with

---

[18] Rom 13

[19] This understanding was tragically abandoned at the Constantinian disaster when the church embraced the state. At this time, the church began to use the power of the state to not only coerce, but kill those who refused to be converted. It was a complete abandonment of Christ's teachings and resulted in much of the religious violence that followed.

those outside the Kingdom. We can, and must, extend forgiveness, love, care and help to those outside of the Kingdom, but they cannot be part of the Kingdom unless they subject themselves to the authority of Christ. We cannot attempt to combine or assimilate the kingdoms of this earth into the Kingdom of God. Nor can we attempt to make the kingdoms of this earth adopt the principles of life within the Kingdom. They simply cannot implement them, for it takes one who is indwelt by the Spirit of God to obey them. We can witness to the other kingdoms by our actions and invite those in these kingdoms to change their citizenship, but we have no real business with the administration of other kingdoms.[20] These other kingdoms, the governments of the world, are fallen and cannot, and will not be, redeemed. All we can hope for is that they will, in some measure, adopt Kingdom practices, but we cannot really *make them 'work,'* or *fix* them. Given the choice, it would be far more effective to build the Kingdom of God rather than devote our lives to the reformation of an earthly kingdom.

The Kingdom of God is also an alternate kingdom, a kingdom distinct from and in competition and conflict with the kingdoms of this world. That this is so is obvious from the fact that we have a King who demands our complete loyalty. Any authority outside of his Kingdom, making a demand on us that violates our King's command must be disobeyed, even to the loss of our own life. Any activity demaned by our King must be obeyed regardless of the demands of other kingdoms, no matter what the cost to us. But in no case does our Kingdom violently oppose the kingdoms of

---

[20]I do not go so far as to say that Christians cannot be involved in government, (however, I do not think it is a good idea and we do better by not being involved) but that we are misguided to think that we can implement much of the Kingdom of God in earthly kingdoms. Given the lack of success we will encounter in our efforts to reform earthly kingdoms, we should carefully consider what we should attempt to reform. Directly building the Kingdom of God would be a better use of our time and have more impact.

this earth.

The Kingdom of God also is an alternate kingdom in regard to its social and economic structures. In it are radically different ethics, economics and social relationships. The kingdoms of this world do not have the same ethics, structures, institutions or relationships. This will become more obvious as we develop our idea of the Kingdom in the chapters that follow.

The Kingdom, then, is more than just the rule of God in our hearts, but the rule of God in our hearts and all our relationships. The Kingdom of God is fundamentally corporate and social. It consists of an interdependent corporate body, the members of which are dependent on God individually as well as corporately. It is a people sharing a history, identity, purpose, influencing one another, formulating common goals and deciding together how to achieve them. The Kingdom stands as a precursor to the final deliverance of God, our salvation, an image of heaven and a witness to the world of the judgment and love of God, and it is by our love that the world knows that we are Christians.

4.3 The Relationship to Trials

Lest we forget, let us remind ourselves of how trials and the Kingdom relate. It is rare indeed when we go through a trial in complete isolation, for we live among people. The Christian lives in a community of believers sharing life's experiences with others. God uses trials in order to refine the character of the citizens of his Kingdom. At the same time he uses them as opportunities for other members of the community to express love to those in need. This is one of the fundamental activities in the Kingdom; people living selfless lives, considering others as more important than themselves and sacrificially providing for the needs of others. In this way the witness of the Church is made powerful and the world outside the Kingdom knows that we are disciples of Christ.

As they see this, many are drawn to Christ and God is glorified.

Trials, rather than being unwelcome intrusions, or things to be avoided, are events that provide a central and fundamental function within the Kingdom of God.

The presence of the Kingdom has a profound impact on our response to trials. One of the reasons why it is so hard for people to believe and accept James' command "to count it all joy when we enter various trials," (Jas 1:2) is that our churches do not implement Kingdom practices.[21] How much easier would it be to embrace trials if we knew that we had brothers and sisters ready to help us in our time of need? No doubt it would radically change our response to trials. But the church is, for the most part, not interested in implementing the Kingdom of God, and the Christian in the midst of a trial is left at the mercy of some other agency such as local or federal government. This should not be.

---

[21] This is an excellent example of the necessity of reading God's Word within the context of a community. If we do not live in a community that is living out the principles and imperatives of God's Kingdom, we have great difficulty in understanding God's word.

Chapter 5

The Kingdom: The Sabbath and Jubilee

To properly understand the Kingdom of God we must take a moment and look at the Jewish Sabbath and Jubilee years. In particular, we will see that it provides an important context for caring for those who are suffering.

When we think of Judaism and the Mosaic Law, we are typically drawn to the temple worship with its system of sacrifices and the extensive dietary and ceremonial purity laws; seldom do we consider the laws regarding interpersonal relationships. Of greatest neglect are the laws concerning the Sabbath year and the Jubilee. This is truly unfortunate for it is in this body of law that we see God's concerns in the social and economic spheres of the kingdom of Israel. By extension, this is doubly important when we consider the gospels and the epistles since they are better understood in light of Sabbath and Jubilee principles. When looked at through this lens, the New Testament comes to life. Not only do Sabbath year and Jubilee principles assist in understanding the New Testament, they also provide a context in which to discuss social and economic justice within the body of Christ, the Kingdom of God, and the world at large. More than that, however, the practice of Sabbath Year and Jubilee principles within the Kingdom of God are what economic and social justice look like.

By carefully examining the Sabbath year and Jubilee we find God expressing his will concerning social and economic justice; something we desperately need in twenty-first century Christianity.

Rather than seen as the least important aspect of Jewish law we should see the Sabbath year and Jubilee as second only to temple worship, which points directly to the final sacrifice to be provided by the Lamb of God. Not only does God set up a revolutionary law governing social and economic relationships, but he frequently condemns the nation of Israel, through his prophets, for their blatant disregard of these practices. God is not simply interested in the salvation of our souls; salvation is not so limited. God's salvation is comprehensive, for the Fall of Man was comprehensive. The Fall precipitated a complete collapse of all aspects of God's creation, all of which needs redemption. God's salvation extends to all of our relationships as well as our very bodies, and beyond that, the redemption of creation itself. God's love is provided indiscriminately to both the just and unjust: the sun rises, the rains come, crops grow, wealth is created, and all men enjoy the physical blessings of God. To those called by God's name, God lavishes the knowledge of himself, his presence, frees us from the power of sin, delivers us from the power of death and the grave, transfers us to his Kingdom and gives a present and future eternal hope. With such generosity, what right do we have denying or refusing to seek social and economic justice for others? Some of the most severe condemnations in both the Old Testament and Gospels are directed to those who deny social and economic justice; God is very interested in these matters.

The theological principles of the Sabbath year and Jubilee are absolutely shattering to twentieth century social and economic understanding. God sets our understanding, our prudence, on its head. With these principles, God put in place, within the very institutions of Israel, new attitudes and practices with respect to the enslaved, poor, indebted, limits to economic growth and limits on the accumulation of wealth, fundamentally challenging and changing human relationships and our relationship to wealth.

5.1 The Sabbath

5.1.1 Creation

The first time we encounter resting or ceasing from work is at the end of the creation account.

> Thus the heavens and the earth were completed, and all their hosts. By the seventh day God completed His work which He had done, and He rested on the seventh day from all His work which He had done. Then God blessed the seventh day and sanctified it, because in it He rested from all His work which God had created and made.
>
> Gen 2:1–3

God here determines that one day of rest out of seven is to be the norm; it is blessed. Notice that setting aside one day out of seven as a day of rest comes immediately after the creation, prior to any recorded interaction with man or laying down of a moral or religious code. A day of rest is religiously primeval. It is good in a fundamental sense.

Certainly, God did not rest because he was tired. But why did God rest and set aside one day out of seven as a day of rest? At a minimum, God rested to reflect on and enjoy his creation. It was also done as an example for mankind. Physical rest and reflection on God are first seen to be the purpose of the Sabbath.

5.1.2 Manna

The next time we find God speaking of the day of rest is in Exodus 16. The Israelites are in their 45th day of freedom from their enslavement in Egypt, located in the wilderness of Sin, and on their way to Sinai where God will give his Law. From the people's complaint it seems that things are pretty grim, with food and water scarce.

> Would that we had died by the LORD'S hand in the land of Egypt, when we sat by the pots of meat, when we ate bread to the full; for you have brought us out into this wilderness to kill this whole assembly with hunger.
>
> Exod 16:3

Most likely, they had taken some provisions from Egypt, but now these were running out. They may have begun to ration what was left and were obviously facing starvation if something were not done soon. From a human perspective the problem must have looked impossible; approximately a million people in a great wilderness had to be fed. But God had already shown himself powerful and faithful to these people during the last two months. He had ended their enslavement and delivered them from Egypt's army; could they reasonably assume that God would abandon them?[1] To this desperate cry and insolent unbelief God graciously provides and at the same time presents his people with a test (Exod 16:4) to reveal their level of obedience to God's simple Sabbath command.

God's provision is remarkable and the test simple.

---

[1] Notice how important trials were in the education of Israel. They spent four hundred years in captivity, were seriously threatened by extinction at the hand of the Egyptian army and here in Exodus 16 were facing starvation. As God graciously provides, despite their unbelief, they are given lessons to see that God is faithful and can be trusted. In each case it is deliverance against all odds, at the last minute.

5.1 The Sabbath

> Then the LORD said to Moses, "Behold, I will rain bread from heaven for you; and the people shall go out and gather a day's portion every day, that I may test them, whether or not they will walk in My instruction. On the sixth day, when they prepare what they bring in, it will be twice as much as they gather daily."
>
> Exod 16:4, 5

The importance of this deliverance and test is emphasized by the drama which attends them and is seen clearly in the communication of the coming provision to the nation.

> Then Moses said to Aaron, "Say to all the congregation of the sons of Israel, 'Come near before the LORD, for He has heard your grumblings.' " It came about as Aaron spoke to the whole congregation of the sons of Israel, that they looked toward the wilderness, and behold, the glory of the LORD appeared in the cloud. And the LORD spoke to Moses, saying, "I have heard the grumblings of the sons of Israel; speak to them, saying, 'At twilight you shall eat meat, and in the morning you shall be filled with bread; and you shall know that I am the LORD your God.' "
>
> Exod 16:9-12

As Aaron was speaking to the people, telling them that God had heard them, the Divine Presence[2] appeared before them all and spoke directly to Moses. God's message was that he would feed them; there will be no mistaking who is responsible for the provision; they will know that their Lord and God has done this.

The following morning the people wake to find a "fine flake-like thing," manna, all over the ground. Puzzled, they ask Moses what it is. He replies,

---

[2] As used here, Divine Presence indicates a unique manifestation of God in his glory and presence. Much more is said about the Divine Presence in the chapter on weakness.

> It is the bread which the LORD has given you to eat. This is what the LORD has commanded, 'Gather of it every man as much as he should eat; you shall take an omer apiece according to the number of persons each of you has in his tent.' ... Moses said to them, "Let no man leave any of it until morning."
>
> Exod 16:15b, 16, 19

There were, however, conditions placed on the use of this gift; they must limit the amount they take to one omer[3] and are not to save any of it for the following day.[4] Amazingly, those who had gathered much had no excess and those who gathered little had not lack. But those who kept some for the following day found it spoiled and full of worms.

On the sixth day they were to gather twice as much as on a regular day, the second omer to be used on the seventh day, a sabbath day, a day of rest.

> Eat it today, for today is a sabbath to the LORD; today you will not find it in the field. Six days you shall gather it, but on the seventh day, the sabbath, there will be none.
>
> Exod 16:25, 26

Despite God's command, some went out on the seventh day looking for manna and found none. For this the people are severely reprimanded.

> It came about on the seventh day that some of the people went out to gather, but they found none. Then the LORD said to Moses, "How long do you refuse to keep My commandments and My instructions? See, the LORD has given

---

[3] An omer is equal to 3/16 to 1/3 of a bushel.

[4] It is striking how closely the principles taught here parallel the principles Christ taught: Don't worry about tomorrow, don't lay up treasure on earth, trust God to provide, be content with what God provides.

> you the sabbath; therefore He gives you bread for two days on the sixth day. Remain every man in his place; let no man go out of his place on the seventh day." So the people rested on the seventh day.
>
> Exod 16:27–30

The first major introduction of the Sabbath comes with the giving of a continuing provision of food as well as an economic lesson. It is interesting to see how the principles are introduced in carefully designed steps. They are not introduced to the provision or the Sabbath all at once, but in steps that emphasize various principles. First, the provision is given along with a lesson that one is to be satisfied with what one has been given. There is also the idea that one can have enough. They are also taught not to hoard. In the second step they are introduced to the Sabbath where they learn the importance of resting from their labor and trusting in God's provision for the Sabbath.

The economic lesson and the lesson of God's faithful provision are not peripheral to the Sabbath, but rather essential. Men are predisposed to trust in their own strength, to look to themselves for their provision. However, we have a loving Father who will provide for us as we obey his commands. Men are also predisposed to accumulate wealth, working as much as possible to acquire it. The concept that it is enough to have our needs satisfied directly challenges this predisposition. The proximity of this concept to the Sabbath reinforces its importance.

5.2 The Sabbath Year and the Jubilee

In Luke 4 Christ announces his ministry and declares himself to be the Messiah.

> The Spirit of the Lord is upon Me, because He anointed Me to preach the gospel to the poor. He has sent Me to

> proclaim release to the captives, and recovery of sight to the blind, to set free those who are oppressed, to proclaim the favorable year of the Lord.
>
> Luke 4:18, 19

The Jew at this time understood that Christ was talking about real poor, the blind and those who were physically oppressed. Unlike those of us living in the modern world, his audience did not spiritualize what he was saying. This is not to say that he was not also addressing the spiritual bankruptcy and oppression of the human condition and the deliverance from this condition by his work on the cross and resurrection, but it is important to see that both Christ and his audience had a concrete social and economic understanding that was based firmly in the Mosaic Law and the prophetic promises. It is to this aspect of Christ's statements that we now turn, for the whole passage above, ending with the phrase "the favorable year of the Lord," introduces the Hebrew Jubilee.[5] This will prove to be extremely important in understanding the Kingdom of God and Christ's ministry since he came to bring in the Kingdom of God. Both the gospels and the epistles are saturated with the theological principles and practices built on the Jubilee and Sabbath year.

The Sabbath year is the seventh year in a "week" of years in which an amazing economic liberation occurs. During the Sabbath year three significant things occur.

First, the land was left fallow. Leaving the land fallow in the Sabbath year is discussed in several places, Exodus 23:1-11 and Leviticus 25.

> When you come into the land which I shall give you, then the land shall have a sabbath to the LORD. Six years you shall sow your field, and six years you shall prune your

---

[5] Yoder, *The Politics of Jesus*, chapter 2

5.2 The Sabbath Year and the Jubilee

> vineyard and gather in its crop, but during the seventh year the land shall have a sabbath rest, a sabbath to the LORD; you shall not sow your field nor prune your vineyard. Your harvests aftergrowth you shall not reap, and your grapes of untrimmed vines you shall not gather; the land shall have a sabbatical year. All of you shall have the sabbath products of the land for food; yourself, and your male and female slaves, and your hired man and your foreign resident, those who live as aliens with you. Even your cattle and the animals that are in your land shall have all its crops to eat.
>
> Lev 25:3–7

Given that Israel was agrarian, leaving the land fallow essentially brought the most significant economic activity of the nation to a halt resulting in enormous economic impact.[6]

Second, Jewish slaves were set free. The freeing of Jewish slaves is found in Exodus 21:2–6, Deuteronomy 15:12–18

> If your kinsman, a Hebrew man or woman, is sold to you, then he shall serve you six years, but in the seventh year you shall set him free.
>
> Deut 15:12

Third, all debts among fellow Jews were forgiven. The forgiving of debts is found in Deuteronomy chapter two.

> At the end of every seven years you shall grant a remission of debts. This is the manner of remission: every creditor shall release what he has loaned to his neighbor; he shall not exact it of his neighbor and his brother, because the LORDS remission has been proclaimed.
>
> Deut 15:1, 2

---

[6]I fear that I may have seriously understated its impact. It was probably more like an economic earthquake.

Slavery among Jews is not to be understood as Roman or early American slavery. This kind of slavery was the result of an inability to repay monetary debts or due to extreme poverty arising from misfortune. Indebtedness, followed by slavery, was not only or even chiefly due to irresponsibility or poor money skills. Debts often occurred due to hardship brought on by circumstances beyond one's control. For example, if a family were to lose its father and/or sons due to an accident, murder or disease the family could become destitute. Theft or natural disaster could also bring about a financial catastrophe from which the family could not recover.[7]

The Year of the Jubilee, occurring once every fifty years, implemented the most radical event. In this year, in addition to the events mentioned above, ownership of the land was returned to those who owned it at the beginning of the Jubilee, 50 years prior. This certainly brought an economic earthquake, shaking the prevailing power structure and distribution of wealth to its core. It essentially leveled the society economically. By so doing, it restructured relationships and affected how people perceived themselves.

5.2.1 Agrarian Economies

To get an idea of how profound these four practices were it is necessary to understand an agrarian society. In such a society all economic activity is focused on achieving a successful harvest. Without an adequate harvest starvation ensues. This is a basic

---

[7]Even in modern America the leading cause of bankruptcy is the loss of health. Divorce or the death of a primary wage earner are also leading causes. To assume that the poor and needy are always found in their conditions by choice or irresponsible behavior is the height of arrogance and insensitivity and should be condemned in the strongest terms. Is it not also proper to forgive even the one who is found in need due to their own failure? Have we always done what was right and proper, has not Christ forgiven us? Specks and logs come to mind if we refuse to forgive. (Matt 7:3)

5.2 The Sabbath Year and the Jubilee   75

economic activity in which failure is accompanied by death. It is not simply one among many economic activities, it is the activity about which everything is directed, and the land is at the center of it all. Without land none of this is possible.

We in the twenty-first century have nothing like it. Life and death still hang on our ability to feed ourselves and there are those whose single focus is growing the food we need, but with the modern revolution in farming this activity is done by very few and largely unseen. Most, in this modern age, give no thought to this essential economic activity; some even suppose that food comes from a grocery store, unaware of the vast effort it takes to get the food from the producers to the store.

In ancient times there were no farm machines to till the ground, plant the seed and harvest the grain; it was a labor intensive activity requiring large numbers of people. A significant portion of this labor pool was made up of sharecroppers, free men at the lower rungs of society as well as Jewish and foreign slaves. In many ways this pool of manpower was as essential as the land itself, for without the human resources the farms could not operate and the harvest fail. To a large farm, the loss of half its labor force would be devastating.

The loans, that is short-term debt, also had an important part to play in this agrarian economy for it provided a farmer a way to stretch from the planting to the harvest. Money would be loaned to buy seed or labor to plant and harvest with the expectation that at harvest time the loans could be retired from the abundance of the harvest. This did not always happen; the father died or became ill, the crops failed from a natural disaster or crop disease, the end result being default.

5.2.2 Economic Impact

We can now see how radical the Sabbath year and Jubilee practices were as they cut to the very heart of all economic activity. Leaving all the land in the nation fallow at the same time effectively shut down the largest part of the nation's economy. No financial or agricultural empires were going to be built or advanced in the Sabbath year.

Freeing of slaves did not have a significant economic impact during the Sabbath year since all the land was left fallow, but the following year the impact would be profound. Those who held large tracts of land were not able to farm it all unless they were able to replace their workforce. They had to hire free men, perhaps the same men they had just freed, whose labor had previously come at no cost. In this we see a redistribution of wealth; one whose labor was free now receives wages. This could seriously limit the economic fortunes of the more fortunate. Freeing of slaves, however, permitted families to reunite and allowed a shuffling of labor within the nation, resulting in access to more labor for some and less for others, thereby having a tendency to economically level the economy.

Releasing all debt also had a profound economic effect. Outstanding debt is an asset if one assumes that it will be repaid; if not, the loan is seen as a gift or charity. Forgiving a debt results in a total loss of the asset and can have serious consequences for the lender. Debt release also effected a redistribution of wealth.

Recall that support for those in need was to be given generously; the giver was not to hold back, nor was he to charge interest if he provided a loan. This created a dilemma for the lender as a Sabbath year approached; the lender would be tempted to withhold help as it approached. As the Sabbath year neared there was obviously less time to pay back the loan and the lender faced greater financial risk. God, knowing this, specifically commanded

5.2 The Sabbath Year and the Jubilee

that the lender was to essentially ignore the approach of the Sabbath year.

> Beware that there is no base thought in your heart, saying, 'The seventh year, the year of remission, is near,' and your eye is hostile toward your poor brother, and you give him nothing; then he may cry to the LORD against you, and it will be a sin in you. You shall generously give to him, and your heart shall not be grieved when you give to him, because for this thing the LORD your God will bless you in all your work and in all your undertakings. For the poor will never cease to be in the land; therefore I command you, saying, 'You shall freely open your hand to your brother, to your needy and poor in your land.'
>
> Deut 15:9–11

Releasing of all debts is in keeping with God's commanded to generously provide for the poor. Normally debt is given to someone who has some expectation of paying the debt back; with the poor there is not such an expectation. But those incurring debt were in need, if not yet poor. Forgiving of all debt is then seen as ultimately implementing God's command of giving, expecting nothing in return.

> Now in case a countryman of yours becomes poor and his means with regard to you falter, then you are to sustain him, like a stranger or a sojourner, that he may live with you. Do not take usurious interest from him, but revere your God, that your countryman may live with you. You shall not give him your silver at interest, nor your food for gain. I am the LORD your God, who brought you out of the land of Egypt to give you the land of Canaan and to be your God.
>
> Lev 25:35–38

This principle is repeated by Christ in the Gospels, but this grace is now extended to all, not just countrymen.

> If you lend to those from whom you expect to receive, what credit is that to you? Even sinners lend to sinners in order to receive back the same amount. But love your enemies, and do good, and lend, expecting nothing in return; and your reward will be great, and you will be sons of the Most High; for He Himself is kind to ungrateful and evil men. Be merciful, just as your Father is merciful.
>
> Luke 6:34–36

The passage in Leviticus 25 continues and provides further instructions about the poor. It begins with an important conditional statement.

> If a countryman of yours becomes so poor with regard to you that he sells himself to you, you shall not subject him to a slaves service. He shall be with you as a hired man, as if he were a sojourner; he shall serve with you until the year of jubilee. He shall then go out from you, he and his sons with him, and shall go back to his family, that he may return to the property of his forefathers.
>
> Lev 25:39–41

It seems that God's preference is for the fortunate to take care of the poor, expecting nothing in return, rather than take them as slaves. In some sense, the fortunate decides whether the person is so poor that he should accept, as a slave, the one selling himself as a slave. The choice to take care of them without insisting they be sold as a slave seems to be preferred. "But if you do then ..." — God is so intent on the dignity of the poor, and on an attitude of grace towards the unfortunate that he commands that if the decision is made to accept one selling themselves into slavery, that the one accepting this person is not to subject the poor to a slave's

5.2 The Sabbath Year and the Jubilee

service, but that of a free hired man. God is here seen going to considerable lengths to take care of the poor. How do we measure up to this standard?

The restoration of the land to its original owners during the year of the Jubilee was an economic sledge hammer leveling all economic empires, small and great. The land lays fallow, all slaves are freed, debts are forgiven, and if this isn't disrupting enough, ownership of the land reverts to its original owners. Some who had started out with little and gained large holdings started over again. Those who had land and lost it now have it back. Families are reunited and joy is heard in the land.

How in the world could they do this? How can we implement the theological principles behind the practices and pour them into modern societies? For a modern American or European we must undergo a radical change of heart. We must abandon conventional wisdom. Jettison just about all we believe about possessions, property, money, the poor and needy. We must throw off man's understanding of prudence and adopt God's understanding. And finally, we Christians must live in functioning communities, rather than as collections of individuals.

What do the Sabbath year and the Jubilee reveal about God's attitude toward economics? If anything is clear it is that God does not want there to be economic empires, entities of highly concentrated wealth and power. We have heard this from Christ.

> Do not store up for yourselves treasures on earth, where moth and rust destroy, and where thieves break in and steal. But store up for yourselves treasures in heaven, where neither moth nor rust destroys, and where thieves do not break in or steal; for where your treasure is, there your heart will be also.
>
> Matt 6:19–21

It is the same principle structurally implemented in the Sabbath year and Jubilee in the kingdom of Israel.[8]

By these principles, God is preventing the centralization of wealth and power. Centralized wealth and power are virtually always abused and used for the benefit of the powerful and their friends. This principle is seldom violated. In 1 Samuel God develops this claim fully as he warns the Israelites of the consequences of monarchy. (1 Sam 8:10–18) Governments are the greatest concentrations of wealth and power that exist.

Contained within the Sabbath year and Jubilee is a most unusual principle, at least from a modern person's perspective. The principle is contentment, the thought that we can actually have enough. This is radical for most of us in the modern world. Today, we can never have enough. Some industries rely heavily on this principle. Consider the computer industry. Every few months the big manufacturers, come out with the latest and greatest and make it so that most have to upgrade simply to maintain backward compatibility, even if they don't need the extra performance. Other examples are available, but this one is sufficient to make the point. Unlike our modern economies, centered on the individual accumulation of wealth and consumption, the Jewish economy was centered on people. Wealth and resources were not ends in themselves, but means to provide for all.[9]

Sabbath year and Jubilee practices brought social and economic justice to the poor and disadvantaged. Clearly, God's in-

---

[8]Perhaps we need to rethink conventional wisdom that says we need a sizable fortune to permit a retirement in absolute comfort and total independence.

[9]It is important to see that the Jewish people did not look to a centralized power to distribute wealth, nor did they abandon the notion of the ownership of property. However, ownership of property was understood to mean stewardship of God's property. Those today, who still believe that there is salvation, social and economic justice, in the modern nation state will continue to be disappointed. Real social and economic justice can only be achieved in the Kingdom of God (the Body of Christ, the Church).

5.2 The Sabbath Year and the Jubilee

terests are not only 'spiritual', for he is concerned with the treatment and care of the disadvantaged, the poor and needy, those on the lower rungs of society. But the care and treatment of the poor and disadvantaged are not things found outside the spiritual realm. Our response to the poor and disadvantaged reveal the depth of our love for others and our love and obedience to God. We do not diminish our personal spirituality by addressing these social and economic issues, for if we are truly spiritual we will be concerned with the same things God is concerned.

Refusing to help those in need caries serious consequences. Look at how the nation of Israel was condemned by God and how Christ condemned the Jews of his day for their refusal to help and their exploitation of the poor and unfortunate. Some of God's greatest condemnations are reserved for this kind of disobedience.

Just how interested is God in these principles and the practices based on them? It is not a passing interest to be sure. God's commitment is revealed in his command that they become a part of the very fabric of the Israelite kingdom through the Law of Moses. These were essential, not optional, and God wanted to make sure they knew his will in these matters. How might we order our lives to ensure that we carry out what is on God's heart?

Chapter 6

The Kingdom: Sabbath & Jubilee Theology

Today it is difficult, if not impossible, to implement many of the specific practices of the Sabbath year and Jubilee, but the theological principles provide us with clear direction for the implementation of practices that demonstrate God's love to the brethren within the Kingdom and those in the world. We have mentioned some of the theological principles above, but in this chapter we will be more deliberate.

6.1 Motivation

God himself provides the example for Sabbath year and Jubilee principles. God liberates, forgives and frees. His provision encompasses the extraordinary and the ordinary; food, air, rain, sun, and he does this for the good and the evil alike. He generously provides, not grudgingly, but willingly. He extends his common grace to all and his special grace to his children, and we are made rich by his gifts.

Our motivation to liberate comes from God's liberation of us. For the Jew, his greatest experience of liberation was his deliverance from bondage in Egypt. "You shall remember that you were a slave in the land of Egypt, and the LORD your God redeemed you; therefore I command you this today." (Deut 15:15, see also Lev 25:42,55)

For the liberation of the poor (their care and deliverance from their need) we hear God saying, "I am the LORD your God, who brought you out of the land of Egypt to give you the land of Canaan and to be your God." (Lev 25:38) Giving to those in need is based on God's example; He gave the land of Canaan to the Jew along with all its abundance and himself as their God. How then can we withhold our bounty from the poor?

Now, in the New Covenant, by virtue of Christ's death and resurrection, our motivation and example are even greater. We have not simply been delivered from physical bondage as the Jew, but the power of sin has been utterly defeated, death has been defeated, we have been completely forgiven, we have been delivered into the Kingdom of God, God now dwells in us as he did in the Temple and we have a sure future and hope; all the things for which the Old Testament saints looked we now have. Liberation and forgiveness have been lavished on us. Seeing this, we have every reason and a divine example to motivate us to practice the principles of the Kingdom.

6.2 Something Else to be Learned

We have frequently mentioned that God uses trials to bring about maturity. The culmination of this maturity is seen in a Christian who demonstrates the character of Christ, one who is being conformed to the image of Christ — a servant. We have not spent a great deal of time on this subject, but as we study the principles of the Kingdom of God we will carefully examine the life and teachings of Christ. As we do, we will find a clear picture of the character of Christ, how lovely is Christ and what it means to be made in his image.

6.3 Comprehensive Salvation

Before we begin this discussion it will be helpful to consider the comprehensive nature of God's salvation, for we often limit its scope.

To begin, it is helpful to consider the consequences of the Fall of Man. These are enumerated below.

1) Man came under God's condemnation. Man's relationship with God was broken. Man is now a rebel. His eternal destiny is hell.

    1.1) Death and physical corruption, disease, old age, etc. are now part of our existence. The body turns to dust.

    1.2) All of man's relationships have been damaged. There are now barriers between men when once there were none.

    1.3) Suffering and difficulty come from the evil acts of men.

       1.3.1) Men enslave one another, abuse one another and kill one another. They bring social and economic injustice.

2) The whole creation, the physical world, has been subjected to slavery to corruption.

    2.1) Men suffer as the fallen creation convulses.

Therefore, given the results of the Fall we see that God's salvation must comprehend at least the following:

1) Man must be reconciled to God. Man must be remade and conformed into the image of Christ.

    1.1) Death and corruption must be defeated. Man must be resurrected to incorruption.

1.2) Relationships among men must be restored. The barriers must be removed.

1.3) Rather than oppress, men must love and do good to all.

2) The creation must be delivered from its slavery to corruption.

2.1) Men must no longer suffer from the convulsions of the fallen creation.

God's salvation must clearly be a comprehensive salvation, one not only involving man's soul, but all of creation.

It is Christ, the creator, who brings salvation to his creation. We must not think that salvation is primarily for the soul, that is, the restoration of man's relationship to God. It extends to all of God's creation. Men are not simply souls with bodies where the body is seen as less important or perhaps even irrelevant. No, we are a composite and God will bring salvation to both the soul and the body in the resurrection. Death and the grave will ultimately be defeated and our bodies will shed their corruption and clothe themselves in incorruption. Not only this, but salvation is extended to all of the physical creation, for it too will be made new being delivered from its slavery to corruption. God's salvation is for the whole creation in all its aspects.

But we must not stop here in our discussion, for we have left out several other ways in which the Fall has corrupted the world. In the Fall all relationships between men were damaged, some entirely broken, and need restored. The restoration of these relationships has always been God's plan and we see his concern for it in the Law of Moses. We see it most clearly, however, in the life of Christ and in the development of his Church. The refrain we hear over and over is there are no longer any barriers between men. All men are considered our neighbor, we are to do good

6.3 Comprehensive Salvation

to all men, even our enemy. Racial, social, national, economic, and religious barriers are meaningless. There is nothing that now separates us.

Beyond this there is another level of salvation that interests God. Great suffering and difficulty come to men from the evil acts of men and the convulsions of the fallen creation. From men come murder, slavery, social and economic exploitation, oppression, persecution and the like. From the convulsions of the fallen creation comes death, destruction, destitution, poverty and famine. It is God's intention that mankind be saved from these things as well, for one day God will put an end to it all. God has not yet implemented the all-encompassing salvation that he has promised, but he has stepped in and brought salvation, first through the work of Christ and then through the Body of Christ now in the world, those who are citizens of the Kingdom of God. In the Kingdom we see God's children bringing God's salvation to the oppressed and needy, first to those in his Kingdom and then to those outside.

This last aspect of salvation is extremely important to God and is well documented in both the Old and New Testaments. In the Old Testament we find teachings on the Sabbath year and Jubilee. These are all about the care of the poor and needy, social and economic justice, the prevention of the accumulation of wealth and the centralization of power that comes from it, an equitable redistribution of wealth and saving ourselves from unlimited production and consumption. In the New Testament we find these principles continued.[1]

---

[1] It is essential to understand that I do not mean to extend the social and economic aspects of God's salvation to society at large. It is possible only within the Body of Christ, those who are members of the Kingdom of God. I do not believe that the competing political and social structures outside of the Kingdom of God can really participate in this salvation. If they do, it is only a poor imitation. Those in the Kingdom of God can,

God's salvation is comprehensive; what we call the spiritual as well as the physical are encompassed by it. In this way, we see that the Kingdom is not simply about "the spiritual," that is, personal salvation or a spiritual union of believers. It certainly encompasses these, but it includes a full-bodied notion of community where forgiveness, love and concrete physical care for others is demonstrated.

6.4 Liberation

The Sabbath year and the Jubilee demonstrate that God does not want the slave to remain perpetually in bondage; he does not want the one under crushing debt to remain crushed; he does not want people to remain in a landless condition and he wants the poor to be liberated from their poverty. The Sabbath year and the Jubilee addressed all of these.

In the New Testament, Christ begins his ministry by speaking to these very matters.

> The Spirit of the Lord is upon Me, Because He anointed Me to preach the gospel to the poor. He has sent Me to proclaim release to the captives, and recovery of sight to the blind, To set free those who are oppressed, to proclaim the favorable year of the Lord.
>
> Luke 4:18,19

It is important to understand that the Jew of this time understood these statements to be dealing with real poor, real captives, real blind people, real oppressed people and a real declaration of a Jubilee. The Jewish nation had known these words since the time

---

of course, extend love, forgiveness and care to those outside the Kingdom, but the intention is not primarily to reform these other kingdoms, but to demonstrate the desirability of the Kingdom of God by our actions, and by this draw them into the Kingdom.

that Isaiah wrote them; they were part of their future hope and here was a man claiming that he was the Messiah, fulfilling this prophecy before them. What was not entirely obvious to these Jews was that he had come to liberate them spiritually as well. They were primarily looking for a Messiah who would restore the Kingdom to Israel.

We do not want to ignore the spiritual aspects of this passage, for Christ came to liberate us from the kingdom of Satan, the power of sin, and our impending eternal punishment, but let us not forget that Christ was also intensely concerned for the poor, the captives, the sick, and in general, social and economic justice.

Christ had much more to say about Sabbath year and Jubilee principles, some of which is negative in nature, for Christ condemns exploitive practices that violate God's commands regarding the poor, oppressed, captive and sick. Christ seems to go out of his way to remind people of their responsibility, and if necessary, their disobedience and confronts them. Some of the more important instances are discussed below.

The Evil Servant, Matt 18:21–35

This parable is part of an answer Christ gave Peter regarding a question about forgiveness.

> Then Peter came and said to Him, "Lord, how often shall my brother sin against me and I forgive him? Up to seven times?" Jesus said to him, "I do not say to you, up to seven times, but up to seventy times seven."
>
> Matt 18:21,22

The parable that follows the question involves a king who has decided to settle accounts with his slaves. Two of his slaves are mentioned, one of which owes him a sum which he could never repay.[2] Seeing that this slave could not pay back the debt, the

---

[2] The situation the slave found himself in was not unrealistic for the day.

king decided to sell the slave and his family to recover some of his loss. Upon hearing this the slave, prostrating himself on the ground, begged for more time. The king, seeing the man's distress, had compassion on him and released him from his debt. However, this same slave, after having been forgiven this huge debt, went out and found a fellow slave who owed him a far smaller sum and demanded payment. When his fellow slave asked for more time, he was refused and placed in debtor's prison until the amount should be repaid. The king, upon hearing this, condemned the evil slave and carried out his original plan.

Christ ends this parable with a dire warning: "My heavenly Father will also do the same to you, if each of you does not forgive his brother from your heart." (Matt 18:35) Not only are we to forgive as often as we are wronged, but we are to forgive, from our hearts, any debt, no matter how large. Here we see a condemnation of the refusal to liberate from debt. This parable is usually spiritualized and *debt* is not seen as actual monetary debt, but only as a wrong suffered. Given the abuse of debt by the rich and their refusal to implement the Sabbath year release from debt, we must acknowledge that debt, as used here, holds both for real monetary debt and wrongs suffered. It is not unlike the use of debt found in the Lord's prayer.

Zaccheus, Luke 19:1–10

Tax collectors were at the lowest social level within Jewish society. The reason was the abuse the tax collectors visited on the population. These men were usually Jews who had bid on, and won, the tax collector's contract from the local authorities. The authorities gave considerable latitude to tax collecting activities permitting tax collectors to take in amounts in considerable ex-

---

During this time, the exploitation of the poor was rampant and the debt the poor could accumulate over time was crushing.

6.4 Liberation

cess of what the authorities required, an obviously exploitive and properly despised practice. By this, the tax collector could amass an enormous fortune at the expense of everyone else. It was a raw use of power used for self-gratification with complete disregard of the effect on others.

Zaccheus, the chief tax collector of Jericho, one of the most hated men in the city, had heard that Christ was to pass by. Wanting to see Christ, but being a small man and not in front of the crowd, he climbed a tree. To his surprise, Christ looked directly up at him and said, "Zaccheus, hurry and come down, for today I must stay at your house." Can you imagine the surprise he must have felt? Zaccheus had obviously heard about Christ and knew a great deal of what he taught. Perhaps he was intrigued and maybe even convicted by some of the things he had heard. By his response we see that he must have already been under conviction. At Christ's command he got down off the tree and gladly received Christ. On the way to his house some in the crowd who saw this exchange became indignant and spoke out, "He has gone to be the guest of a man who is a sinner." Upon hearing this Zaccheus stopped and spoke to the Lord in front of the crowd.

> Behold, Lord, half of my possessions I will give to the poor, and if I have defrauded anyone of anything, I will give back four times as much.
>
> Luke 9:8

Christ replied, "Today salvation has come to this house, because he too, is a son of Abraham." Zaccheus understood that it was not enough to simply find salvation for himself; as he received liberation and forgiveness he knew that he would have to engage in the liberating practices that he had heard Christ teach. He had heard that Christ was interested in the proper treatment of the poor and disadvantaged. He therefore, gave half his wealth away to the poor, liberating them from their poverty, and used the rest to make restitution. Zaccheus' faith was not dead but alive, being demonstrated in the concrete principles of the Sabbath year and Jubilee. His true spirituality overflowed into action.

Devouring Widow's Houses, Mark 12:40; Matt 23:14
Here, Christ condemns the religious practices that were designed to extract wealth from the needy. Rather than liberating, they were placing people in financial need. In this case, it was a means of taking the wealth and property of widows, some of the most vulnerable people in society. We see a similar mechanism in the practice of *corban* (Matt 15:1–9, Mark 7:1–13) where an older child could declare that all of what he had would be given as an offering to the temple, thus leaving nothing for the care of his elderly parents, thereby, failing to obey the commandment to honor mother and father.

A Proper Kingdom Dinner, Luke 14:12–14
These two verses come from a much longer record of a Sabbath meal at a Pharisees' house. (Luke 14:1–24) The encounter is extraordinary and we will consider it in some detail, beyond what is needed to make the point made in verses 12–14. By this time Christ is on the outs with the Pharisees and they are watching his every move. Perhaps by accident, or more probably by design, a man with dropsy sat in front of Christ. Taking the challenge, Christ asks the Pharisees and scribes whether it is lawful to heal on the Sabbath. Refusing to answer, Christ heals the man and sends him away and asks whether anyone at the table would not pull out an ox that had fallen into a well on the Sabbath? Again there is no answer. They have failed to capture Christ; his understanding of the Sabbath is correct and theirs is wrong and they know it, even if they don't like it.

After this confrontation Christ proceeds to give a lesson on pride and humility by telling a parable. In this parable a guest

6.4 Liberation

comes to a party, and thinking too highly of himself he takes a seat of honor. Later on another comes to the party, one whom the host considers more important. To accommodate the new arrival, the guest who took the seat of honor is asked, in front of all those present, to sit in a position of lesser importance.[3] In a gathering such as this there is always a considerable amount of posturing and glory-seeking; men making sure they get the recognition they think they deserve. Knowing that many of those at this meal have had these same thoughts, and may even have acted on them, makes the parable all the more challenging to those present. The principle being taught follows necessarily. "For everyone who exalts himself will be humbled, and he who humbles himself will be exalted." (Luke 14:11)

The Pharisee had, as is usual, invited his friends and acquaintances, people who could repay his generosity. Knowing this, and wishing to communicate an important Kingdom principle, Christ simply states, without couching it in a parable, how one gives a meal in the Kingdom. Christ's words are so penetrating that we include them here.

> When you give a luncheon or a dinner, do not invite your friends or your brothers or your relatives or rich neighbors, otherwise they may also invite you in return and that will be your repayment. But when you give a reception, invite the poor, the crippled, the lame, the blind, and you will be blessed, since they do not have the means to repay you; for you will be repaid at the resurrection of the righteous.
>
> When one of those who were reclining at the table with Him heard this, he said to Him, "Blessed is everyone who will eat bread in the Kingdom of God!"
>
> Luke 14:12–15

---

[3] Christ may have been recounting an actual occurrence at this or some other meal that the people at this meal were aware.

At least someone at the meal seemed to understand what Christ was saying. What he failed to understand was that the Kingdom was breaking out before his very eyes and the man bringing it in was sitting before him.

There is so much here, but look who are to be invited. We are to invite those who cannot repay, the truly needy, those needing real physical and monetary aid, liberation of the kind that they desperately need.[4] Ordering our lives in this way, and demonstrating faith and love of this type, is what James and John talked about. This is living faith and love, faith and love with works.

The Rich Man and Lazarus, Luke 16:19–31

There are several lessons to be learned from this parable but we will narrow our focus on just one. The status of the rich man and Lazarus is presented in verses 19 and 20.

> Now there was a rich man, and he habitually dressed in purple and fine linen, joyously living in splendor every day. And a poor man named Lazarus was laid at his gate, covered with sores, and longing to be fed with the crumbs which were falling from the rich mans table; besides, even the dogs were coming and licking his sores.
>
> Luke 16:19,20

The implication is that the rich man did little if anything for Lazarus, he simply ignored him despite passing by him every time he went in or out of his gate. The rich man showed a callous indifference. Liberating Lazarus from his obvious need was not a consideration. In light of the Sabbath year and Jubilee practices, this denial of assistance to a fellow Jew was a gross violation of the Mosaic Law and rightly condemned.

---

[4]Please understand I am not neglecting spiritual need or removing it to a lesser level. I am only emphasizing physical care at this time just as Christ is doing.

6.4 Liberation

As happens to all men, Lazarus dies and is followed in death by the rich man. After his death, the rich man finds himself in torment and Lazarus in Paradise, Abraham's bosom. Their conditions are now reversed. The rich man suffers the punishment that God reserves for those who close their hearts to the needy and refuse to liberate them. This is worked out in detail in Matt 25:31-46, a scene of God's final judgment of the nations where the ultimate destiny of all is decided. Notice the criterion for judgment. Those who had been engaged in liberation are accepted, those who were not are rejected. Notice, also, how personally Christ takes this. Those who had engaged in liberation of the unfortunate were considered by Christ as having done the acts to himself.

> ... Truly I say to you, to the extent that you did it to one of these brothers of Mine, even the least of them, you did it to Me.
>
> Matt 25:40

while those who had refused were considered to have refused to do these things to Christ.

> ... Truly I say to you, to the extent that you did not do it to one of the least of these, you did not do it to Me. These will go away into eternal punishment, but the righteous into eternal life.
>
> Matt 25:45,46

Let us not be confused by this passage: practicing liberation is not what saves us, but it is what those who are really saved practice. The proper question is, "What does it mean to be saved?" It is not simply having a proper doctrinal understanding of salvation followed by a public confession and baptism. Satan and his servants have excellent doctrine and have at times even confessed Jesus as the Christ while he was on the earth. The point is this, if good works do not follow upon conversion, then you are evidently not one of God's children. Faith without works is dead, and this not only includes the fruits of the spirit understood as godly character, but the extension of material support to the needy as well. (Jas 2:15,16 and 1 John 3:16–18) This is what salvation looks like.

The Unfaithful Steward, Luke 16:1–13

In this parable, a master had found out that he had an unfaithful steward. Upon realizing that he had been found out, the steward devises a plan to deliver himself from his predicament. Being a manager of his master's financial affairs, his plan is to settle his master's accounts in an equitable manner in hopes of being graciously received by these former creditors after he is fired by his current master. It appears that he had demanded payment in excess of what was required by his master and was pocketing the excess. By reducing the creditors' payments to what was actually owed, he was able to both reduce his master's accounts receivables and endear himself to those creditors whom he hoped would give him a job or take him in after his current master had removed him. For this the steward is praised. He had finally dealt justly practicing Sabbath year and Jubilee principles.

Now let us turn to the early church and the apostolic writings and find out what they have to say on this matter.

The Early Church, Acts 2:43–45; Acts 4:32–35

In the beginning of Acts we have the inception of the early church and we find them practicing Sabbath year and Jubilee principles from the very start. It seems to have been the most natural thing to do given the voluminous instruction Christ had given on these matters. In Acts chapter two we find that

> Everyone kept feeling a sense of awe; and many wonders and signs were taking place through the apostles. And all those who had believed were together and had all things in

6.4 Liberation

> common; and they began selling their property and possessions and were sharing them with all, as anyone might have need.
>
> Acts 2:43–45

Later in Acts chapter four we find the disciples engaging in the same practices.

> And the congregation of those who believed were of one heart and soul; and not one of them claimed that anything belonging to him was his own, but all things were common property to them. And with great power the apostles were giving testimony to the resurrection of the Lord Jesus, and abundant grace was upon them all. For there was not a needy person among them, for all who were owners of land or houses would sell them and bring the proceeds of the sales and lay them at the apostles feet, and they would be distributed to each as any had need.
>
> Acts 4:32–35

These early Christians were living exactly as Jesus had taught. This was faith with works. There was not a needy person among them. Can we say that of our churches today?

It is crucial that we see the cause and effect. The apostles' witness to the resurrection of Christ to the world was with power because there was not a needy person among them. Those around them knew these people were Christians. People could not live like this unless something extraordinary had happened to them. It was just as Christ had said,

> A new commandment I give to you, that you love one another, even as I have loved you, that you also love one another. By this all men will know that you are My disciples, if you have love for one another.
>
> John 13:34,35

In our churches today, we do not need 'relevance,' hot music, theater and ministries that care for 'felt needs,' but rather we need to live radical lives of forgiveness, servanthood, mutual submission, caring for the brethren. If we did we would be more than relevant, and powerful in our witness to the world.

The Gift to the Jerusalem Church, 2 Cor 8,9
Paul, seeing that the church in Jerusalem was undergoing considerable persecution and in serious need, sought, from among the churches he was traveling, a monetary gift for the Jerusalem church. Here was a real physical need that could be addressed by a monetary offering. Once again we see living faith with works, works of material assistance.

Withholding Help, James 2:15,16; 1 John 3:17,18
These two passages are perhaps the most searing, apart from the words of Christ, on the subject of material and physical care. Withholding material assistance is condemned in no uncertain terms.

> What use is it, my brethren, if someone says he has faith but he has no works? Can that faith save him? If a brother or sister is without clothing and in need of daily food, and one of you says to them, "Go in peace, be warmed and be filled," and yet you do not give them what is necessary for their body, what use is that? Even so faith, if it has no works, is dead, being by itself.
>
> Jas 2:14,17

In 1 John we find a similar remark, but in this case with regard to love.

> But whoever has the world's goods, and sees his brother in need and closes his heart against him, how does the love of God abide in him? Little children, let us not love with

word or with tongue, but in deed and truth.

I John 3:17,18

It is difficult to say anything beyond what is said in these passages, but lest we have missed it, we must see that love based in true spirituality ultimately drives us to help others physically, materially and monetarily. Saying, "I will pray for you" or having warm thoughts toward others in need is completely inadequate and properly condemned.

Misuse of Riches, James 5:1–6
James has more to say on this topic. In addition to what he has said already, James has one last word on the misuse of riches, condemning it with considerable intensity.

> Come now, you rich, weep and howl for your miseries which are coming upon you. Your riches have rotted and your garments have become moth-eaten. Your gold and your silver have rusted; and their rust will be a witness against you and will consume your flesh like fire. It is in the last days that you have stored up your treasure! Behold, the pay of the laborers who mowed your fields, and which has been withheld by you, cries out against you; and the outcry of those who did the harvesting has reached the ears of the Lord of Sabaoth. You have lived luxuriously on the earth and led a life of wanton pleasure; you have fattened your hearts in a day of slaughter. You have condemned and put to death the righteous man; he does not resist you.
>
> James 5:1–6

Many of us read this and find consolation saying, "I'm glad that I am not like this man." But we must honestly ask, "Does any of this apply to us?" We may not have withheld wages, but have we stored up treasure for ourselves, have we lived luxuriously and led a life of pleasure denying ourselves little or nothing? Have we, in an effort to "get the best deal," essentially robbed another of a fair price or fair wage? For many of us in the Western world our answer must be yes. Certainly we have neglected the needs of others, perhaps not deliberately, but simply due to apathy.

6.5   Forgiveness

Forgiving debt was an essential part of the Sabbath year. It meant a new start for those who had fallen on difficult times, perhaps due to crop failure, loss of a husband or some natural disaster. It also prevented them from having to sell themselves into slavery; however, if this happened they would have been set free in the Sabbath year.

In the New Testament we find forgiveness extended to include all people at all times, the Sabbath year never ends.

No Limit to Forgiveness, Matt 18:23–35, Luke 17:3,4
We have already looked at the parable of the evil servant in Matthew 18 and seen his unwillingness to forgive. At the end of the parable we find this frightening warning.

> And his lord, moved with anger, handed him over to the torturers until he should repay all that was owed him. My heavenly Father will also do the same to you, if each of you does not forgive his brother from your heart.
>
> Matt 18:34,35

Recall that the context of Matthew 18:34,35 is the forgiveness of monetary debt. Recall also that when Peter first asked Christ how often we should forgive our brother, Christ replied that, "we are to forgive seventy times seven." Christ was clearly indicating that forgiveness is always extended. We find a similar passage in Luke 17.

6.5 Forgiveness

> Be on your guard! If your brother sins, rebuke him; and if he repents, forgive him. And if he sins against you seven times a day, and returns to you seven times, saying, 'I repent,' forgive him.
>
> Luke 17:3,4

We again see the requirement to always forgive those who repeatedly sin against us.

The Lord's Prayer, Matt 6:9–15, Luke 11:1–4
In Matthew 6:9–15 we have Christ's instructions for prayer.

> Pray, then, in this way:
> Our Father who is in heaven,
> Hallowed be Your name.
> Your Kingdom come.
> Your will be done,
> On earth as it is in heaven.
> Give us this day our daily bread.
> And forgive us our debts, as we also have forgiven our debtors.
> And do not lead us into temptation, but deliver us from evil. For Yours is the Kingdom and the power and the glory forever. Amen.
>
> Matt 6:9–13

The only part that Christ provides commentary on is the one on forgiveness. Once again we see the frightening warning.

> For if you forgive others for their transgressions, your heavenly Father will also forgive you. But if you do not forgive others, then your Father will not forgive your transgressions.
>
> Matt 6:14,15

This is an extremely simple prayer, but it perfectly captures how and what we should pray for. It also teaches us how to order our lives, what to focus on and what is on God's heart. And finally it shows us that God demands that we forgive all, should we call him our Father.[5]

Father Forgive Them, Luke 23:34

The greatest act of forgiveness is that which God extends to us by virtue of the death and resurrection of Christ. We might meditate on this act of forgiveness for an eternity and still not know its depths. But the profundity of this forgiveness is deepened when we consider how Christ prayed for those who were responsible for his crucifixion and immediate suffering.

> Father, forgive them; for they do not know what they are doing.
>
> Luke 23:34

Likewise, we find Stephen, the first martyr, praying the same thing just before he dies at the hands of his persecutors, "Lord, do not hold this sin against them!" (Acts 7:60)

Forgiveness is for all, at all times, and we have no reason to deny it to others, even as they kill us, given what God has done for us and forgiven us, both in his common and special grace. Let us not forget that the forgiveness we extend is not only for wrongs done against us, but for any sort of debt owed us, monetary or otherwise.[6]

---

[5] A similar warning is found in Mark 11:25, "Whenever you stand praying, forgive, if you have anything against anyone, so that your Father who is in heaven will also forgive you your transgressions."

[6] This is not to say that we should never expect to have a monetary debt repaid if we have agreed that the loan should be paid back. But even in these cases we should act with mercy, just as God is merciful towards us, should we see that the debt is unreasonable due to some new circumstance. Or, perhaps we just need to be merciful, even if there is no special need. When we do

Extending forgiveness, especially from the heart, can be extremely difficult. But do it we must. It must be extended to all, at all times. Make no mistake, a life committed to this kind of forgiveness is an extraordinary life and impossible to live out in our own strength. Our only hope is to live in obedience to God, continue in prayer, devotion to the Scriptures, and be controlled by the Spirit of God, complemented with excruciatingly honest self-examination.

6.6 Generosity and Compassion

Compassion and generosity are essential components of the Sabbath year and Jubilee. Forgiving of debt and the release of slaves are both compassionate acts as the one freeing and releasing sees the human hardship and tragedy involved in such situations. But compassion does not remain a warm fuzzy feeling of good will toward another; it goes into action, even generous action.

In regard to freeing slaves we find that the releasing master is to help the freed slave get a new start. Sufficient means to begin anew must be given. Simple freedom is completely inadequate. God's material blessing to the master must be extended to the material provision made to the slave upon his release.

> If your kinsman, a Hebrew man or woman, is sold to you, then he shall serve you six years, but in the seventh year you shall set him free. When you set him free, you shall not send him away empty-handed. You shall furnish him liberally from your flock and from your threshing floor and from your wine vat; you shall give to him as the LORD your God has blessed you.
>
> Deut. 15:12–14

---

forgive we must forgive from our hearts. God is not only interested in the proper act, but the proper attitude of heart.

For most of us today it would be enough to simply release the slave. God, however, does not stop there, he wants the slave to be given every advantage to make a new start. After all, what is freedom worth if one is not given the means to assert it?

6.6.1 Compassion

In the New Testament we find many lessons on and instances of compassion. Matthew 12:7 (and similarly, 9:13) records one such lesson.

> But if you had known what this means, 'I desire compassion, and not a sacrifice,' you would not have condemned the innocent.
>
> Matt 12:7

Christ's comment arises from a confrontation with the Pharisees regarding Sabbath practices. On a certain Sabbath, Christ and his disciples became hungry and subsequently entered a field and began eating the heads of the grain. Upon seeing this, the Pharisees challenged Christ; how can you violate the Sabbath law? This violation, however, had no basis in the law of Moses; Jewish scholars had added this prohibition. To this, Christ replied that compassion is to be desired rather than a commitment to the arbitrary traditions of men. Importantly, the word used here for compassion does not simply mean a feeling of compassion, but is rather active in nature. It is seen as the emotion that necessarily precedes an act of compassion.

Christ is also seen having compassion on, and then acting compassionately towards, people whom he sees as sheep without a shepherd (Matt 9:36, Mark 6:34), crowds needing to be fed (Matt 14:14; 15:32, Mark 8:2), toward the blind (Matt 20:34) and the sick (Mark 1:41), a grieving mother (Luke 7:13), and the rebellious city of Jerusalem (Matt 23:37) just prior to his supreme

6.6 Generosity and Compassion

act of compassion, death on the cross.

We also see compassion leading to action expressed in the parables of the Good Samaritan (Luke 10:33) and the Prodigal son (Luke 15:11–32).

In Colossians 3 we find Paul commanding us to put on a heart of compassion and forgiving all.

> So, as those who have been chosen of God, holy and beloved, put on a heart of compassion, kindness, humility, gentleness and patience; bearing with one another, and forgiving each other, whoever has a complaint against anyone; just as the Lord forgave you, so also should you. Beyond all these things put on love, which is the perfect bond of unity. Let the peace of Christ rule in your hearts, to which indeed you were called in one body; and be thankful.
>
> Col. 3:12–15

Before continuing, contemplate for a moment what is being said here. It is absolutely extraordinary. Imagine living with brothers and sisters in Christ who lived in such a manner, it would be that next to heaven itself. And imagine the power that such a body of Christians would have to affect their world. By the work of Christ and the power of God's Spirit, this is the Kingdom breaking out on earth giving us an image, even if imperfect, what heaven will be like, and moving with power in the world as we saw in the early church in Acts 4. May we ask God to give us a vision and a commitment to live like this.

6.6.2 Generosity

Generosity is that quality of compassion in action that gives these acts a golden luster. It is more than doing the right thing, but doing it in excess. Christ's commands in this regard are more than most can understand, let alone obey. We are to give to him who asks (Matt 5:42) — we give indiscriminately. We are to give expecting nothing in return (Luke 6:35,36) — sheer insanity. Could he really mean this? And we are to give to those who cannot repay us (Luke 14:12–14) — fiscal irresponsibility. No, this is neither insanity nor irresponsibility; Christ is not telling us to do something that violates common sense; this is common sense, this is real wisdom in action. But why should we do this? Because this is exactly the way that God has and continues to deal with us. What can we give back to God that could even remotely compare in value to what he has done for us? Absolutely nothing.

That this is wisdom is sure, but it is clearly not man's wisdom, but is rather seen as foolishness by men. But is not this always the case?

> But a natural man does not accept the things of the Spirit of God, for they are foolishness to him; and he cannot understand them, because they are spiritually appraised.
>
> 1 Cor 2:14

6.7 Economics: New Testament Emphasis

We have looked at the economics of the Sabbath year and Jubilee within the context of the Old Testament in considerable detail and will now turn our attention to how these principles play out in the New Testament.

6.7.1 Fallow Land

Leaving the land fallow was a cessation of economic activity permitting a refocusing of ones labors leaving time to pursue God, family and community interests more intently, and necessitating that one trust God more fully for their material provision. After all, much of one's economic activity and labor ceased. Seen in this light we can see how many New Testament passages parallel

6.7 Economics: New Testament Emphasis

the command to leave the land fallow in the Sabbath year. In a profound sense leaving the land fallow embodies, at least in part, the command to stop worrying about our provision and be about building the Kingdom of God. (Matt 6:33)

In Matt 6:19–34 (parallel passage Luke 12:13–34) we have one of the central passages of the Sermon on the mount that is directly applicable to our topic. The passage in Luke begins with a request from a person in a crowd following Jesus to have his brother divide the family inheritance with him. To this request Christ pointedly replies, "Beware, and be on your guard against every form of greed; for not even when one has an abundance does his life consist of his possessions." (Luke 12:15) This was a most appropriate answer, for by asking Christ's assistance in such a matter in front of a crowd reveals that his fellow was far too concerned with wealth.

Christ then presented a parable about a very productive rich man who went to great lengths to store up his treasure, the material wealth in which he trusted. In the midst of his work, God came to require his life. Now who was to get his riches? For what had he spent his time and energy? He had sought to ensure his security by his own hand and had not become rich toward God for he had neglected the Kingdom of God. He had not left his field fallow. The sad end for such a person is; "So is the man who stores up treasure for himself, and is not rich toward God." (Luke 12:21) I cannot help but think of upscale Americans spending their time and energy chasing wealth to ensure that they retire in ease, neglecting the Kingdom of God and saving themselves by their own hand.

But one may ask, "Was not this man prudent?" or "You don't mean to say we should be lazy?" or "What should he have perused?" And finally, "How will I be provided for if I should endeavor to be rich toward God seeing this means leaving land fallow?" To all these questions and more Christ gives a wonderful reply.

> For this reason I say to you, do not worry about your life, as to what you will eat; nor for your body, as to what you will put on. For life is more than food, and the body more than clothing. Consider the ravens, for they neither sow nor reap; they have no storeroom nor barn, and yet God feeds them; how much more valuable you are than the birds! And which of you by worrying can add a single hour to his life's span? If then you cannot do even a very little thing, why do you worry about other matters? Consider the lilies, how they grow: they neither toil nor spin; but I tell you, not even Solomon in all his glory clothed himself like one of these. But if God so clothes the grass in the field, which is alive today and tomorrow is thrown into the furnace, how much more will He clothe you? You men of little faith! And do not seek what you will eat and what you will drink, and do not keep worrying. For all these things the nations of the world eagerly seek; but your Father knows that you need these things. But seek His Kingdom, and these things will be added to you. Do not be afraid, little flock, for your Father has chosen gladly to give you the Kingdom.
>
> Luke 12:22–32

Several things must be emphasized. First, do not worry, God knows we need food and clothing; but see, he takes care of the animals and we are far more valuable than they. Second, we do not have the power to really ensure our provision; we cannot even do a little thing like extend our life a single hour. Third, seeing how faithfully God provides for his creation, how could we consider, even for a moment, that he would not provide for us.[7] Fourth,

---

[7] God will certainly provide, but he may not provide at the level we desire.

6.7 Economics: New Testament Emphasis

we must leave our fields fallow, decide not to continue to pursue comfort and riches, and instead seek the Kingdom of God.

In the passage above we hear God's words echoed as they were given to the Hebrews regarding his sure provision in the Sabbath year, the year of the Jubilee, and the following year while they were waiting for the harvest to come in.

> But if you say, "What are we going to eat on the seventh year if we do not sow or gather in our crops?" then I will so order My blessing for you in the sixth year that it will bring forth the crop for three years. When you are sowing the eighth year, you can still eat old things from the crop, eating the old until the ninth year when its crop comes in.
>
> Lev 25:20–22

It must have seemed completely unrealistic to expect to live on the produce of one year for full three years. But we are talking about God, not just anyone, and those who obey him and leave their land fallow will be taken care of. But notice, with what should we expect or be content? Is it a nice house, a wonderful job where everyone appreciates us, superb health? What we are promised is a relationship with God himself, life with our brothers and sisters in the Kingdom of God, for God has gladly given us the Kingdom (Luke 12:32). Given these, how could life get any better. Food and clothing ought to be enough.

> If we have food and covering, with these we shall be content. But those who want to get rich fall into temptation and a snare and many foolish and harmful desires which plunge men into ruin and destruction. For the love of money is a root of all sorts of evil, and some by longing for it have wandered away from the faith and pierced themselves with

---

We must first be satisfied with God himself and then gratefully accept the level of his provision.

many griefs.

1 Tim 6:8–10

But what does it mean to seek the Kingdom of God? Do we pray, witness, study our Bibles, cultivate a deep and meaningful devotional life? Pray for God's will to be done in the world? Yes, by all means, but we cannot stop with these because we have been created for good works, we must take our faith and love and make them living by liberating, spiritually and materially,[8] those we can, and extending forgiveness to all, doing all we can to bring in the Kingdom of God.

Christ provides the meaning for seeking the Kingdom of God in the final two verses of this passage.

> Sell your possessions and give to charity; make yourselves money belts which do not wear out, an unfailing treasure in heaven, where no thief comes near nor moth destroys. For where your treasure is, there your heart will be also.
>
> Luke 12:33,34

This cuts right across the grain of our modern understanding of wealth management in 21st century America. Those who say Christ is something less than an absolute radical are simply wrong. He who has ears to hear let he hear.[9]

Christ makes a similar demand in Luke 14:33 while laying down the requirements for discipleship.

> Now large crowds were going along with Him; and He turned and said to them, "If anyone comes to Me, and does not

---

[8] I am talking about the provision of material needs, not political liberation. The state, that is a government, cannot bring this kind of liberation and forgiveness. I do not even think that it is a good use of our time to try to reform the state. Only God's Kingdom can really accomplish these.

[9] Pertinent to this discussion are Phil 3:7, "But whatever things were gain to me, those things I have counted as loss for the sake of Christ," and Heb 11:26, speaking about Moses "considering the reproach of Christ greater riches than the treasures of Egypt; for he was looking to the reward."

6.7 Economics: New Testament Emphasis

> hate his own father and mother and wife and children and brothers and sisters, yes, and even his own life, he cannot be My disciple. Whoever does not carry his own cross and come after Me cannot be My disciple. For which one of you, when he wants to build a tower, does not first sit down and calculate the cost to see if he has enough to complete it? Otherwise, when he has laid a foundation and is not able to finish, all who observe it begin to ridicule him, saying, 'This man began to build and was not able to finish.' Or what king, when he sets out to meet another king in battle, will not first sit down and consider whether he is strong enough with ten thousand men to encounter the one coming against him with twenty thousand? Or else, while the other is still far away, he sends a delegation and asks for terms of peace. So then, none of you can be My disciple who does not give up all his own possessions.
>
> Therefore, salt is good; but if even salt has become tasteless, with what will it be seasoned? It is useless either for the soil or for the manure pile; it is thrown out. He who has ears to hear, let him hear.
>
> Luke 14:25–35

Notice the wording in verse 33, "none of you can be my disciple who does not give up all his own possessions." It is a categorical denial of the possibility of being a disciple. We can get an idea of what this means by looking at the life of the Church in the New Testament. In the book of Acts we find that no one considered what they possessed as their own. They did not deny that a person could exercise control over the property that God had given them,[10] but they understood that all that they had was owned by God and made it available to any who had need, to such an

---

[10] They would not understand our notion of private property. As they understood it, we are stewards of what God has given, and he has charged us with the disposal of his gifts in a manner that glorifies him.

extent that there were no needy among them. They did not close their heart toward their brothers and sisters in need.

How might we leave our land fallow today? Most of us do not have farms but we do have time and energy, our "land". Might we decide not to take that second job, that promotion, that business opportunity that beacons to a brighter financial future and devote more time and energy to building God's Kingdom? If we do not, we might have to trust God for our provision, or perhaps our economic future would not seem so secure. But what of it? Do we think that we can ensure our future or save ourselves by our own hands? Why not leave our land fallow and seek the Kingdom of God and let God provide as he sees fit?

6.7.2 Debt Release

The release form debt was an important part of the Sabbath year, providing a new start for those who had fallen on bad times. It must be recalled that debt was not accumulated so easily or frivolously as it is in modern times. Debt usually came under conditions of extreme need. Perhaps there was a local crop failure, the animals on a farm died from anthrax, the father or sons on the farm had died making it impossible to harvest the crops, and so on. Debt was, therefore, taken on by those with serious needs.[11] Under these circumstances one can see how appropriate forgiving of debt was.

In the New Testament, during the life of Christ, the rich and powerful Jews, as well as the Romans and the local indigenous kings had found ways to take advantage of the poor, driving them into debt and taking their property, essentially making the poor perpetual indentured servants, if not outright slaves. Even the Pharisees and Sadducees, the religious and national leaders of the

---

[11] Recall, however, that the preferred way to handle this was to simply give to the poor (Lev 25:39–41) rather than turn them into slaves or provide loans.

6.7 Economics: New Testament Emphasis

Jewish nation, had their schemes for enlarging their wealth. It is into this world Christ comes and levels some of his strongest condemnations.

In these conditions we find Christ in his lesson on prayer (Matt 6:9–15), the Lord's prayer, saying "forgive us our debts, as we also have forgiven our debtors." (Matt 6:12) and clarifying with, "For if you forgive others for their transgressions, your heavenly Father will also forgive you. But if you do not forgive others, then your Father will not forgive your transgressions." (Matt 6:14,15). Christ here includes all types of debts, monetary and wrongs suffered; remember that he is addressing people within a particular social and economic context and he does include monetary debt. This is further supported by the confrontations and parables that follow in his ministry.

For example, in the parable of the evil servant in Matt 18:23–35, on which we have spent considerable time, we see condemnation, in the strongest terms, for a refusal to forgive debt.

In the parable of the unfaithful steward (Luke 16:1–13) we find the steward restoring justice to his master's creditors by releasing them from the unreasonable charges for goods which he had inflated. It was a form of debt release.

In Luke 12:30–33, a passage we have just looked at, we find a command to redistribute capital to the poor. Although this is not directly debt relief, it certainly would prevent some poor from entering debt and perhaps enable other poor to extricate themselves from debt.

Although few of us lend money in large amounts, all of us find ourselves providing a loan to people in need. Sometimes it is appropriate that the loan should be repaid, but at other times, even for a reasonable loan which was given with the expectation of repayment, we need to simply extend forgiveness. Mercy and grace need to operate freely.

Modern western capitalism is, to some extent, built on excessive debt and other non-Christian principles. It is, in the short term, a powerful mechanism to continuously expand markets as is needed by western capitalism. This system looks nothing like the economics presented in the New Testament and should be opposed. A good place to start is to teach our children and others of the evils and find creative ways within the church to work around the system that endeavors, with all its might, to drive us into its misguided way of life.

6.7.3 Contentment: Having Enough

Contentment and having enough are centered in the practices and principles of the Sabbath year and Jubilee. There is no headlong rush to continually grow the economy or accumulate wealth. The Old Testament practices, in some ways, enforced a level at which one considered themselves to have enough. It was difficult to move beyond a certain level of affluence. But these limitations and principles were not simply for the development of personal righteousness, although this was part of it. What they also accomplished was the transfer of wealth and resources from those who had an abundance to those who had little. We see that contentment and believing we can have enough work both personally and corporately.[12]

The out-flowing of wealth and resources is also seen as central in the New Testament. We have already seen it in many parables and encounters in Christ's life. For the church, it is as people see that we love one another, that is care for one another, that our witness is powerful (Acts 4:32–35). This is exactly what happened in the Church in Jerusalem just after it started. The witness of

---

[12]By committing to the concepts of contentment and having enough we more easily embrace Sabbath year and Jubilee principles which actually permit this transfer of wealth.

6.7 Economics: New Testament Emphasis

the apostles was powerful because there were no needy among them. Wealth flowed from those who had to those who had not.

The principles of contentment and having enough are antithetical to modern economics, of which the two main assumptions are scarcity and unlimited need. These ideas drive us and our economies toward unlimited growth and to ever greater levels of consumption. We are told that we must have the latest and the greatest, not only for our own gratification, but we are told that to refuse to continue our consumption would be irresponsible for that would slow down economic growth. "Do your civic duty and get out there and shop." Some industries possess such economic power that they do not so much make the pitch that we buy the latest and the greatest, rather they force us. This has been the case in the computer industry where some manufacturers have refused to include backward compatible features making it essential to get the latest hardware or software. Obviously there is tremendous pressure to reject contentment and the belief that one can have enough.[13]

If we are to implement the Sabbath year and Jubilee principles in our day we must say no to these pressures. Neither economic growth, nor our desire for more things are worthy of our focus. To engage in practices based on Sabbath year and Jubilee principles we must have income above what is necessary to live on. The implication is that we must live on less than what we earn. If we reject the principles of contentment and having enough we will fail in implementing the Kingdom.

Having said this, with what should we be content? What does God consider to be enough? This is extremely important given the level at which we are able to live in modern Western societies. We have already seen the answer, it is found in Matthew 6 and it is

---

[13]In light of this we must give considerable thought as to how we must change our life. This is a real challenge.

food and clothing. This is confirmed by Paul in second Timothy.

> If we have food and covering, with these we shall be content. But those who want to get rich fall into temptation and a snare and many foolish and harmful desires which plunge men into ruin and destruction. For the love of money is a root of all sorts of evil, and some by longing for it have wandered away from the faith and pierced themselves with many griefs.
>
> 2 Tim 6:8–10

The modern Western economic experience is singular, both in time and space. Nothing like it has ever occurred. But in most of the world, even now as in ages past, many live below, at, or just above the level of food and clothing.

This has important implications for both those who have abundance above food and clothing and those who are entering a trial full of economic misfortune. For the one who has more than food and clothing, especially in light of the Sabbath year and Jubilee principles, they must ask, "If I am to be content with food and clothing, how much of my wealth should I reasonably hold onto above these basics and still consider myself obedient to God?" This is not an academic question, it must be answered. Too much is at stake, most importantly, the witness of the Kingdom of God to the world. On the other hand, the one entering, or in the midst of a trial, must realize that God will not feel as though he has failed if they should come to food and clothing as their maximum provision.

But how in the world can one be content with food and clothing? Isn't there more to life than just these? There is indeed, but it is not more things, but God himself. It boils down to what we value, eternal things or the temporal. Few of us give serious thought about what God, in Christ has done for us, how magnificent it is to simply know God and walk this life with him, what a miracle it is that God dwells in us, that he has given us the fellowship of brothers and sisters in the Kingdom that he is bringing into the world, and given us a sure and glorious hope. If we understood, really understood, what it is that God has given us we would be overcome with gratitude; food and clothing would be more than enough, and we would be embarrassed to ask him for anything else.

6.7.4 The New Testament

It is hoped, that by now the reader is convinced that Christ came to bring the Kingdom of God on earth, that it is breaking out even now, even if not in its fullest expression. Some, however may still have some reservations and may point out that there is not the same preoccupation with Sabbath year and Jubilee principles in the epistles as is found in the Gospels. They claim that there is not a similar emphasis to what Christ said in the gospels. To this complaint let us consider the early church. (Acts 2:43–45, Acts 4:32–35) The church in Jerusalem was the earliest possible church, springing up only a short while after the crucifixion, and in the absence of any apostolic teaching or working out of the theological principles that were to come later. All these people had to go by was what Christ had just taught them. When we see how they organized themselves we find that they took Christ completely at his word, understanding him to have meant exactly what he had said. They immediately set about building a community based on voluntary association, where people gave to others in need out of their own possessions, for not one of them claimed that anything belonging to him was his own. Nowhere was coercion used; a person could dispose of their possessions as they saw fit. These people practiced Sabbath year and Jubilee principles with a passion. It was done to such an extent that there was not a needy person among them. The result was life in a wonderful community and a powerful witness to the world outside the community, just as Christ had promised.

> Everyone kept feeling a sense of awe; and many wonders and signs were taking place through the apostles. And all those who had believed were together and had all things in common; and they began selling their property and possessions and were sharing them with all, as anyone might have need.
>
> Acts 2:43–45

Later in Acts chapter four we find the same practices.

> And the congregation of those who believed were of one heart and soul; and not one of them claimed that anything belonging to him was his own, but all things were common property to them. And with great power the apostles were giving testimony to the resurrection of the Lord Jesus, and abundant grace was upon them all. For there was not a needy person among them, for all who were owners of land or houses would sell them and bring the proceeds of the sales and lay them at the apostles feet, and they would be distributed to each as any had need.
>
> Acts 4:32–35

Some may say that this may have gone on for a while, but ceased fairly soon thereafter. This, however, does not square with the historical record.[14] If we look at the apostolic writings and other extra-biblical writings, we find considerable evidence that the churches kept up these practices. With the Constantinian disaster, where the official Christian church was made one with the state, we see a reduction or cessation of these practices. But that part of the church that went on to embrace the power of

---

[14] Verduin, *The Anatomy of a Hybrid* and Lohfink, *Jesus and Community*

the state does not, nor has it ever represented the Church of Christ. Throughout much of the darkness of the Constantinian tragedy we find the Church breaking out, and more often than not, implementing Kingdom economic practices.

As to the New Testament, beyond the gospels we do not see an explicit preoccupation with Sabbath year and Jubilee principles even though there are several pointed passages addressing these matters in James and I John as we have already seen.[15][16] But is this really surprising? I think not. How much more could be said on these matters than what Christ had said? Do his teachings really need to be expounded upon because of their obscurity? Is there some hidden theological knowledge that keeps us from applying them? No! When Christ had finished teaching on these topics there was really no more to be said; what had to be done was go out and live them. This is exactly what the early church did, and in the epistles we see these principles being assumed, with everything taking place in this context.[17]

6.8 The Impact on Kingdom Understanding

The principles we have just studied have a profound impact on our modern understanding of the Kingdom of God. We see that the Kingdom of God is not just a spiritual kingdom, at least in

---

[15]The notable exceptions found in James and I John seem to highlight the lack of an explicit emphasis on the Kingdom. Is there a new language or vocabulary that arises in which these principles are taught? There is in fact a new language that appears in the epistles, namely the Church and the Body of Christ.

[16]Eph. 4:28 is an extraordinary passage being addressed to a thief. In it the thief is admonished to work and not sin so that he will be able to share with those in need. It is clear evidence of the emphasis of caring for those in need.

[17]A specific application of these principles is discussed by Paul 2 Cor 8,9, where he gives considerable time to the discussion of taking up an offering for the church in Jerusalem.

the sense that we often narrowly define spiritual (that is, personal salvation), but it is concerned with economics, and social and economic justice both having a profound impact on how we interact with both people and things. We must still be concerned with personal righteousness, but not to the exclusion of the principles introduced here. In fact, our practice of these principles is seen as proof of our right standing before God; it is a demonstration of a living faith rather than a dead faith.

Obviously, we cannot implement the Sabbath year and the Jubilee practices directly, but we can and must order our lives within the Kingdom of God to implement practices relevant to our cultural setting based on the principles of the Sabbath year and Jubilee.

Let us consider one last passage before leaving this topic lest we think that Christ was not interested in the physical treatment of others. In this passage, Christ gives us a glimpse of the great judgment of God where the eternal destinies of men are determined. The criterion for judgment is our treatment of the hungry, thirsty, naked, prisoner and sick. The implications are frightening. These words are incredibly powerful.

> But when the Son of Man comes in His glory, and all the angels with Him, then He will sit on His glorious throne. All the nations will be gathered before Him; and He will separate them from one another, as the shepherd separates the sheep from the goats; and He will put the sheep on His right, and the goats on the left. Then the King will say to those on His right, 'Come, you who are blessed of My Father, inherit the kingdom prepared for you from the foundation of the world. For I was hungry, and you gave Me something to eat; I was thirsty, and you gave Me something to drink; I was a stranger, and you invited Me in; naked, and you clothed Me; I was sick, and you visited Me; I was

6.8 The Impact on Kingdom Understanding

> in prison, and you came to Me.' Then the righteous will answer Him, 'Lord, when did we see You hungry, and feed You, or thirsty, and give You something to drink? And when did we see You a stranger, and invite You in, or naked, and clothe You? When did we see You sick, or in prison, and come to You?' The King will answer and say to them, 'Truly I say to you, to the extent that you did it to one of these brothers of Mine, even the least of them, you did it to Me.' Then He will also say to those on His left, 'Depart from Me, accursed ones, into the eternal fire which has been prepared for the devil and his angels; for I was hungry, and you gave Me nothing to eat; I was thirsty, and you gave Me nothing to drink; I was a stranger, and you did not invite Me in; naked, and you did not clothe Me; sick, and in prison, and you did not visit Me.' Then they themselves also will answer, 'Lord, when did we see You hungry, or thirsty, or a stranger, or naked, or sick, or in prison, and did not take care of You?' Then He will answer them, 'Truly I say to you, to the extent that you did not do it to one of the least of these, you did not do it to Me.' These will go away into eternal punishment, but the righteous into eternal life.
>
> Matt 25:31–46

Christ is not here teaching a gospel of works, rather he is teaching us that faith without works is dead. If we do not love as God loves, extending love and care to those in need, then we are not his child and have no place in the Kingdom to come. He who has ears to hear let him hear.

Chapter 7

The Kingdom: Further Foundations

In the last two chapters we presented a central aspect of the Kingdom, Sabbath year and Jubilee principles. Without a firm understanding of these principles, the works of Christ in salvation and the bringing in of the Kingdom God are poorly understood, and for the purposes of this work, neither do we understand the proper context of our trials. There are, however, other important aspects of the Kingdom and it is to these we now turn.

7.1 The Love of God: Agape

God is love. (1 John 4:8) Love is not simply attributed of God; we do not simply say that God is loving, but rather God *is* love. In some sense it is more fundamental. God is not made up of some substance called love, but love is so bound up in his essence that the words we must use to describe him are *God is love*. But what does this mean? How do we understand this?

Human language completely fails to fully capture the divine and the infinite. Nevertheless, we are able to understand much by the analogical capacity of language. By using what we see and know now we can, by analogy, understand, in a limited capacity, what God is actually like. What we have is an arrow pointing toward the perfection of God's love. We do not, in any sense, fully apprehend it, but we can sense the perfection of God's love. But this is not adequate. How do we break out of the limitations of language and know more fully the love of God? The answer is to *look* at God's love and to love as God commands.

It is only as we turn and look to Christ that we can understand God's love. Our understanding does not come to us in words as much as it does by the very acts[1] of Christ himself. Our understanding is completed, not by reasoning from propositions[2] with deductive logic, but by existential knowledge; we see God loving and understand. Real knowledge of love is gained from acts of love.

God's love is further explained as we observe Christians loving as Christ loved, and further still as we love. Where language and reason fail, action brings light. The image of God loving is then seen and God's love understood by the demonstration of Christ's love and likewise by his children's acts of love. With these thoughts in mind let us examine some of Christ's teachings and works of love.

---

[1] Love is never only a feeling or a state of mind. Love and action always go hand in hand. If we say we love but, do not move to action, we lie (1 John 3:17,18). It is like faith and works (Jas 2:18–26). Should we say that we have faith but do not do the works of Christ, we lie. It is impossible to separate love and acts of love.

[2] It is true that reason and propositional logic must be present at the start or there is nothing to begin with, but they are unable to bring us to a mature understanding. I believe that this is the case with most of the Christian life. Christ stated that we will understand as we obey, which itself is action, not simply proper knowledge.

7.1 The Love of God: Agape

7.1.1 The Teachings

It is often thought that the Mosaic law consists only of a complex labyrinth of rules and regulations, but the core of the Law is love.

> "Teacher, which is the great commandment in the Law?" And He said to him, " 'You shall love the Lord your God with all your heart, and with all your soul, and with all your mind.' This is the great and foremost commandment. The second is like it, You shall love your neighbor as yourself.' On these two commandments depend the whole Law and the Prophets."
>
> Matt 22:36–40

If the core of the Mosaic law is love, how could it hold a lesser place in the New Covenant?[3] Love is not one important thing among many, it occupies the center.

The Prodigal Son. Luke 15:11–32
The occasion of this parable is the grumbling of the Pharisees and scribes at the beginning of Luke 15.

> Now all the tax collectors and the sinners were coming near Him to listen to Him. Both the Pharisees and the scribes began to grumble, saying, "This man receives sinners and eats with them."
>
> Luke 15:1,2

This was all Jesus needed to give a lesson in love; "So He told them this parable, saying ...". The religious leaders did not see God's love extending to sinners in this way and were indignant that Jesus would contaminate himself with these wretches. However, neither God nor the Son were so inclined, rather, for them,

---

[3] I have heard it said, "Love God and do what you want." This may seem a little extreme unless we understand what it means to love God. If we love God, what we want will be what he wants.

it was all about wretches, of whom the scribes and Pharisees were numbered, but refused to acknowledge, being convinced of their own righteousness established by their works.

In this parable we see a beautiful picture of God's love. In it, the younger of two sons demands to be immediately given his inheritance. Amazingly the father gives the inheritance to his son who promptly leaves home, lives a wretched sinful life, at the same time squandering the inheritance, and finds himself destitute, tending swine, without enough food to eat.

In the Jewish tradition, a son could receive his part of the inheritance either at his father's death or while he was still alive. If he received it while his father lived, he was only permitted to exercise control over his inheritance after his father's death; to do otherwise was to treat his father with contempt. As we see, this son has done his father a great injustice; he treats his father as if he were dead by not only taking possession of the inheritance, but by exercising control over it while his father yet lived. The outcome of his rebellion is his descent to the lowest point that a Jew might go, living outside of the Jewish homeland, tending a herd of swine.

Importantly, the father permits the son to exercise his free will without interference. It really is extraordinary given the cultural context of the day. The father could have refused to give the inheritance, or after it was given, could have refused to let his son depart with it. But never is a serious protest raised. Imagine the condemnation the father's peers must have heaped upon him; "How could he be so irresponsible to permit his son to indulge in this sort of behavior?" The father is obviously not seeking to secure his reputation as he lets his son depart with his inheritance.

Eventually the son "came to himself," a phrase indicating repentance, and decided to come back to his father. He knew that he had done a terrible thing to his father and God, and came back

7.1 The Love of God: Agape

with an attitude of real repentance asking only to be received as a slave. He understood his rebellion, the extent of his rebellion, and that he has forfeited any right or claim to sonship or the treatment expected by a son.

Before the son even got to the house, the father saw him from a distance. At this point the father had many courses of action open to him. He could have waited for the son to come to the house and verbally ripped him apart and sent him away, or after his tirade, sent him to the slaves' quarters. He could also have done something less severe such as given him a severe talking to and told him to get into the house, and exacted his pound of flesh in some other, more creative way.

However, the father saw the son from afar; the father has been looking and waiting for his son; he had not written him off. He desperately wanted his son to come home. With this simple observation, the father's response is not unexpected, but it does defy a normal human response — the father took off after the son.

> So he got up and came to his father. But while he was still a long way off, his father saw him and felt compassion for him, and ran and embraced him and kissed him.[4]
>
> Luke 15:20

The son, most likely, completely surprised, goes on and confesses to his father.

> Father, I have sinned against heaven and in your sight; I am no longer worthy to be called your son.
>
> Luke 15:21

The father did not even respond to this or give him the expected "talking to." He knew his son's heart. He immediately accepted his son, as a son, put shoes and a robe on him and proceeded to have a celebration, "for this son of mine was dead and

---
[4] A kiss, in this context, as the Jew understood, indicated forgiveness.

has come to life again; he was lost and has been found." (Luke 15:24)

The father's response is nothing like what one might expect, and in it Christ is communicating how God loves the sinner who repents and comes to him. Christ came to save sinners, not the righteous. Although the parable is used to describe God's love for the lost it also speaks to us and how we are to love, for we are commanded to love as God loves. (Matt 5:48) This is an impossible task unless it is done in the power of God.

The Good Samaritan. Luke 10:30–37
This parable is given in reply to a lawyer's question, "Who is my neighbor?" Christ subsequently proceeds to blow apart everyone's presuppositions.

In the parable, a man, presumably a Jew, was traveling from Jerusalem to Jericho. This man was attacked by thieves, robbed, beaten and left for dead. In time, both a priest and a Levite, traveling the same road and seeing this man, simply walked by doing nothing. Eventually a Samaritan, hated more than a Gentile by the Jew, came and had compassion on the injured man, taking care of his wounds, putting him on his donkey and bringing him to an inn where he could recover. Before leaving, he gave the innkeeper money to cover any further expenses. He also told the innkeeper that he would come back and pay any additional costs.

After telling the parable, Christ interrogated his audience:

> Which of these three do you think proved to be a neighbor to the man who fell into the robbers hands? And he said, "he one who showed mercy toward him." Then Jesus said to him, "Go and do the same."
>
> Luke 10:36,37

Given the Jewish audience, this was an extraordinary story; a Samaritan was the hero and the cream of the Jewish religious

7.1 The Love of God: Agape

leadership were contemptible. Telling a story where a Samaritan was helping a Jew was crossing an inviolable barrier, and yet we see Christ doing it. Most amazingly, the point of the parable is that all men, even enemies, are our neighbors and we are to extend love and care to them as well. This is nothing new; we have already heard Christ say essentially the same thing in an earlier context.

> But I say to you who hear, love your enemies, do good to those who hate you, bless those who curse you, pray for those who mistreat you.
>
> Luke 6:27, 28

Paul says much the same in Romans 12:14–21. It is essentially a summary of the Sermon on the Mount.

In these parables and others, in addition to specific encounters in Christ's life, we see God's love taught and lived out and we find that God's love, agape love, is characterized in the following way: unconditional, indiscriminate, bold, operates when it is inconvenient, assumes risk, takes time, expensive to the one loving, and jeopardizes social status.[5] It looks nothing like the love that finds its source in man; only God is the author of this love.

Paul sums up agape love in 1 Corinthians 13.

> Love is patient, love is kind and is not jealous; love does not brag and is not arrogant, does not act unbecomingly; it does not seek its own, is not provoked, does not take into account a wrong suffered, does not rejoice in unrighteousness, but rejoices with the truth; bears all things, believes all things, hopes all things, endures all things. Love never fails
>
> 1 Cor 13:4–8a

---

[5]Kraybill, *The Upside-Down Kingdom*

7.1.2 Christ: Love Explained

Philippians chapter two instructs us how to love one another in the Kingdom.

> ... make my joy complete by being of the same mind, maintaining the same love, united in spirit, intent on one purpose. Do nothing from selfishness or empty conceit, but with humility of mind regard one another as more important than yourselves; do not merely look out for your own personal interests, but also for the interests of others.
>
> Phil 2:2–4

A group of people living this way paints an incredibly beautiful picture, something irresistible. It was found as such by those who observed the early church. It really was irresistible, sweeping through the Roman empire like fire. The people described above are united in purpose and love; selfishness and conceit are not found among them. Instead, humility abounds and each considers the needs of others as more important than their own. This is love in action in a community. But this does not describe a community that man would build, or even could build, if he were so inclined. This community exists because of God's love. This is a community living in love, love demonstrated by God himself.

Paul continues and gives us the exemplar for the love he has just described.

> Have this attitude in yourselves which was also in Christ Jesus, who, although He existed in the form of God, did not regard equality with God a thing to be grasped, but emptied Himself, taking the form of a bond-servant, and being made in the likeness of men. Being found in appearance as a man, He humbled Himself by becoming obedient to the point of death, even death on a cross. For this reason also, God highly exalted Him, and bestowed on Him the

7.1 The Love of God: Agape

> name which is above every name, so that at the name of Jesus every knee will bow, of those who are in heaven and on earth and under the earth, and that every tongue will confess that Jesus Christ is Lord, to the glory of God the Father.
>
> Phil 2:5–11

This is Christ loving us. God the Son, Christ, the second Person of the Trinity, one in essence with God the Father and God the Holy Spirit, possessor of the glory and power of the Godhead, emptying himself, freely choosing to lay aside, for a time, his visible glory, the exercise of his divine prerogatives and submit himself to God the Father, becoming a bond-servant, and choosing to be made in the likeness of man, the creature. Christ remained fully God, but he also became fully man to bring man back to himself and redeem the whole creation. We do not have a high priest who cannot identify with us, but one who was tempted in all ways as we are. He suffered hunger, lack of sleep, the pain of a blow. He knows fully what it is to be a man, but a man without sin. For love he emptied himself; whatever lengths were necessary, no matter how high the cost, he paid it for our sake. Doing the Father's will by saving us was more desirable to him than retaining equality with God. Don't let these words leave your thoughts too quickly. Imagine it, God the Son subordinated himself to our needs! It is an arresting thought, almost frightening if we really understand who it is that loves us so.

But Christ is not done, for having emptied himself he humbled himself becoming obedient to death. God the Son humbled himself, subordinated himself to the Father's plan that he should die to bring man back to him. Christ humbled himself before the Father and all of mankind. But he did not die just any death, but a death on a cross, a cursed manner of death. And all this was done because of God's love for us. This is our supreme example of love that points the way to how we must love.

7.1.3 Suffering Love: Nonviolence

Christ's love was a suffering love, a love that was willing to suffer at the hands of the one to whom the love was directed regardless of the level of violence sustained. Love has no room for a violent response.

There were many temptations for Christ to take up power and violence to bring in the Kingdom and restore justice and peace, but he chose not to use violence, not even in the smallest way, for "while being reviled, He did not revile in return; while suffering, He uttered no threats." (1 Pet 2:23a) And it is through peace that he brought justice.

> A bruised reed He will not break
> And a dimly burning wick
> He will not extinguish;
> He will faithfully bring forth justice.
>
> Isa 42:3

Christ could have called six legions of angels instead of going to the cross, he could have called his followers to take up arms and set up his Kingdom, he could have used violence, but he did not. Instead Christ "kept entrusting Himself to Him who judges righteously." (1 Pet 2:23b) And notice, it is by nonviolent means that Christ brings forth justice.

Christ embraced the Father's way — a way of suffering and nonviolence. This was the way to real power, for he made us "alive together with Him, having forgiven us all our transgressions, having canceled out the certificate of debt consisting of decrees against us, which was hostile to us; and He has taken it out of the way, having nailed it to the cross. When He had disarmed the rulers and authorities, He made a public display of

7.1 The Love of God: Agape

them, having triumphed over them through Him." (Col 2:13b–15) Violence could not have done this, only the power of God's love.

We not only have Christ as our example of nonviolence, but we also have his teachings commanding us to be nonviolent. Matthew chapter five[6] is perhaps the most well-known, but also the most "reinterpreted" to avoid what is painfully obvious.

> You have heard that it was said, 'An eye for an eye, and a tooth for a tooth.' But I say to you, do not resist an evil person; but whoever slaps you on your right cheek, turn the other to him also. If anyone wants to sue you and take your shirt, let him have your coat also. Whoever forces you to go one mile, go with him two. Give to him who asks of you, and do not turn away from him who wants to borrow from you.
>
> Matt 5:38–42

Regarding our enemies we see an even more challenging command.

> You have heard that it was said, 'You shall love your neighbor and hate your enemy.' But I say to you, love your enemies and pray for those who persecute you, so that you may be sons of your Father who is in heaven; for He causes His sun to rise on the evil and the good, and sends rain on the righteous and the unrighteous. For if you love those who love you, what reward do you have? Do not even the tax collectors do the same? If you greet only your brothers, what more are you doing than others? Do not even the Gentiles do the same? Therefore you are to be perfect, as your heavenly Father is perfect.
>
> Matt 5:43–58

---

[6] See the parallel passage in Luke 6:27–36.

To our enemies, we are to respond with suffering love, not violence. As Christ hung on the cross he asked the Father to forgive those who had crucified him. While were yet sinners (enemies of God) Christ died (loved) for us.

Lest we think that only Christ taught this, or that nonviolence is only for the "really committed" listen to what Paul has to say.

> Bless those who persecute you; bless and do not curse. Rejoice with those who rejoice, and weep with those who weep. Be of the same mind toward one another; do not be haughty in mind, but associate with the lowly. Do not be wise in your own estimation. Never pay back evil for evil to anyone. Respect what is right in the sight of all men. If possible, so far as it depends on you, be at peace with all men. Never take your own revenge, beloved, but leave room for the wrath of God, for it is written, "Vengeance is Mine, I will repay," says the Lord. "But if your enemy is hungry, feed him, and if he is thirsty, give him a drink; for in so doing you will heap burning coals on his head." Do not be overcome by evil, but overcome evil with good.
>
> Rom 12:14–21

This is essentially the same thing that Christ said in Matthew five. Even Peter teaches the same.

> To sum up, all of you be harmonious, sympathetic, brotherly, kindhearted, and humble in spirit; not returning evil for evil or insult for insult, but giving a blessing instead; for you were called for the very purpose that you might inherit a blessing. For, The one who desires life, to love and see good days, must keep his tongue from evil and his lips from speaking deceit. He must turn away from evil and do good; He must seek peace and pursue it. For the eyes of the Lord are toward the righteous, and His ears attend to

7.1 The Love of God: Agape

> their prayer, but the face of the Lord is against those who do evil.
>
> 1 Pet 3:8–12

In 1 Peter 2:22 we find Peter quoting Isaiah 53:9 "His grave was assigned with wicked men, yet He was with a rich man in His death, because He had done no violence, nor was there any deceit in His mouth." Peter quotes this while telling us to patiently endure suffering as Christ did in his Passion. Not even under conditions as bad as this are we to be violent.

Furthermore, the use of violence is inconsistent with the fundamental nature of a Christian — a servant priest who exercises no power and authority over others. Recall that the Levites, the priests of the Old Covenant, were not engaged in warfare. (Num 1:47–54)

We must not understand Christ's and the apostle's commands to nonviolence, or the ethics of Christ in general, to only apply to 'private' ethics. The Scripture knows of no such thing as a division between private and public ethics. Given the historical, social and political context[7] during the first century it is impossible to believe that the speakers and hearers understood themselves to be discussing private ethics. How is it possible for an enemy of mine, who is also an enemy of my government, be any less of an enemy, as defined in Matthew five? And how is it that I may kill this enemy external to my country, but not an enemy found in my own country. The logic, even beyond the historical context, simply does not work.

But perhaps we still think that nonviolence was not to con-

---

[7] The Roman government was a government of the rich. The common person had no stake in it. Furthermore, the wars of the state were the 'Emperors' wars. Once again, the common person having no stake in the war. When we insist on making a distinction between public and private ethics we are imposing an Enlightenment social liberalism on the Biblical text.

tinue on into the "mature" Church age. Maybe this is the way out? Alas, no such escape is possible, for the early Church took the teachings of Christ, Paul and the rest of the Apostles at face value and did not practice violence nor accept one into their assembly who was a soldier, a maker of arms or any violent person. Neither did they compel by force those who did not agree with them. Theirs was a voluntary association. They lived lives described in Matthew 5 and Romans 12. It was not until the Constantinian disaster that what was called the "official church" combined with state power and embraced and used violence in its own name for its ends. And it did so with a vengeance, often killing those who would not bow to their power. But the true Church, those both within and without the officially sanctioned church, remained faithful and endured, suffering in love the violence visited upon it by the "fallen church," that is the official state church.[8] The true Church, by the state church called "heretics," never really went away, but remained and are with us still, always a thorn in the side of the "fallen church" reminding it of the example of Christ's suffering love.[9]

Violence, understood in the broadest terms, encompasses an enormous diversity. In the passages above, the Western mind is likely to consider only physical violence, and that, mainly as it is used in armed conflict. Christ and the apostles certainly included this, but it by no means exhausts our understanding of violence. We are to refuse verbal, and emotional as well a physical violence.

---

[8] To call the state church fallen may be a little severe since there were some within it that protested its conflation with the state and its interests. But as an institution, I think it fair to call it fallen.

[9] The distinction I am making here is that between the church, of what ever name and composition, that embraced state power, and the Church, also of whatever name and composition, that refused to be so combined and remain faithful to Christ's example. One can find a discussion of this in *The Anatomy of a Hybrid* by Leonard Verduin and related works mentioned in this book.

7.1 The Love of God: Agape

It is often this kind of violence that we find in our families and workplaces and it often precedes physical violence. We are to be nonviolent in the smallest things, even in the answer given in response to the little irritations and injustices we suffer from other people. In all of our relationships our response to violence must be love, and suffering if need be.

At the time of the Constantinian disaster the Church embraced the power of the State and at the same time embraced violence, something that is completely foreign to the Body of Christ. And because of it the Church lost much of its real power. It simply became another oppressor. Whereas pagan Rome sought to make all bow to its pagan state religion, now the new Christian Roman empire sought to make all bow to its Christian state religion. The old tyrant was simply replaced by a new one. Christianity was now just another tyrant and it had lost most of its ability to witness to the fallen world and was seen outside of Christendom as simply another center of power grabbing what it could. This was not the witness Christ intended for the Church.

The American Evangelical church has made a similar mistake. We do not embrace Constantinianism, that is a full-blown state church, but we do embrace violence used by the state on our behalf, seldom if ever condemning the use of violence by our government. We condone the use of force by our government on our behalf regardless of the consequences or the underlying causes, even if our nation is receiving evil for the evil we have done in the past. This is not to justify those who attack us, but evil begets evil, the inevitable moral causality in the fallen world. As the world around us observes us, and the actions of the state we support, they do not see the love of Christ, only the raw naked power we demand that the government exercise on our behalf to ensure our freedom to worship.[10] Suffering love isn't even on the screen

---

[10]It is as if we worship the freedom to worship. We must secure it at all

and we have no witness to the world. It is an enormous tragedy at many levels and remains largely unseen by those who should know better.[11]

7.1.4 Rejection of Reciprocity

Within interpersonal relationships, reciprocity is one of the most fundamental principles embodying much of what we understand regarding moral causality.[12] In its most generous form we do good so that we might receive good. In its most malevolent form we justify the use of violence in response to the violence done to us. It is in this latter form, perhaps better called retaliation, that reciprocity drives the escalation of violence in wars and personal relationships until violence is maximized. Reciprocity is fundamental, expected, and most often practiced in its negative form.

Reciprocity may be what underlies most human relationships but it is not by God's design, but by man's rebellion against God. In the New Testament we find Christ putting an end to both positive and negative reciprocity. Reciprocity is not for the one living in the Kingdom of God.

In the Kingdom, Christ teaches us to forget about doing good in order to expect good in return. Reciprocity limits doing good only to those who can repay. We are rather to do good to all.

> You have heard that it was said, 'You shall love your neighbor and hate your enemy.' But I say to you, love your enemies and pray for those who persecute you, so that you may be sons of your Father who is in heaven; for He causes

---

costs, no matter how many have to die for it. I can hardly think of anything more un-Christlike.

[11]There are many excellent books on Christian nonviolence. Among them are *Nevertheless, What would You Do, The Politics of Jesus* and *When War is Unjust*, all by John Howard Yoder and *Jesus and the Nonviolent Revolution* by Andre Trocme

[12]Kraybill, *The Upside-Down Kingdom*

7.1 The Love of God: Agape

> His sun to rise on the evil and the good, and sends rain on the righteous and the unrighteous. For if you love those who love you, what reward do you have? Do not even the tax collectors do the same? If you greet only your brothers, what more are you doing than others? Do not even the Gentiles do the same? Therefore you are to be perfect, as your heavenly Father is perfect.
>
> Matt 5:43–48

We find a similar passage in Luke with even greater emphasis on not expecting anything in return.

> Give to everyone who asks of you, and whoever takes away what is yours, do not demand it back. Treat others the same way you want them to treat you. If you love those who love you, what credit is that to you? For even sinners love those who love them. If you do good to those who do good to you, what credit is that to you? For even sinners do the same. If you lend to those from whom you expect to receive, what credit is that to you? Even sinners lend to sinners in order to receive back the same amount. But love your enemies, and do good, and lend, expecting nothing in return; and your reward will be great, and you will be sons of the Most High; for He Himself is kind to ungrateful and evil men. Be merciful, just as your Father is merciful.
>
> Luke 6:30–36

Notice that we are to treat others the same way we want them to treat us, but we extend this treatment to everyone, not limiting it to those who can treat us the way we would like to be treated. If we limit our good works to those who can repay we are no better than the worst of society: sinners and tax collectors. There is nothing laudable about doing good to our family, close neighbors, friends and associates from whom we can expect good in return.

And for the Christian, it in no way demonstrates the love of God to the world since it is behavior common to all, even the evil.

Recall the command to the Pharisee who had invited Christ to dinner.

> When you give a luncheon or a dinner, do not invite your friends or your brothers or your relatives or rich neighbors, otherwise they may also invite you in return and that will be your repayment. But when you give a reception, invite the poor, the crippled, the lame, the blind, and you will be blessed, since they do not have the means to repay you; for you will be repaid at the resurrection of the righteous.
>
> Luke 14:12–14

The emphasis here is important, for doing good to those who cannot repay is not simply suggested as something we ought to do once in a while or left to chance. It is rather done deliberately, intentionally. "When you give a dinner do not invite your friends, but those who have no means to repay you." It indicates that this is to be a central part of our life, behavior that is not simply tacked on, but an essential characteristic.

What is radical and catches the world's attention are good works done to those from whom we can expect nothing in return, because the world does not practice this. The world sees no virtue in this. It is this kind of good works when practiced in a community, such as the early church, that there is the possibility of there being no needy. And it is this kind of good works that will make our witness to the world powerful and attractive because it mirrors the way that God loves mankind.

The outcast and the poor certainly have no means to return our favor because they lack the means. Our enemy, on the other hand, often has the means, but refuses to return good because they hate us. Doing good to our enemy is yet another level up from doing good to those who cannot repay us. Actively loving

7.1 The Love of God: Agape

our enemy is godlike and the most extraordinary of all Christian behavior.

With our enemy there is another dimension to the relationship that brings in the possibility of negative reciprocity. They have done some evil against us, usually in some form of violence. The human law of reciprocity tells us that retaliation is justified, and perhaps exactly what is needed, but not so in the Kingdom. Not only is the Christian not supposed to retaliate, but he is to do something positive — return good.

Lest we think that Christ was the only one who taught this consider Paul.

> Bless those who persecute you; bless and do not curse. ... Never pay back evil for evil to anyone. Never take your own revenge, beloved, but leave room for the wrath of God, for it is written, "Vengeance is Mine, I will repay," says the Lord. "But if your enemy is hungry, feed him, and if he is thirsty, give him a drink; for in so doing you will heap burning coals on his head." Do not be overcome by evil, but overcome evil with good.
>
> Rom 12:14,17,19–21

This is extremely difficult. Doing good to the poor is much easier since we can at least feel good about helping someone in need; they might even be grateful. But doing good to an enemy who is abusing us ... what do we get out of it? We don't even get to have warm fuzzy feelings about a job well done. We just have to take it and return good for the evil, bless them and pray for them. They don't even get what they deserve. Yes, that's right, but neither have we gotten what we deserve; it's about mercy and as we show mercy the world sees God's mercy.

The greatest refusal to retaliate was Christ's, exceeding anything we might do, as day exceeds night, becoming our example of non-retaliation, nonviolence and doing good in return. Christ suffered the abuse of the Jewish leadership, the scorn of Rome, a travesty of a trial, disfiguring beatings, execution on a cross and did not retaliate. But most of all, he willingly paid the punishment I deserved, returning the greatest good that could be done, and did not retaliate against me for my rebellion that took him to the cross. And at the cross we find him praying, "Father, forgive them; for they do not know what they are doing." (Luke 23:34)[13]

Consider for a moment how broadly we must apply this refusal to retaliate. When we think about non-retaliation our thoughts most often turn to extreme cases like those found in persecution, genocide and perhaps criminal behavior. What we have covered certainly applies to these, but the more frequent application is in our daily relationships at all levels. Most of our time is spent either at work or at home and we have many opportunities to refuse retaliation, retaliation often in small ways, but retaliation nevertheless. How often does someone return a sharp word? How often does someone ignore or deny your need or request? How often are you slighted? How often have you been looked over despite your superior abilities and performance? Many times, if you have lived very long. To all these and more God demands that we do not respond in kind. But the command does not stop there; it is not enough to refuse to retaliate, but we must do good in return, blessing them and praying for them, for "you are to be perfect, as your heavenly Father is perfect." Living in the presence of our enemies, refusing retaliation and returning good is godlike living; man would never do this, it is as foreign to us as breathing water. Only men filled with God's Spirit can do it, and when it is done it is the most powerful thing that God can do through us in this world. In this we truly demonstrate God's love to those around us.

---

[13] We find Stephen praying similarly in Acts 7:60

7.2 A New Way: No Barriers, No Divisions

The practice of religion is radically different in the Kingdom that Christ brought. In the Old Testament the Jew occupied a very privileged position having been given the Law of God, but now, in Christ, the promise to Abraham that all nations would be blessed by his seed is fulfilled and the Gentile is included. Not only this, but there is no longer any relevant distinction between Jew and Gentile. But even more than this, there is no longer a distinction between slave and master, man or woman, etc.; all are equal before Christ and in submission to one another. This is a radical leveling, a destruction of all divisions, even social, economic and national. With respect to relationships this does not do away with our respective functions which remain unique, but as we stand before Christ there are no relevant distinctions and with respect to love and how we consider one another, there is no notion of superiority, but rather mutual submission.

Christ is our greatest example of living without barriers. Christ healed Gentiles, he fed their multitudes, he stayed with Samaritans, he ate with sinners and tax collectors, he permitted a prostitute to anoint him for burial, he touched the unclean and he permitted women to be an integral part of his ministry. At every turn Christ was crossing barriers, it seems as often as he could, showing us that they were no longer meaningful.

Hand in hand with crossing barriers is a willingness to be numbered among the outcast and the undesirable and letting go of our reputation. In many ways our reputation is a source of pride and we must not save it at the cost of our obedience to Christ. It is far better to be numbered with Christ and the other outcasts than to be one of the beautiful people sought out by the proud and self-willed.

7.3 Servanthood

Servanthood forms the basis of relationships within the Kingdom of God. Our Lord taught this himself and provides our greatest example.

> You know that those who are recognized as rulers of the Gentiles lord it over them; and their great men exercise authority over them. But it is not this way among you, but whoever wishes to become great among you shall be your servant; and whoever wishes to be first among you shall be slave of all. For even the Son of Man did not come to be served, but to serve, and to give His life a ransom for many.
>
> Mark 10:41–45

Notice carefully that we are not even to exercise authority over one another. Structures of power and authority are not to be part of human relationships within the Kingdom of God.

From John's gospel we have another lesson in servanthood.

> Do you know what I have done to you? You call Me Teacher and Lord; and you are right, for so I am. If I then, the Lord and the Teacher, washed your feet, you also ought to wash one another's feet. For I gave you an example that you also should do as I did to you.
>
> John 13:12–15

Christ is not calling us to serve from power and authority, but from the very bottom, doing things that a Jewish master could not even command his Jewish slave. Not only this, but Christ teaches us in Matthew 23 that we are to have no titles, for One is our Father, One is our Teacher and One is our Leader for we are all brethren. Those who function as leaders and teachers must only lead where God has already lead and teach what God has

7.3 Servanthood

already taught, and even then only by persuasion and prayer, not coercion and force.

But how is it that power and authority cannot form the basis of our relationships? Don't some need to be in authority? How can anything get done? Does it even make sense? Certainly not if we understand relationships in terms of our modern culture. For the children of God gentleness, persuasion and intercessory prayer on the behalf of others are the tools of leadership. Does God force us to believe and behave in specific ways?[14] No, of course not. Then how can those called by his name coerce and force others to do anything? When Paul says that all authority has been given to Christ he really means all. Power and authority are not for us.

And so we find ourselves in complete dependence upon God to achieve his ends. Our task is to be faithful, serve others, care for the poor and needy, spread the gospel and become more like Christ. It is not our task to secure outcomes and results. No only this, but it is sinful for us to try, for this is God's task and we dare not trespass.[15]

How then is it possible that human relationships can function. How can we live in a community without exercising power and authority? God himself provides, bringing salvation to all our relationships, for he has remade those who are his children and is conforming them to the image of his Son. The basis of relationships is now love and forgiveness. Mutual submission in love and humility makes it possible. It is exactly what God's salvation

---

[14]God can and does work circumstances to move us in the direction he desires, but he does not destroy our volition, by force. We may choose to obey or disobey.

[15]Within the Church, even our discipline is more passive than active and is done by the corporate body. In cases where a Christian refuses to repent of a serious sin they are to be banned from church fellowship until they come and repent. Although it is passive, it is the most effective means of bringing them to repentance. Our goal is for their salvation. Banning comes only at the end of a long process of persuasion done in love and humility.

looks like.

God truly has brought salvation to us, saving our souls, bodies and relationships. How blessed we are to be God's children, being able to live is such a glorious manner. What freedom we enjoy.

7.4 Conclusion

As we have seen, life in the Kingdom of God is not only about personal salvation and righteousness, but about life in a community that demonstrates the love of God to the world. As we understand the Kingdom, we find that godly economics and social and economic justice are a necessary result of a life transformed by God, and demonstrates a living faith. These are not to be seen as tacked-on activities done because we are social progressives, but done in obedience to God's command, having seen him do the same to us and then caring for others in a similar manner.

The fear among many conservative Christians today is being labeled a 'liberal'. Tremendous social and cultural baggage comes with this label, much of it very undesirable from a Christian perspective: abortion, sexual promiscuity, homosexuality, etc.[16] However, of late, it is the liberals who have made the strongest case for social and economic justice, the very things that Christians should be concerned with as we go about preaching salvation in Christ.[17]

We Christians should not be afraid of being misunderstood or mislabeled, for there is a world of difference between our motives and methods and those who go by the name liberal, as defined

---

[16] Of course, not all who call themselves liberal embrace these practices. However, a large majority who use this label do embrace them. Hence the aversion.

[17] To be fair, there have always been Christians who have helped the poor and outcasts of society. Since the early 1500's the Anabaptists have been quite consistent in this practice, and stand out as a particularly good example. However, they are not alone and many other examples exist.

7.4 Conclusion

above. The traditional liberal looks to the government to save them and take care of the poor. The Christian is not so inclined and understands that there is no salvation in the government and that Kingdom practices can only be implemented within the Kingdom. Even if governments are able to implement these practices they will only be poorly approximated, and in time will be abused and turned to evil.[18] We look to God's Kingdom to care for the poor and the outcast. We should ignore our fears and go out and do God's business.

As to the Sabbath year and Jubilee principles, if we fully understand them, we find that the socialists and communists were not only terribly misguided, but were far too timid in their socio-economic revolution; God's way is far more radical, but this should come as no surprise. God does not insist on socialism or communism,[19] but by the example of his statutes in the Mosaic Law and the example of Christ in the New Covenant, he creatively restructures economic and social relationships to ensure that there are no needy and prevents the fortunate from becoming enslaved to their wealth. As the early church practiced these principles there were no needy found among them.

We must understand that these principles cannot be successfully practiced by those outside the Kingdom of God. Christian ethics can only be followed by those who have been remade by Christ. Those outside the Kingdom can only approximate this way of life. This is not to say that we should not help the government, under which we find ourselves, to adopt some of these

---

[18]Just look at Social Security and Medicare. These are not about helping people, but getting and maintaining political power. Neither are they sustainable.

[19]God also does not insist on free market capitalism. In fact, many of its basic foundations violate Christian principles. We are rather seen as stewards of God's provision, disposing of God's bounty in ways that honor and glorify God.

principles, but we must not be deceived into believing that we can extend the Kingdom of God to those outside the Kingdom of God as long as they refuse to acknowledge Christ as their king. The most effective thing we can do for those outside the Kingdom is to live out Kingdom practices within the Kingdom of God (the Body of Christ, the Church), preach the gospel, extend love, forgiveness and material help. In other words, be faithful to what God has already commanded: life in the Kingdom and missionary activity. Trying to reform government is not effective. Spend your time building the Kingdom of God.

The Kingdom is also characterized by a revolution of forgiveness and love. It is not forgiveness and love as men practice it, but as God practices it. Forgiveness is perpetually given no matter what has been done to us. Love is extended not only to our family and friends, but also to our enemies to whom we also do good.

As to religion, we do not obey traditions of men, but the commands of God. And with respect to divisions, they are no longer relevant; the distinctions between Jew and Gentile, male and female, black and white, European and Asian, slave and free have no meaning at all in the Kingdom of God. And not only this, we are all in mutual submission to one another, considering the needs of the other more important than our own.

As respecting trials we see that they are essential for the operation of the Kingdom of God, they are not peripheral, but at the center of Kingdom activity. By them we are refined and made more fit for life in the Kingdom, and by them, those who have the means demonstrate their love to those in need by caring for them, thereby powerfully witnessing to the world.

> A new commandment I give to you, that you love one another, even as I have loved you, that you also love one another. By this all men will know that you are My disciples,

7.4 Conclusion

if you have love for one another.

John 13:34,35

These are *essential* activities within the Kingdom and trials form their basis.

Chapter 8

The Nature and Purpose of Trials

The primary purpose of man is to glorify God, and the glorification of God is largely accomplished by conforming us to the image of his Son and advancing his Kingdom in the largest possible sense. It is to his glory that God uses trials and it is not possible to come to a proper understanding of trials, nor any other part of our lives, without this foundation. Understanding this, we can answer all our why's and submit to whatever God has in store for us. God, however, does not limit his revelation to this only, but goes into considerable detail telling us what he is accomplishing in trials.

It is here that we turn to a more personal discussion of trials. What has preceded, the study of the Kingdom of God, has given us an excellent foundation in the corporate aspect of trials, and as we have seen, one central purpose of trials is the building up of the Kingdom by demonstrating our love for one another as we care for those in trials. The early Church was powerful because of their love; there were no needy among them. Additionally, those in need saw God's love in the lavish giving of their brethren, thereby seeing that God really is love and that his promise to care for them was to be trusted. But notice, this could only happen in a community. It cannot be done alone. But now, let us look at trials from a more personal perspective.

Ultimately, God desires that we become a mature Christian, someone conformed to the image of his Son and he wants us to build his Kingdom. Only a person being conformed to the character of Christ can properly glorify God, inhabit and build his Kingdom. Nothing else will do and it is through trials that much of the difficult work of conforming is accomplished. As I reflect on my own life, it would seem that nearly all of this ongoing work has been accomplished through trials.

Regarding trials, two concepts, the strategic and the tactical, have proven very helpful. A tactical view is one that considers the goals and objectives for a specific trial; who needs to be moved in a particular direction, what is being accomplished, what occasioned the trial, what moved God to let it enter our lives and did God take a direct hand in it or is it a trial that he permitted? These tactical questions may be asked, but we are seldom, if ever, permitted to know the answers. However, we are certain of the strategic goals and objectives, no confusion exists with these. Whatever the trial, we know with certainty that God is glorifying himself, conforming us to the image of his Son and building his Kingdom. We also know that in our trials Christ will disclose himself to us as we obey. (John 14:21) Our tactical knowledge may not be complete, for God has determined, in nearly all cases, that we will not possess complete tactical knowledge, but God does give sufficient knowledge to permit a rational person to embrace trials for extremely good reasons.

8.1 The Nature of Trials

8.1.1 Characteristics of Trials

When we consider trials many things come to mind; emotional and physical pain, loss, uncertainty, lack of control, etc. In all these the word weakness most accurately describes the condition in which we find ourselves. We have lost power and are unable to drive events in the direction we wish. This forces us into a position of dependence, dependence on God and those around us, a position we find terribly unsettling and humbling.

Despite being uncomfortable with weakness and the dependence that follows it is exactly what we need, for it reflects our true condition at all times, even times of plenty and ease. Never are we in control; the belief that we control our destiny and deliver ourselves by our strong right arm are illusions, a great self-deception; never are we self-sufficient, we are ever at God's mercy for our breath, health and his sustaining power over the universe whereby all things are held together. We are pathetically weak and trials simply emphasize our condition and destroy our pride.

What, may we ask, do weakness and the resultant dependence achieve? Much in every way. As we are disabused of our reliance upon ourselves we can finally begin to appropriate real power, the power of God, so that we may glorify him, be conformed to the image of Christ, build his Kingdom, and in this find fulfillment, contentment and purpose. It is from a position of weakness that power comes.

The apostle Paul relates an encounter with weakness, weakness occasioned by a chronic physical ailment. After praying several times for it to be removed, Christ comes to him and tells him that "My grace is sufficient for you, for power is perfected in weakness." (2 Cor 12:9a) Power perfected in weakness, amazing! As we give up on our power and accept the weakness with which we are encumbered, God's power can operate to achieve what is truly of value: glorifying God, building his Kingdom and making us into the image of Christ. Being told this, Paul gives a perfectly rational reply: "Most gladly, therefore, I will rather boast about my weaknesses, so that the power of Christ may dwell in me. Therefore I am well content with weaknesses, with insults, with distresses, with persecutions, with difficulties, for Christ's sake; for when I am weak, then I am strong." (2 Cor 12:9b,10) Knowing what Christ has just spoken, the only rational response is to be content with trials, even making them our boast, for by them God's power breaks out into our lives and then into the world.

A condition of weakness then is an excellent, even desirable, condition in which to find ourselves. Not something to be avoided, but welcomed and an occasion for contentment. Think on this for a moment; this is absolutely extraordinary, a revolution in how we understand our lives. But it makes perfect sense only in the economy of God, and brings freedom, peace and purpose, to even the most troubled life. God's wisdom, love and grace toward us are beyond our ability to fathom. To such grace our response must be worship: "Worthy are You, our Lord and our God, to receive glory and honor and power; for You created all things, and because of Your will they existed, and were created." (Rev 4:11)

8.1.2 Two Primary Types

Trials can be separated into two basic types according to the circumstances in which they arise; trials common to all, herein called general trials, and trials that arise from persecution, known in the gospels as our cross. Although these two types of trials occur under very different conditions, they nevertheless can appear quite similar. Not only this, but God's purpose in them is similar, though not identical, and our response to them should not differ,

8.1 The Nature of Trials

at least in our joyful embrace of them.

General Trials

All of mankind, Christian and non-Christian alike, are subject to general trials, but they are not distributed equally among all people; some have far more than others. For the Christian, these trials are divinely appointed[1] and given for our growth and maturity in Christ. These trials often involve, in some way, our financial status, possessions, health, relationships, authority, the environment, strife within a government and strife between governments. Death and dying are trials we all experience. Dying, especially from a disease, can be a very long and difficult trial lasting many years. All have lost loved ones. We have all heard of or experienced the loss of possessions. All have had health problems to one degree or another and our relationships with other people often provide the most fertile ground for trials. Floods, earthquakes, storms and the like have caused great misery and governments have brought untold heartache and suffering.

General trials have a common cause, the fall of man; our sin, my sin and yours. These are things we have brought on ourselves because we have rebelled against God. Death, the most feared trial[2], is earned, "... for the wages of sin is death." All who have ever lived must collect their wages. But not all must die the second death, being cast into the lake of fire, for Christ has restored the way to God.

Creation groans under the rebellion of man and the earth convulses. Death and decay have entered the world, men hate one another and commit evil acts against one another, nations perse-

---

[1] Recall from the chapter on the sovereignty of God that some trials are deliberately brought to us by God while others are permitted to come to us. God, however, redeems them both.

[2] Death is not feared by the Christian. See Paul in Romans 16.

cute their citizens and nations war against other nations bringing misery on a vast scale. Everything decays and riches saved for a rainy day evaporate. And trials abound, for man would rather worship the creature rather than the creator. We would be masters of our own destiny, but we pay a heavy price.

Thankfully, despite our responsibility for the general trials that come to us, God in his love redeems them and uses them to conform us to the image of Christ and build his Kingdom. God takes the evil we have wrought and glorifies himself and brings a blessing.

> And we know that God causes all things to work together for good to those who love God, to those who are called according to His purpose. For those whom He foreknew, He also predestined to become conformed to the image of His Son, ...
>
> Rom 8:28,29

Cross Bearing

Cross bearing, that is persecution, plays a central role in the life of a Christian. It is, like general trials, something we are to joyfully embrace, and something to be expected, for we have been called to it.

> Consider it all joy, my brethren, when you encounter various trials, knowing that the testing of your faith produces endurance. And let endurance have its perfect result, so that you may be perfect and complete, lacking in nothing.
>
> Jas 1:2–4

Cross bearing, however, is not to be understood as a difficult illness, relationship or some other trying circumstance. Nor is it understood to be self-denial. As used by Christ, it is suffering persecution for his sake.

8.1 The Nature of Trials

Early in the gospel of Matthew we find Christ teaching us about persecution — cross bearing.

> Blessed are those who have been persecuted for the sake of righteousness, for theirs is the Kingdom of heaven. Blessed are you when people insult you and persecute you, and falsely say all kinds of evil against you because of Me. Rejoice and be glad, for your reward in heaven is great; for in the same way they persecuted the prophets who were before you.
>
> Matt 5:10–12

James says much the same thing.

> Consider it all joy, my brethren, when you encounter various trials, knowing that the testing of your faith produces endurance.
>
> Jas 1:2,3

And Peter echoes James,

> ... But to the degree that you share the suffering of Christ, keep on rejoicing, so that also at the revelation of his glory you may rejoice with exultation.
>
> 1 Pet 4:13

Contrary to a typical human response we are told to rejoice and be glad, for testing produces endurance; we share in the suffering of the prophets and our reward is great, for we will inherit the Kingdom of heaven. (Matt 5:10–12)

Christ teaches further that we cannot be a follower of him if we do not take up our cross.

> He who loves father or mother more than Me is not worthy of Me; and he who loves son or daughter more than Me is not worthy of Me. And he who does not take his cross and

follow after Me is not worthy of Me. He who has found his life will lose it, and he who has lost his life for My sake will find it.

Matt 10:37–39

Then Jesus said to His disciples, If anyone wishes to come after Me, he must deny himself, and take up his cross and follow Me. For whoever wishes to save his life will lose it; but whoever loses his life for My sake will find it. For what will it profit a man if he gains the whole world and forfeits his soul? Or what will a man give in exchange for his soul?

Matt 16:24–26

Christ's words fell hard on the ears and hearts of his listeners, and so should they fall on us if we understand them. Imagine hearing these words as they heard them: A man whom they had known for years was demanding complete and uncontested allegiance. Not even the closest family tie could interfere, you had to relinquish any claim upon your life and had to suffer persecution with him. Your identification with him had to be complete. So serious and inflexible are the demands that Christ cautions us to stop and consider the cost before we follow him. (Luke 14:25–35) What kind of man would demand so much? Who would be so bold? No mere man could legitimately demand this, but God incarnate could and does even today.

Christ does not permit a multilevel discipleship with varying degrees of commitment; either you are totally his or you are none of his. If a relationship with another competes with your relationship with Christ, you cannot be his disciple. If you are unwilling to deny yourself, you cannot be his disciple. If you are unwilling to take up your cross, you cannot be his disciple. If you will not follow him — believe wholly in him and live as he lives — you cannot be his disciple. If you should seek to save your life for your

8.1 The Nature of Trials

own ends, you will lose it. If you follow him as he demands, and in the process lose your life — give up all claims — you will find it. Either lose your life or find it, there is no middle ground. How different this is from the modern call to follow Christ.

Christ is not asking us to do anything that he has not already done. His love for the Father was unrivaled. As to self-denial "... although he existed in the form of God, did not regard equality with God a thing to be grasped, but emptied himself, taking the form of a bond-servant, and being made in the likeness of men. Being found in appearance as a man, he humbled himself by becoming obedient to the point of death, even death on a cross." (Phil 2:6–8) As to suffering he was "A man of sorrows and acquainted with grief." (Isa 53:3) Christ, as always, is our example.

Persecution is common and expected in the life of a Christian. Christ himself taught that "A slave is not greater than his master. If they persecuted Me, they will also persecute you; if they kept My word, they will keep yours also." (John 15:20) He also said, "Truly I say to you, there is no one who has left house or brothers or sisters or mother or father or children or farms, for My sake and for the gospel's sake, but that he will receive a hundred times as much now in the present age, houses and brothers and sisters and mothers and children and farms, along with persecutions; and in the age to come, eternal life. But many who are first will be last, and the last, first." (Mark 10:29–31) Paul tells us that "... all who desire to live godly in Christ Jesus will be persecuted." (2 Tim 3:12) And Peter says "... do not be surprised at the fiery ordeal among you, which comes upon you for your testing, as though some strange thing were happening to you;..." (1 Pet 4:12) ; "Therefore, since Christ has suffered in the flesh, arm yourselves for the same purpose,..." (1 Pet 4:1); "For you have been called for this purpose, since Christ also suffered for you, leaving you an example for you to follow in his steps." (1 Pet 2:21) Persecution is a normal part of Christian life; its absence is a matter of great concern.

To these passages we may add several more:

> Therefore do not be ashamed of the testimony of our Lord or of me His prisoner, but join with me in suffering for the gospel according to the power of God,...
>
> 2 Tim 1:8

> For to you it has been granted for Christ's sake, not only to believe in Him, but also to suffer for His sake, experiencing the same conflict which you saw in me, and now hear to be in me.
>
> Phil 1:29,30

> Suffer hardship with me, as a good soldier of Christ Jesus.
>
> 2 Tim 2:3

To gain further insight let us examine suffering in Christ's life. Christ suffered as he paid the penalty for our sins on the cross, and at the hands of men. We do not suffer in the same way so as to bring salvation, in a final sense, to mankind, but, we can, in a limited sense, bring redemption to the world through our suffering. As we suffer patiently with Christ in persecution, and perhaps even martyrdom, we bear witness of God's and our love for the world. Historically, we find that persecution and martyrdom are extremely effective in winning souls to Christ. To keep people from being converted, it was not unusual for executioners to prevent the martyr from speaking to the crowd. Love in the face of persecution is profound and powerful. It is said that the the Church is built on the blood of the martyrs. As we participate in persecution we share in the sufferings of Christ and their redemptive capacity.

Christ suffered at the hands of men because they hated him. Men love darkness rather than light for their deeds are evil. (John

8.1 The Nature of Trials

3:19) Christ shined a bright light on their deeds and they hated him for it. Christ represented the Father, the source of all authority, but men would be gods unto themselves and admit no higher authority. But Christ lived a life of love and self-sacrifice. This alone is enough to cause some men to rage.

Men are rebels, at war with God. It is what we are, and those who represent God will be recipients of men's hatred. (John 15:18–25)

In all the persecution he suffered, Christ suffered willingly and did not fight back.

> ...and while being reviled, He did not revile in return; while suffering, He uttered no threats, but kept entrusting Himself to Him who judges righteously; and He Himself bore our sins in His body on the cross, so that we might die to sin and live to righteousness;...
>
> 1 Pet 2:23,24

> He was oppressed and He was afflicted,
> Yet He did not open His mouth;
> Like a lamb that is led to slaughter,
> And like a sheep that is silent before its shearers,
> So He did not open His mouth.
>
> Isa 53:7

By suffering in this way, Christ demonstrated, in the most powerful manner possible, his love and obedience to the Father and his love for us. In the same way, as we willingly suffer persecution, we accomplish similar things; we demonstrate our love for and obedience to God and our love for men.

We must also remember that Christ, for the joy set before him, endured the cross. The joy before him was the redemption of the world, the restoration of all things. (Heb 2:12) To endure, we too must keep the joy set before us firmly in sight, for we will see Christ as he is, live eternally with him, in incorruptible bodies, in a world made new.

As we suffer willingly we choose not to defend ourselves. We choose not to control the situation and place ourselves entirely into God's hands. We choose not to avenge ourselves and we show mercy to our persecutor. In martyrdom we give our life for our persecutor. By our death they see our singular love for God, our obedience to him and our love for them. We lay down our lives voluntarily and there is no mistaking whose child we are. We triumph. We are more than conquerors.

But what is the nature of our triumph? Over what are we conquerors? It is not the type of triumph that the world would identify. We triumph over their evil, we refuse to return evil for evil. Our love for our persecutor triumphs over their evil. Our love remains and becomes a witness of God's love for them. In the steadfastness of our commitment to God's truth and refusal to accept their understanding, we condemn the powers of the world, refuse to acknowledge their priority and judgments. Our obedience to God, and refusal to return evil for evil or to deny Christ, triumphs over the persecutor's desire to see us disobey. But most importantly, we are not separated from the love of God — in this our triumph is greatest. God will permit nothing to separate us from his love. God's conquest of us is proven. We are proven faithful, we are fulfilled, we identify with the sufferings of Christ.

But more is going on as we suffer persecution for Christ's sake. Our faith is confirmed. We stand with Christ. We show our solidarity with him, we believe in him and all that he is and we stand with him in his love for others. We share in his sufferings. The bonds between those who suffer hardship together grows strong, and in the sharing of the experience a closeness develops that only comes from shared hardship. This is why Paul would count all things as loss in view of the surpassing value of knowing Christ

8.2 The Purpose of Trials

and the fellowship of his sufferings. (Phil 3:7–11)

When we stand with Christ in persecution we affirm him and all he stands for. To avoid persecution we must in some way deny him, even if not publicly. We are ashamed of him, we do not love Christ, God and our fellow men. We think only of ourselves and we place ourselves on God's throne. Lest we are tempted to refuse to stand with Christ in suffering let us recall the warning recorded by Matthew.

> But whoever denies Me before men, I will also deny him before My Father who is in heaven.
>
> Matt 10:33

God has clearly ordained trials; both persecution and trials common to all, none of us will escape them. And we would not want to avoid them given what God accomplishes in them, both for himself and us. But lest the reader has become discouraged from this discussion let us be encouraged by Paul's words regarding our hope.

> Therefore we do not lose heart, but though our outer man is decaying, yet our inner man is being renewed day by day. For momentary, light affliction is producing for us an eternal weight of glory far beyond all comparison, while we look not at the things which are seen, but at the things which are not seen; for the things which are seen are temporal, but the things which are not seen are eternal.
>
> 2 Cor 4:16–18

8.2 The Purpose of Trials

8.2.1 General Considerations

On the subject of trials, the two passages below are perhaps the best general summaries to be found. Both our response to and the purpose of trials are made clear.

> And not only this, but we also exult in our tribulations, knowing that tribulation brings about perseverance; and perseverance, proven character; and proven character, hope; and hope does not disappoint, because the love of God has been poured out within our hearts through the Holy Spirit who was given to us.
>
> Rom 5:3–5

> Consider it all joy, my brethren, when you encounter various trials, knowing that the testing of your faith produces endurance. And let endurance have its perfect result, so that you may be perfect and complete, lacking in nothing.
>
> Jas 1:2–4

Consider first the passage found in Romans. Verses three through five are preceded by a central truth; we have been justified by faith and thereby have peace with God. To be justified by faith and not by the works of the Law, thereby having peace with God is good news of the highest degree. But we receive more for we also exult, that is rejoice, in our trials. All lives are filled with trials and in the world's economy trials are to be avoided, not exulted in, and have little or no redeeming qualities. The Christian, however, rejoices in his trials. To be sure, we carry into our trial the joy of our justification by faith and the joy of our future hope, but we also rejoice at the appearance of a trial; the trial itself is an occasion for joy. This should not be surprising since Christ himself told us to rejoice when we are persecuted.

> Blessed are you when people insult you and persecute you, and falsely say all kinds of evil against you because of Me. Rejoice and be glad, for your reward in heaven is great; for in the same way they persecuted the prophets who were

8.2 The Purpose of Trials

> before you
>
> Matt 5:11,12

and Paul concurs

> ... Most gladly, therefore, I will rather boast about my weaknesses, so that the power of Christ may dwell in me. Therefore I am well content with weaknesses, with insults, with distresses, with persecutions, with difficulties, for Christ's sake; for when I am weak, then I am strong.
>
> 2 Cor 12:9,10

and the Apostles' response to persecution is

> So they went on their way from the presence of the Council, rejoicing that they had been considered worthy to suffer shame for His name.
>
> Acts 5:41

The reason the Christian rejoices is that in the Christian's life God sanctifies, by his grace, all trials using them to glorify himself and bless us. Trials, for those not of Christ's Kingdom, often crush and, at times, utterly destroy the individual. They break over them in an overwhelming flood leaving nothing but heartache in their path. The Christian, living in Christ's Kingdom, has a very different experience, one of triumph, victory. Certainly trials can be horribly difficult and overwhelm for a time, but the Christian is assured, he knows that the outcome is certain, that God has redeemed the trial and turns it into victory: glory for himself and a benefit to the Christian.[3] This victory is so complete that the Christian looks upon the trial and rejoices for he knows the end to

---

[3] Remember the benefit to us is conforming us to the image of Christ and knowing him more perfectly. It is essential that we remember this as we suffer the really hard trials, trials that *seem* to have no redemptive value.

which it is directed. The world apart from Christ knows nothing of this victory and it is ours only through the grace of God.[4]

Christians are assured that trials bring about endurance (perseverance). Notice the confidence with which this is stated in the passages above, "... we know ...", not we suspect or are reasonably certain. The trials are not mysterious, confusing, arbitrary acts of God or nature. We know what they work in us and the ends to which they are directed. This confidence is provided for at two levels, first God tells us in his word what he is doing, and second we learn from our experience that God is faithful to accomplish what he has set out to do.

Trials are the instruments God uses to bring endurance. That endurance is needed is obvious for life is difficult; the sin of man brings great heartache, the creation is fallen, our own heart often pulls us away from God and men who hate God persecute those who love him. If we do not have endurance we will falter and abandon our faith. Endurance of any kind is always developed by repeated exercise of the appropriate type. Physical endurance is built by repeated physical exercise, mental endurance is built by repeated mental exercise and spiritual endurance is built by trials. No other means are as effective. To think that we could achieve spiritual maturity without the discipline of trials is ignorance or self-deception of the highest degree. Unfortunately, many Christians consider this principle to be bad news, believing that if this is the case they can do without endurance; it is not worth the trouble. Those who believe this are terribly mistaken.[5]

The nature of endurance is better understood by considering the word from which it is built. The root word in endurance is

---

[4]This victory comes by submitting to God's plan, not taking matters into our own hands. We are not looking for a victory as it is understood by the world, but in a more substantial victory, a lasting victory.

[5]Similarly, do we really think that we can truly know Christ and not share in the fellowship of his sufferings? The idea is preposterous.

8.2 The Purpose of Trials

taken from the art of refining metals and refers to enduring trials without loss or deterioration. Just as gold or silver suffers no loss or deterioration as it is heated, so the Christian suffers no loss — not of anything which he holds dear — or deterioration of character, quality of or joy of life, relationship with God, fulfillment, or any other thing we might care to consider. The Christian suffers the trials without murmuring or discontentment, sure in the knowledge of what God is doing and the final outcome.

Proven character is the fruit of endurance. By repeated faithful endurance of trials our character is refined and we are conformed to the image of Christ.

> For those whom He foreknew, He also predestined to become conformed to the image of His Son, so that He would be the firstborn among many brethren;...
>
> Rom 8:29

As to what we are to become, God's ultimate goal is for us to exhibit the character of Christ. Christ's character then, as presented in the gospels and elaborated in the epistles, is normative for us his followers. As our character is conformed to that of Christ's we are able to truly glorify God, love and serve others, to live in peace, in so far as it depends on us, and be peacemakers ourselves. We come more and more to live like citizens of the Kingdom of God.

Our character is proven in another sense as well. As we examine ourselves we often wonder about the depth of our commitment to Christ and whether we really believe his message. Trials provide the ideal occasion to test our faith and see if it is real. This evidence is of great importance to us since it confirms to us that we really do believe; it makes it even more real and valuable to us. It is a disclosure of our character to ourselves and is one of the things that keeps us going. Our character is also proven to those about us, Christians and non-Christians alike. For our fellow Christians, they find encouragement as they see us faithfully endure and obey and they are given an opportunity to glorify God. For the non-Christian we provide an occasion for them to see the depth of our commitment to Christ. The love and personally character we display in the trial (especially martyrdom), the obedience to God we exhibit and our total commitment to Christ is often overwhelming for them and they come to Christ as a result. This has happened more times than could be counted and was the reason so many were converted to Christianity in the first three centuries.

Now proven character brings hope. The truth and reality of our faith are confirmed and become even more substantial to us and our future hope becomes far more real providing great comfort and spurring us on to greater obedience. The longer we live and the more we learn from our trials, the more important our relationship with Christ becomes; our love of the things of this world diminishes and we see more clearly the value of the hope that has been given to us. As our hope thus develops we find more and more comfort from it and find our endurance greatly increasing.[6]

And let endurance have its perfect result, so that you may be perfect and complete, lacking in nothing. (Jas 1:4) The end result of our trials is that we should be fully mature Christians.[7] That we can be mature Christians is clearly indicated in this passage. By implication, we should not forever remain weak and uncertain in our faith, but should move towards maturity. To define this maturity we could simply compile a list of characteristics a mature Christian should exhibit. A far better way is to consider the

---

[6] Our hope is the resurrection of the body, eternal life in the presence of God, the ultimate defeat of death, complete freedom from sin, the redemption of the creation and the restoration of all things.

[7] This does not mean perfection but maturity. As time passes, we should look more like Christ.

8.2 The Purpose of Trials

character of Christ, our exemplar. This is quite appropriate since it is to the image of Christ that we are being conformed.

As to the blessings, some think that the gains provided to us are only a future reward, derisively called "pie in the sky." The benefit to us, however, is not only future but immediate; our endurance and confidence in God are strengthened, we learn obedience in our suffering, we are further conformed to the image of Christ and our relationship with Christ is deepened. As Christ learned obedience through suffering (Heb 5:8) so also do we. This has great importance in light of John 14:5,

> He who has My commandments and keeps them is the one who loves Me; and he who loves Me will be loved by My Father, and I will love him and will disclose Myself to him.
>
> John 14:5

As we obey Christ he discloses himself to us. For this alone we should rejoice when trials appear. If trials bring greater obedience, which in turn bring a greater disclosure of Christ to us, why would we not rejoice at the coming of a trial? We fail to rejoice only if we do not understand this or do not truly value knowing Christ, in which case we are most likely not one of his. But we receive even more, for as we know Christ more fully, we more fully experience eternal life, even in our present life, for Christ in his high priestly prayer, says that

> This is eternal life, that they may know You, the only true God, and Jesus Christ whom You have sent.
>
> John 17:3

If this does not quicken a Christian's pulse, I have no idea what would. This is truly glorious and utterly undeserved. God has done this for sinful wretches. What amazing love.

8.2.2 A Father's Discipline

The letter of Hebrews was written during a time when persecution was a serious concern. Times of trials not only provide Christians with opportunities to identify with Christ, but also to abandon their faith. The passage found in Hebrews 10:19—12:13 addresses this concern, being an exhortation to faithfully endure, given the serious consequences of abandoning our faith.

Chapter ten begins with a discussion of the inadequacy of the Law to sanctify and the adequacy and scope of Christ's offering. We now have confidence to enter the holy place (this is absolutely astounding) by the blood of Christ, and we are enjoined to hold fast the confession of our hope without wavering and encourage one another to love and good deeds. The exhortation to endure begins with verse 26.

> For if we go on sinning willfully after receiving the knowledge of the truth, there no longer remains a sacrifice for sins, but a terrifying expectation of judgment and the fury of a fire which will consume the adversaries. Anyone who has set aside the Law of Moses dies without mercy on the testimony of two or three witnesses. How much severer punishment do you think he will deserve who has trampled under foot the Son of God, and has regarded as unclean the blood of the covenant by which he was sanctified, and has insulted the Spirit of grace?
>
> Heb 10:26–29

The warning arises from the dire consequences of abandoning our faith, abandonment made evident by a habitual and willful sinning after claiming to have come to Christ. Falling away is a real danger.[8] For those who have abandoned their faith there

---

[8]The warning is clearly written to a true Christian; this person has received the knowledge of the truth and been sanctified by the blood of the covenant.

8.2 The Purpose of Trials

only remains "a terrifying expectation of judgment and the fury of a fire which will consume the adversaries." (Heb 10:27)

The author of Hebrews continues his exhortation by reminding them of "the former days, when, after being enlightened, you endured a great conflict of sufferings ... knowing that you have for yourselves a better possession and a lasting one." (Heb 10:32-34) At some point in the past their faith was vibrant and sincere and they fully understood its value and the hope that was theirs. Surely this should serve to encourage them to endure, to not "throw away their confidence."

> Therefore, do not throw away your confidence, which has a great reward. For you have need of endurance, so that when you have done the will of God, you may receive what was promised.
>
> Heb 10:35,36

The writer again reminds them of the seriousness of abandoning their faith; God has no pleasure in the one who does not endure. But the author, intent on exhortation, expresses confidence in them considering them "not of those who shrink back to destruction, but of those who have faith to the preserving of the soul." (Heb. 10:39)

Often the best encouragement is to be found in examples of those who have lived as we ought, and the author prepares an unparalleled historical review of those who have had faith to the preserving of the soul. The review is comprehensive beginning with Abel and ending with the vast multitude who were persecuted, "not accepting their release, so that they might obtain a better resurrection," (Heb 11:35) "of whom the world was not worthy." (Heb 11:38) In all cases these endured, some under horrible conditions, despising the world's riches and comforts and

---

An excellent discussion of this whole topic is presented by Robert Shank in *Life in the Son*

looking forward to the city made by God and a reward from his hand.

It is significant that this review contains only persons from the Old Testament. The Old Testament saints faithfully endured without having received the promise of the Messiah; his coming and the salvation he would bring were yet future and still they endured, believing in God's promise. Those of us living after Christ's coming have a far more privileged position; Christ has come and his salvation is realized and God's Kingdom has broken out into the world. If those who had not received the promises endured, surely we who live in their fulfillment would be even more inclined to do so.

This great cloud of witnesses should not only encourage us but spur us to action and

> ... lay aside every encumbrance and the sin which so easily entangles us, and let us run with endurance the race that is set before us, fixing our eyes on Jesus, the author and perfecter of faith, ...
>
> Heb 12:1,2

So often there is a sin or encumbrance that causes us to stumble and lose faith; often something we value is the problem. These sins and encumbrances are not to be tolerated, but removed. Vigilance against things that entangle is needful if we are to endure. Endurance, however, is not something that we can ensure by our own strength and actions; we must have God's power. It is on Christ then that we fix our gaze, the author and perfecter of faith. And he is the most perfect example of endurance because he,

> ... for the joy set before Him endured the cross, despising the shame, and has sat down at the right hand of the throne of God. For consider Him who has endured such hostility

8.2 The Purpose of Trials

> by sinners against Himself, so that you will not grow weary and lose heart.
>
> Heb 12:2,3

Because of Christ's redemptive work we are now sons with all the privileges and benefits of sonship even to being heirs with Christ. (Rom 8:16,17) As sons who have not yet been perfected, we are also recipients of God's instruction and discipline and at times scourging. A loving father not only provides positive encouragement, but also discipline. If fatherly discipline is absent there are only two possibilities; either the father does not love the son or one is not in fact a son. Given that God is a responsible loving father who faithfully disciplines his children, it must be that if discipline is absent then we are not his child. The absence of discipline is a very bad sign.

It is partly in this way, by Godly discipline, that Christ is the perfecter of our faith for "it is for discipline that we endure" (Heb 12:7). And it is through discipline that we grow.

> ... He disciplines us for our good, so that we may share His holiness. All discipline for the moment seems not to be joyful, but sorrowful; yet to those who have been trained by it, afterwards it yields the peaceful fruit of righteousness.
>
> Heb 12:10,11

Even though discipline is difficult to endure, the end result is to share in God's holiness, to become holy. If we are willing to endure, holiness and peace await us.

On this side of eternity we will forever be in need of spiritual growth for our flesh is not yet redeemed. In some cases we need training or education, for we lack understanding, but in other cases we may willfully disobey and need to be punished — scourged. In either case, our father takes it upon himself to discipline us in ways that glorifies himself and benefits us. God takes it upon himself to order our lives for the perfecting of our faith.

All our trials should be seen in light of this great truth, for our trials are part of God's discipline and instruction. All our trials have been ordained and provided for by our loving Father to make us holy. There is great commonality between this passage in Hebrews and those above in James and Romans; our trials are for our growth and maturity, to be conformed to the image of God's Son. But the passage in Hebrews brings the matter to us in a more personal way. God, our loving Father, takes it upon himself to train us in righteousness. The trials that come to us are not part of some mysterious uncontrollable force, nor a chaotic hurtling series of events, nor are they part of some inscrutable plan we have no hope of understanding; no, all that happens in our life is purposeful, provided by our Father who loves us perfectly and orders all our ways. Knowing this, why would we not embrace our trials joyfully? The only thing that would subvert his love is our rejection of it, resulting in "a terrifying expectation of judgment and the fury of a fire which will consume the adversaries."

8.2.3 Specific Reasons

We know the strategic reasons why we endure trials; to glorify God, be conformed to the image of Christ and build the Kingdom, but we are also informed, in a general sense, of the tactical aspects. Unfortunately, we are usually unable to make use of this since we are seldom informed as to the exact nature of the tactical reasons for our particular trial. This is not to say that it is useless to consider the tactical reasons, for God does, at times, reveal them to us. This is particularly the case when our trials come to us as a result of sin in our lives.

What follows is a presentation of the more important specific tactical reasons. However, it is not a complete list.

In 2 Corinthians 12 we find Paul relating an encounter with

8.2 The Purpose of Trials

Christ where he is informed that the infirmity in his flesh is given to protect him from becoming proud. The basis of this pride was the vision of the third heaven which God had revealed to him. Without this chronic trial he would have succumbed to spiritual pride, making him useless to God and perhaps even shipwrecked in his own faith. God, knowing this, with great love, did what was necessary to protect Paul from himself. It is very doubtful that this has only happened once, and many may suffer trials for similar reasons, the trials becoming precious wounds from a faithful, loving Father.

The trials of Job arise from a conflict in heaven, Job, in some sense, being secondary to the real conflict. The conflict is between Satan and God. Satan comes to challenge God regarding the basis of Job's obedience. Satan claims that Job only loves God because God has done good things for him; if God will withdraw his blessing Satan predicts that Job will curse God. God accepts the challenge and permits Satan to bring suffering to Job. However, in all this Job does not act as Satan expects although Job becomes very confused and despondent. In the conclusion God is vindicated and Job is restored to his former position many times over.

We learn several things from Job's life and trial. First, we see that trials can be occasioned on heavenly conflict, not anything that happens on earth. Even then we know that God will use it to refine us and glorify himself. Second we see that trials can come to the best of us; Job, by God's own evaluation, is the best man on earth; "For there is no one like him on the earth, a blameless and upright man fearing God and turning away from evil." (Job 2:3) Third, God does not owe us an answer for what happens in our life. We must accept what he permits. At the end of the trial we find Job becoming despondent, confused and not a little put out with God; things are not working out as they are supposed to, at least not as he expects. God appears to Job, and rather than tell him why the trial has come he makes Job, by a series of questions, acknowledge that he has no right to challenge God. Only submission is proper. It is at this time that God restores his fortunes.

In the life of Joseph we find God saving the beginnings of an entire nation from famine. Because of jealousy, Joseph is sold into slavery by his brothers, where, at the bottom of his trials, he ends up in prison. From here he miraculously becomes second in command to the king of Egypt. The story is extraordinary and we see the sovereign hand of God at work in many places. The important thing for us to take away is that God was working all the time, no matter how bad it became, to accomplish his divine purpose.

Although we could continue this discussion, we will end with Christ's healing of a blind man. After healing the man, Christ's disciples ask him the reason for the man's blindness: was it due to his sin or his parents sin? To this Christ replies that it was not due to sin but rather that God might be glorified. The reason for the blindness was that God might be glorified by this specific event. We could extend this principle in many ways, but we are not to think that any and all illnesses will be healed so as to glorify God. This was not the case for Paul, in fact God himself gave him the physical ailment. What we must understand is that whatever the trial, it may have been given to bring glory to God in some very specific manner. This is beyond the general way that God glorifies himself in all the affairs of men, in this instance God is uniquely bringing glory to himself.

The specific reason for a trial is often not revealed to us as it was to Paul, Joseph or the blind man. But this we do know, God brings them in his love and care for us and his intention is that he be glorified, we be conformed to the image of Christ and his

8.2 The Purpose of Trials

Kingdom built.

Chapter 9

The Nature of Maturity

9.1 The Imperative

The end to which all things is directed is the glory of God, and the bringing in of the Kingdom of God is one of the most important ways this is done. And as God brings men and women into his Kingdom, his Kingdom is built. However, it is not enough to simply redeem us and place us into his Kingdom; God's intention is to conform us to the image of his Son as we cooperate with the power of the Spirit of God who lives within us. Only those who are living lives that, in a real way, resemble Christ's life can live in this Kingdom. Those who do not see the need, or simply refuse to live like Christ and yet believe they are in the Kingdom of God, are terribly mistaken.

In Romans we find Paul telling us of God's plan to conform us to the image of Christ.

> For those whom He foreknew, He also predestined to become conformed to the image of His Son, so that He would be the firstborn among many brethren; ...
>
> Rom 8:29

Paul's teaching follows naturally from what Christ had already taught — he calls us to follow him and he calls us to be holy as our Father in heaven is holy. (Mark 8:34–38, Luke 9:23–27, Matt 10:37–39, Matt 16:24–26)

This is more than just a call to simply follow; if you follow me you must be like me; it is an imperative. It is impossible to be a follower of Christ if you do not live like Christ.[1] The word *follow* implies far more than simply going where he went, or believing what he believed. The context is that of a disciple, and a disciple was to adopt the beliefs, values and way of life, of his teacher. It is imperative that we understand that we are to follow how Christ lived, and not only have his 'doctrine.' I do not mean to reduce the importance of proper knowledge, but if proper knowledge does not bring about proper behavior then we are mistaken that we have proper knowledge. This unhealthy emphasis on proper doctrine has plagued Western Christianity since the days of the Reformation.[2]

To conform us to the image of Christ, God uses a great many means, but our focus here is on trials, and in trials we find God working the most profound changes in our character. But we must now ask, "What is the image of Christ?"

9.2 The Nature of Christ

Interestingly, we have already spent a considerable amount of time on this subject as we examined the Kingdom of God. As we developed the principles of the Kingdom of God in the New Testament, we studied the life and teachings of Christ; Christ is our

---

[1] On this earth we are to make steady progress in our emulation of Christ, but we will never become fully like Christ. However, even here our goal is to be as much like Christ as possible.

[2] From the early 1500's, a notable exception was and continues to be many from the Anabaptist tradition.

9.2 The Nature of Christ

exemplar. We saw how Christ was committed to the principles of the Sabbath year and Jubilee, that is, economic and social justice. We examined his indiscriminate love and forgiveness, his kindness and gentleness, his inclusion of all, his compassion and care of the poor, outcast, sick, sinner, tax collector, his condemnation of the rulers for their exploitation of the disadvantaged, his demand for social and economic justice, that the reach of the Kingdom and its practices were for all men at all times, and his example of and demand for servanthood. To look at the life of Christ and seriously consider how he lived and what he taught is to understand what it means to be conformed to the image of Christ.

If we had to use a single word to describe what Christ, in his humanity, exhibited it must be servanthood. This is exactly what Paul is telling us in Philippians 2. In all things Christ served, even to the laying down of his life. (Mark 10:45). If we should want to gage the depth of our maturity, perhaps we should examine how well we are serving Christ and others.

With respect to love, the love Christ showed to both men and women is unexcelled. He is kind, gentle and compassionate, but he does not stop there; his love turns to action. He is always humble and is never arrogant or acts unbecomingly. He never seeks his own need and does not take into account a wrong suffered (1 Cor 13:4–8). He always has time for all who come to him, from the child to the Jewish scholar. When exhausted and in need of rest, he puts aside his own needs and tends to the needs of others (Mark 10:45). And he included all by breaking down all barriers. But most importantly for us, he endured the cross to transfer us from the kingdom of darkness to the kingdom of light.

To further develop what is the image of Christ we could examine many passages, but the encounter with the woman at the well contains much of what we see in Christ's life in one significant event and is worth closer examination.

The Woman at the Well

Christ's encounter with the woman at the well (John 4:3–42) is often discussed, but we need to consider it once more, for Christ's compassion and loving action are powerfully demonstrated. In it we see Christ at work, his character on display and we see what it means to be like Christ. To put the meeting in the proper perspective we must review the historical context.[3]

That part of ancient Israel known as Samaria was conquered by the Assyrians in 722/721 B.C. After the conquest, there followed a mass deportation of Jews; only a small remnant was left behind. As was often done by conquerors at this time, the Assyrians replaced those deported with people from other lands; in this case Gentiles. The Jewish remnant intermarried with the Gentile settlers and adopted much of their culture and religious beliefs resulting in a religion consisting of a mixture of Judaism and paganism; a religion that orthodox Jews held in contempt along with those who believed it. Jews considered the Samaritans little different from Gentiles. In fact, John tells us that "Jews have no dealings with Samaritans." (John 4:9) It is through this region and people that Jesus is journeying.

Christ, on his way to Galilee from Judea, had to pass through Samaria. Along the journey a stop was made at the city of Sychar where Jesus, being tired and thirsty, sat down by a well around noon, the hottest part of the day. As Christ was waiting for his disciples to return from procuring food in the city, a Samaritan woman came to the well to draw water.

Christ asked this woman for a drink of water. She was quite rightly surprised by this request; Christ's dress identified him as a Jew and she was well aware of the animosity between Jews and

---

[3]This information also relates to the parable of the good Samaritan and that the good news is to go out to the Samaritan and the Gentiles as well as the Jew. We see a precursor to the Great Commission.

9.2 The Nature of Christ

Samaritans. Her reply expressed her surprise "How is it that You, being a Jew, ask me for a drink since I am a Samaritan woman?" We cannot tell whether her question contained any indignation or condemnation, but Christ graciously ignored this comment for he was intent on revealing to her that he is the Messiah, the answer to her deepest needs. His response was perfectly designed to lead her where she needed to go. "If you knew the gift of God, and who it is who says to you, 'Give Me a drink,' you would have asked Him, and He would have given you living water." The woman did not yet know that Christ was speaking figuratively and she pointed out that he had no means of drawing water and expressed her puzzlement; where does one get this water?

Christ replied that "Everyone who drinks of this water will thirst again; but whoever drinks of the water that I will give him shall never thirst; but the water that I will give him will become in him a well of water springing up to eternal life." This water possesses truly unique qualities; it has the power to slate ones thirst forever and become the source of eternal life. This is water indeed and the woman seemed genuinely moved to receive it for she asked "Sir, give me this water, so I will not be thirsty nor come all the way here to draw."

Christ had her attention and the woman had some sense that something important was being said, but she did not yet know how important. Christ now goes much deeper, he intends to further reveal her need, but he does so in a most gracious manner. He asks "Go, call your husband and come here." Her response is simple, but true, "I have no husband." With any other man this would have been sufficient to end the discussion. But this is the Messiah speaking to her and he intends to see her delivered to his Kingdom and his knowledge is far more than any man's. "You have correctly said, I have no husband; for you have had five husbands, and the one whom you now have is not your husband;

this you have said truly." was his reply. We are uncertain how it is she came to have five husbands, whether it was from divorce or extraordinarily unfortunate occurrences, but we now know that she is living in adultery.

The woman must have been shocked. This Jewish man, whom she had never seen before, knew things about her that he could not reasonably know. Not only this, he knows that she is living in adultery and he, being a Jew, is sitting there graciously conversing with her when he might just as well have been condemning her. Further, why would such a man with this knowledge even have begun a conversation with her? What of his reputation among his people, for "Jews have no dealings with Samaritans." She still does not know that this is he who was sent, "for God so loved the world." He has come to seek and to save those who are lost.

The woman now knows that she is speaking to a holy man who possesses knowledge beyond other men and her questions turn to how one should worship God; should God be worshiped on mount Gerazim as the Samaritans believe or in Jerusalem as the Jews insist? Christ makes it clear that the proper place of temple worship is in Jerusalem, but he has far more to say about the worship of God; "... an hour is coming, and now is, when the true worshipers will worship the Father in spirit and truth; for such people the Father seeks to be His worshipers. God is spirit, and those who worship Him must worship in spirit and truth." Christ reveals so much here. He gives a faint indication of the mystery to be revealed; salvation has come to the Gentile as well as the Jew.[4] There will no more be a distinction between Jew, Samaritan and Gentile. And he has given this message to an adulterous Samaritan woman, a woman who would be held in

---

[4]This story is one of the clearest demonstrations of the mystery to be revealed — the new covenant is for all, not just the Jew — that we find in the Gospels.

9.2 The Nature of Christ

contempt by any other Jew. Words simply fail to describe the grace, love and kindness of God the Son.

The woman is now more convinced than ever that the man before her is no ordinary man, and by her next comment she seems to be wondering if the man before her is the Messiah. "I know that Messiah is coming (He who is called Christ); when that One comes, He will declare all things to us." Think of the anticipation and the excitement in her heart as she awaits his reply; Could this really be the Messiah? Could he bring meaning to this broken life of mine? Am I a fool to think that if the Messiah should come that he would speak to me? The amazing reply comes, "I who speak to you am He." It is more than she could have hoped for, it is to the Messiah she now speaks and a flood of emotions crash over her. What can she do?, Who can she go tell?, she must do something! Forgetting the task at hand she runs into the city and tells them "Come, see a man who told me all the things that I have done; this is not the Christ, is it?" and the men come out to speak with the Messiah.

At about the time she leaves Christ at the well, the disciples come back and are amazed to find Christ concluding his conversation with a strange Samaritan woman. While the disciples offer Christ the food they went to procure, the men of the city begin to make their way to him. In response to the disciples' offer Christ makes an unusual reply "I have food that you do not know about?" Christ, in a manner common to him, is preparing the disciples for a lesson. "My food is to do the will of Him who sent me and to accomplish His work." At this moment it is the harvesting for salvation of the field of men now approaching him. Christ does indeed harvest this field and over the next two days, as he stays with them, many come to believe in him.

What happens here is extraordinary:

- Christ humbles himself to speak to a common woman, one

he knows is an adulteress.

- Christ's words are gentle and kind.

- Christ's love is extended to a people thought previously outside of God's blessing.

- Christ has no concern of what others will say about him. No concern for reputation.

- Christ even spends two days with these people, with many coming to him in belief. He is staying with and eating with Samaritans! This is certainly the first indication of the mystery to be revealed; salvation has come to the Gentile as well as to the Jew.

Much of what we have already discussed in the chapters on the Kingdom is here, servanthood, indiscriminate love, love for the outcast and despised and the breaking down of barriers, and it demonstrates how we must live as we are conformed to the image of Christ.

Chapter 10

Weakness and Strength

God's attitude with respect to weakness and strength can be seen in the following passages.

> ... God has chosen the foolish things of the world to shame the wise, and God has chosen the weak things of the world to shame the things which are strong, ... so that no man may boast before God.
>
> 1 Cor 1:27,29

> Thus says the LORD, "Cursed is the man who trusts in mankind and makes flesh his strength, and whose heart turns away from the LORD."
>
> Jer 17:5

The fact is we are weak. Amazingly, most of us don't realize it. Weakness is to be preferred over strength, at least the strength of this world. Weakness is the way to God's power, power to accomplish his will for his glory.

Our contemporary world, however, has no interest in weakness. Weakness of any kind is to be avoided and power is to be sought at all costs. As a society, we seek to control and have power over everything we touch; the politician is to care for every need and solve every social and economic problem; the scientist is to have all knowledge of material things and complete mastery over the the physical world; the doctor is to protect us from all sickness and disease; Madison Avenue tells us that we can all look like Greek gods and goddesses and have the power that derives from such an appearance. In the Western world, every problem must yield to our methods and every mystery explained. In America, nearly every geopolitical problem finds its solution in the use of military power. Absolutely nothing is to be beyond our control; all we need is the will to solve, explain, fix. This attitude prevails despite the fact that the politician seems only to make things worse; the scientist brings us only the empty philosophy of scientific materialism and more effective means of destroying ourselves; the doctor gives us ways to enhance our health and lengthen our days so that we can indulge ourselves more; Madison Avenue gives us an utterly empty, vapid and debased popular culture. The exercise of our power leaves a bitter taste — we deceive ourselves, having only an illusion of power.

The vast majority of those who go by the name of Christian also have little use for weakness. A particularly virulent strain of Christianity tells us that we are to be rich and healthy at all times, that is, possessors of monetary and physical power, despite what our Lord and his apostles taught.

With respect to wealth, did our Lord not say, "So then, none of you can be My disciple who does not give up all his own possessions." (Luke 14:33), and "Do not store up for yourselves treasures on earth, where moth and rust destroy, and where thieves break in and steal." (Matt 6:19). And with respect to weakness Paul says, "If I have to boast, I will boast of what pertains to my weakness." (2 Cor 11:30)

Among many, even those who are considered to be within Christian orthodoxy, the belief in power rather than weakness is more refined, but no less unhealthy. This is consistent with the American mindset that with the right methodology (exercise of power in the proper way) we can make our churches grow (wrongly assuming that growth is the point) and successfully live the Christian life. We embrace the exercise of violence to protect ourselves in our interpersonal relationships rather than choosing nonviolence and trusting in God. Rather than lay up treasure in heaven we lay up treasure on earth, trusting in our own power, storing up enormous wealth to ensure an idle old age, thereby, ignoring God's command not to store up treasure on earth.[1] (Matt 6:19–21,33) Most of us trust in our own strength even for our daily provision; just consider how we respond when we lose our job; shock and fear overcome us at the loss of our ability to take care of ourselves. We act as if we have only ourselves to rely on; God's provision is almost an afterthought.[2] Unfortunately, power rather than weakness is preferred.

By contrast, weakness is highly valued in God's economy, for through weakness God's power is released into our lives and then into the world. More properly stated, the acknowledgment of our utter and complete weakness is valued, for we are indeed weak.

---

[1] Think about how much money, time and effort are needed to avoid working, say, past the age of 55 or 60. Retirement at this early an age could not be considered 50 years ago. Only the very rich were able to do so. Remember also that the requirement to provide for all your own expenses in retirement has arisen as children have abandoned their parents in old age and as the expectation grew that if the individual could not amass a large enough fortune to take care of themselves they must rely on the government.

[2] It must be stated that the fear that accompanies the loss of a job is made worse by the absence of properly functioning churches. If our churches were committed to taking care of the needy in a manner similar to the early church, people would be less inclined to despair, for they could actually see a way for God's love and care to come to them.

We are not powerful. By weakness, the sin of pride is defeated, and the power of God is set free in our lives to transform us, and more importantly, enable us to glorify God. When we are aware of our weakness, God is properly lifted up and we are properly subordinated leaving little room for pride. Pride is the first sin and a theft of God's glory. As long as we rely on our own strength or the strength of others, God's power cannot operate through us and we are trapped in our weakness and are ineffective in our service to God and remain unable to glorify him.

The world sees the path of weakness and sees in it the path to defeat. It is foolishness. Fitting is the passage from Corinthians.

> But a natural man does not accept the things of the Spirit of God, for they are foolishness to him; and he cannot understand them, because they are spiritually appraised.
>
> 1 Cor 2:14

The world despises God's means and ends, for they simply cannot understand them.

The Christian, on the other hand, sees power in the path of weakness, but not personal power or power for its own sake or for personal use. It is power to bear fruit to God's glory (John 15:8). It is power to withstand the attacks of the evil one (Eph 6:10,11). It is power for our struggle "against the rulers, against the powers, against the world forces of this darkness, against the spiritual forces of wickedness in the heavenly places," (Eph 6:12) and it is power for the destruction of spiritual fortresses (2 Cor 10:4). Make no mistake about it, the path of weakness is not some effeminate, ineffective religious experience, but the release of God's very power into the world to defeat and gain victory over the real powers, in God's name, for his glory.

10.1 The Necessity of God's Power

Our need for God's power should be obvious but let us explicitly enumerate some of the more important reasons.

Salvation

Most importantly, we need God's power for salvation; not only for our salvation, but for the world's. The power that accomplishes this is not a power that we exercise, but rather power from which we benefit. Saving ourselves from God's wrath and restoring the way to God is something to which we cannot make even the slightest contribution, for there are none righteous, no one understands, no one seeks God. All turn aside. We have become useless. (Rom 3:10–12)

For Knowledge and Being Filled

In Ephesians chapter three we have one of Paul's beautiful prayers for the church.

> For this reason I bow my knees before the Father, from whom every family in heaven and on earth derives its name, that He would grant you, according to the riches of His glory, to be strengthened with power through His Spirit in the inner man, so that Christ may dwell in your hearts through faith; and that you, being rooted and grounded in love, may be able to comprehend with all the saints what is the breadth and length and height and depth, and to know the love of Christ which surpasses knowledge, that you may be filled up to all the fullness of God.
>
> Now to Him who is able to do far more abundantly beyond all that we ask or think, according to the power that works within us, to Him be the glory in the church and in Christ Jesus to all generations forever and ever. Amen.
>
> Eph 3:14–21

The heart of this prayer is that we be strengthened with power through his Spirit so that Christ may dwell in us, and being rooted and grounded in love, able to comprehend, in all its ways, the incomprehensible love of Christ so we may be filled up with the fullness of God.

This is an extraordinary prayer and worth further examination.

Strengthened with power — Paul prays a number of things beginning with the request that we be strengthened with power through the Spirit. Real power only comes from God and things as valuable as those prayed for here do not come by our strength.

That Christ may dwell in us — It is only as Christ dwells in us that we have power to live the life God wants. What a blessing for us to have such intimate fellowship with the Creator.

Able to comprehend the love of Christ — Notice the prerequisite to understanding Christ's love; we must be rooted and grounded in love. One who does not love will not understand Christ's love. But it is by the power of Christ that we can love and then understand his love. It is not possible to fully understand Christ's love; Paul's desire is for us to comprehend the incomprehensible. Christ's love is so deep that no matter what we now know, it is, and will remain, utterly incomplete. What love would move God to lay aside his glory, take the form of a man, live in obscurity for thirty years, suffer the hatred and scorn of men, die a cursed death at the hands of men and suffer the punishment due men for their rebellion against him to save these very same men?

To be filled up with the fullness of God — Clearly, words are failing the apostle; he is trying to put into words what cannot be fully expressed. We must live out the Christian life to begin to understand. Christ discloses himself as we obey.[3] (John 14:21)

---

[3]Christ's disclosure does not come to us as we study, but as we live in obedience.

10.1 The Necessity of God's Power

Barnes in his commentary provides an excellent discussion on the meaning of this phrase.

> It means here, "that you may have the richest measures of divine consolation and of the divine presence; that you may partake of the entire enjoyment of God in the most ample measure in which he bestows his favors on his people."
>
> (3) It was to be with "all" the fullness of God; Not with partial and stinted measures of his gracious presence, but with a "all" which he ever bestows. Religion is not a name. It is not a matter of form. It is not a trifle. It is the richest, best gift of God to man. It ennobles our nature. It more clearly teaches us our true dignity that all the profound discoveries which people can make in science; for none of them will ever fill us with the fullness of God. Religion is spiritual, elevating, pure, godlike. We dwell with God; walk with God; live with God; COMMUNE WITH GOD; ARE LIKE GOD. WE BECOME PARTAKERS OF THE DIVINE NATURE 2 Pet. 1:4; in rank we are associated with angels; in happiness and purity we are associated with God![4]

The benediction expresses Paul's confidence in God. Although Paul knows that language is inadequate to express what he wants, he is confident that God understands, for he is able to do far more abundantly beyond all that we ask or think. Not only this, but God wants to bless us abundantly with the most meaningful and precious thing — himself.

For Life and Godliness

It is simply impossible to live a life honoring to God without God's power, even after becoming one of God's children. Although we have been delivered to the kingdom of light we are still

---

[4] Barnes, *Barnes' Notes on the New Testament*, Discussion on Eph 3:19

clothed with our fleshly bodies and cannot faithfully obey without supernatural help. Being the gracious God that he is, we see "that His divine power has granted to us everything pertaining to life and godliness, through the true knowledge of Him who called us by His own glory and excellence." (2 Pet 1:3)

God, by his power, has provided everything for life and godliness; we lack absolutely nothing.

To do God's Works and thereby Glorify Him

In Ephesians 2, and elsewhere, we find that we have been created unto good works, works that bring glory to God. Good works are to be the heart beat of our lives as we function in our most elemental Christian capacity — a servant.

But to do good works we must have the power of God which is only made available by abiding in Christ, for apart from him we can do nothing. Abiding may sound mysterious, but it is doing his will, being devoted to prayer, immersed in his word, yielding to the Spirit, obeying his commands and fellowshipping with his people. (John 15:5)

Paul himself would not attempt to labor apart from God's power, but strived according to it, being confident that it worked mightily within him. (Col 1:29) And Peter exhorts us to serve by the strength that God supplies. (1 Pet 4:11)

To Build a Proper Foundation

Foundations are that upon which all things stand. Have we built our lives on sand or rock? Have we built a ministry on the foundation of our own power? Have we built a company or built a family in our own strength? God forbid that we should, for great will be its fall. Only the foundations of God's power, and obedience to the commands of Christ are sufficient.

Even Paul, in his ministry, did not rely on his strength even though his training and intellect were vast. While ministering,

10.1 The Necessity of God's Power

he chose not to use superiority of speech, wisdom or persuasive words, and instead, communicated one thing — Christ and him crucified. He came in weakness, speaking the only message necessary and relied on God's power to do the rest.

> And when I came to you, brethren, I did not come with superiority of speech or of wisdom, proclaiming to you the testimony of God. For I determined to know nothing among you except Jesus Christ, and Him crucified. I was with you in weakness and in fear and in much trembling, and my message and my preaching were not in persuasive words of wisdom, but in demonstration of the Spirit and of power, so that your faith would not rest on the wisdom of men, but on the power of God.
>
> 1 Cor 2:1–5

Men bringing God's word to the world are not to use their own wisdom and powers of persuasion, but rather to bring it in the power of the Spirit of God. Otherwise, the hearer's faith and the preachers ministry may rest on sand rather than rock. This critiques, rather negatively, the methods of Christian marketing.

To Fight the Battle

To see the need for God's power in our life it is helpful to understand the nature of the battle in which we are engaged. If we fail to understand this, we will fight the wrong battle with the wrong weapons.

The struggle in which we are engaged is not against flesh and blood; our adversaries are far more powerful. We struggle against rulers and powers of the world forces of darkness and spiritual forces of wickedness in heavenly places. (Eph 6:12)

Many think that the battles and powers we physically observe are the focus of real power and action. On the contrary, what we see with our eyes is minor league action. The important powers are spiritual, not physical. The power we see in the world is a consequence of the spiritual. Likewise, the battles we see in the world are not the ones we must win; we must rather win the battles in the spiritual realm. It is there where victory and loss obtain the greatest consequences.

Seeing that our battle in not with the physical things in this world we have weapons not of this world, weapons which are divinely powerful for the destruction of fortresses. The things we destroy are speculations and lofty things which hide the knowledge of God and we take our very thoughts captive to the obedience of Christ. (2 Cor 10:3–6)

Swords, guns, tanks, battleships and the like are worthless against the world forces of darkness, and the destruction of fortresses. We must use the weapons God supplies.

> Finally, be strong in the Lord and in the strength of His might.Put on the full armor of God, so that you will be able to stand firm against the schemes of the devil. For our struggle is not against flesh and blood, but against the rulers, against the powers, against the world forces of this darkness, against the spiritual forces of wickedness in the heavenly places. Therefore, take up the full armor of God, so that you will be able to resist in the evil day, and having done everything, to stand firm. Stand firm therefore,having girded your loins with truth, and having put on the breastplate of righteousness, and having shod your feet with the preparation of the gospel of peace; in addition to all, taking up the shield of faith with which you will be able to extinguish all the flaming arrows of the evilone. And take the helmet of salvation, and the sword of the Spirit, which is the word of God.
>
> Eph 6:10–17

Notice that there are no offensive weapons except the Word of God. Our sword is God's truth which is sharper than a two edged sword, dividing the thoughts and intension's of the heart. (Heb 4:12) We go out into the battle as servants, coercing no one, exercising no authority (Mark 10:42–45), considering others as more important than ourselves (Phil 2:2–4) and go about tearing down fortresses.

Be strong in the Lord and in the strength of his might. This is what we must do. The battle is beyond us, we cannot wage this war in our own strength. Only by God's power may we prevail.

To Endure Trials

Enduring in trials is terribly difficulty, especially if they are severe and linger long. But we know that we are to be "... strengthened with all power, according to His glorious might, for the attaining of all steadfastness and patience; ..." (Col 1:11) We do not have to do it alone or in our own power.

For the timid and afraid among us Paul gives this encouragement; "... do not be ashamed of the testimony of our Lord or of me His prisoner, but join with me in suffering for the gospel according to the power of God,..." (2 Tim. 1:8) Certainly, trials are difficult, but we have the wonderful heritage of brothers and sisters in Christ who have joined in Christ's sufferings. God's power is available to us so we might join in the suffering of persecution and so fill up what is lacking in Christ's afflictions. (Col 1:24)

10.2 God's Predisposition to Use the Weak

God is predisposed to use those who know they are weak and are perceived as weak by the world. In fact, God deliberately uses the weak.

> For consider your calling, brethren, that there were not many wise according to the flesh, not many mighty, not

many noble; but God has chosen the foolish things of the world to shame the wise, and God has chosen the weak things of the world to shame the things which are strong, and the base things of the world and the despised God has chosen, the things that are not, so that He may nullify the things that are, so that no man may boast before God.

1 Cor 1:26–29

God shares his glory with no one and his choice of the weak ensures that everyone knows that God's will is accomplished with God's power. It is not that the powerful could in fact do it, they could not, but his deliberate choice of the weak leaves no doubt about the source of power.

The Apostles

Consider the apostles. With the exception of Paul, the apostles were uneducated, and simple men; hardly a group man in his wisdom would choose to bring God's message and turn the world upside down. But who would doubt by whose power the world was changed? It was not by the cleverness of men, but the power of God. (2 Cor 2:2–5)

Gideon Judg 6:11—7:25

In the Old Testament, as well as the New, we find God using the weak and unlikely. During the period of the Judges we find God choosing Gideon, a farmer, an uncertain and hesitant leader. However, he believed God and carried out the the task God set before him. That Gideon did not hold himself in high esteem, is clear from his reply to the angel of the Lord when told he was to deliver Israel from the oppression of Midian.

Gideon did not come from a great and powerful family, well connected to the paths of power, and Gideon was not the first among his own father's household. He was painfully aware that he could not do this in his own power. (Judg 6:15) God, knowing

10.2 God's Predisposition to Use the Weak   199

his weakness, assured him that he would supply the power. (Judg 6:16)

Not only was Gideon weak in the eyes of the world, but his plan and method of battle were simply contrary to all human wisdom. No one would devise such a plan. Twenty two thousand warriors responded to Gideon's call to battle, surely a welcome development seeing that the opposing army was 135,000 strong. But God's plan was to both deliver Israel and ensure that Israel, and those around them, knew that they were delivered by God's hand. Therefore, twenty two thousand men was far too many.

> ... The people who are with you are too many for Me to give Midian into their hands, for Israel would become boastful, saying, My own power has delivered me.
>
> Judg 7:2

At God's command Gideon gave an opportunity, for those who are afraid, to depart and return home; the twenty two thousand become ten thousand, "but the people are still too many." The ten thousand were further reduced in number when the ten thousand came to drink by separating "everyone who laps the water with his tongue as a dog laps." Only three hundred remained; surely an impossibly small number to take on an army of 135,000. And yet God made it clear that he was the one who was to provide the victory.

> ... I will deliver you with the three hundred men who lapped and will give the Midianites into your hands; ...
>
> Judg 7:7

The battle plan was, perhaps, the most unusual ever devised. The three hundred remaining men were to take glass lanterns and trumpets and surround the enemy's camp during the night. At Gideon's command the three hundred smashed their lanterns and blew their trumpets and in the enemy camp panic and confusion reigned, and "the Lord set the sword of one against another even throughout the whole army and the army fled." In the end, no one misunderstood, all knew that God had brought the victory.

God's use of Gideon, an unlikely leader, and a "foolish" method is *normative* in the Scriptures; God does it nearly all the time.

David

The second king of Israel was a poet, lyricist, musician, shepherd and the youngest of his father's house; an unlikely candidate for a king. There is one thing that David understood well — power came not from him, but from God. The earliest occasion we see this understanding displayed comes when David makes known to king Saul his desire to confront the Philistine champion Goliath. David, as a shepherd, was prepared for battle since he had to protect his flock from many predators, such as lions and bears. To this end he carried a sling, a simple but difficult weapon to use skillfully. It is said that many hours, perhaps most of one's youth, were needed to become skillful with a sling. Yet David does not rely on his skill to defeat the champion. He tells king Saul that

> "Your servant has killed both the lion and the bear; and this uncircumcised Philistine will be like one of them, since he has taunted the armies of the living God." And David said, "The LORD who delivered me from the paw of the lion and from the paw of the bear, He will deliver me from the hand of this Philistine." And Saul said to David, "Go, and may the LORD be with you."
>
> 1 Sam 17:36,37

David understood that neither in the past with the lion and the bear nor now against the giant was it his skill that had delivered him, but God's power. As far as David was concerned, the battle was God's; he was only a vehicle through which God would exercise his power; his contribution was obedience.

10.2 God's Predisposition to Use the Weak

Not only did David have a proper understanding of his own weakness, but he refused to take up power when the opportunity arose. To see this it is instructive to see how David became king.

For refusing to carry out God's command to completely destroy the people of Amalek, Saul had been rejected by God as king over Israel. A short time after informing Saul that God had rejected him as king, Samuel, the prophet, anointed David as king. This was done in secret in David's father's house. David, however, does not ascend to the throne at this time. God has his own schedule and plan and David does not take matters into his own hands despite the fact that God's prophet Samuel, the only one who could rightly anoint his as king had done so. David chooses not to take up the power at his disposal even though he is now the rightful king of Israel.[5]

Despite the rejection of Saul as king, he remained in power for a time. After his rejection, God withdrew his Spirit, and at times Saul was overcome with terrible fits of violence. In order to alleviate this condition a musician was called. Someone in the king's household recommended David (the rightful king of Israel), a young man skilled on the harp. David took up this task and greatly helped the king. (1 Sam 16:12–23) It was some time after he took on this duty that he defeated Goliath[6].

Despite the comfort he provided, Saul came to perceive David as a threat; perhaps this was occasioned by the obvious blessing of God in his life in the defeat of Goliath. During one of his fits, Saul threw a spear at David intending to kill him. Saul attempted this

---

[5]David exhibits an important character trait; he refuses to take up power into his own hands to deliver himself. This is just like Christ, the apostles and the early Church.

[6]It is very interesting that while in the king's household helping Saul with his fits of violence, and in the defeat of Goliath, David is the rightful king of Israel. Imagine being placed into the same situation and not taking power into your own hands.

twice. Becoming ever more afraid of David, and apparently not willing to kill him outright or sensing futility, he appointed David as a commander in his army, a commander of one thousand men. David, being blessed by God and dreaded by Saul, prospered at this new task and became beloved by all Israel and Judah. God was preparing the way for the revealing of the rightful king to Israel.

Saul's efforts to remove David were not working, and in desperation he commanded his sons and servants to kill David. Providentially, God provided a friend for David in Jonathan, Saul's son, who informed him of the plot, giving David time to escape with those loyal to him. David fled from Saul and spent time in the wilderness of Israel and in Philistia, all the while with Saul's army hot on his heels.

During this time, David had two opportunities to kill Saul. The first occasion was in a cave where David and some of his men had hidden themselves. Amazingly, Saul came into the cave to relieve himself. David was able to get so close to Saul that he was able to cut off a piece of his clothing. This he used as proof, while confronting Saul at a distance, that he was indeed close enough to take Saul's life. Despite the urging of his men, David did not take Saul's life.

> Far be it from me because of the LORD that I should do this thing to my lord, the LORD'S anointed, to stretch out my hand against him, since he is the LORD'S anointed.
>
> 1 Sam 25:6

The second occasion was in the middle of Saul's camp late one night. David and one of his men came to the very center of Saul's camp where Saul himself was sleeping. Once again David chose not to take Saul's life; all he took was the spear and the jug of water lying near Saul to be used as proof that he had been close enough to take Saul's life. Once again, David mercifully spares

10.2 God's Predisposition to Use the Weak

Saul. Upon being prodded to kill Saul David replied,

> ... Do not destroy him, for who can stretch out his hand against the LORD'S anointed and be without guilt? David also said, As the LORD lives, surely the LORD will strike him, or his day will come that he dies, or he will go down into battle and perish. The LORD forbid that I should stretch out my hand against the LORD'S anointed; ...
>
> 1 Sam 26:9–11

In this reply we gain significant insight into David's reasons for not taking Saul's life. God had made Saul king and he was going to have to remove him; David would not undo God's work. Despite having God's anointing as king of Israel and knowing that God had removed Saul as king, David did not grab the power given to him and take matters into his own hands.

Moses

Moses, a Jew, under divine providence, came to live and grow up in the court of Pharaoh as the adopted son of Pharaoh's daughter. Again, providentially, his mother was chosen to be his nurse. As Moses grew up, it is very likely that his mother told him of the God of Abraham, Isaac, and Jacob, the one true God, and how the Jews were his people, for when Moses became a man he took note of the oppression of his people and seeking to lessen their burden murdered an Egyptian taskmaster. The murder was clearly premeditated. Pharaoh, upon hearing of this act, sought to put Moses to death, but Moses escaped into the land of Midian where he attached himself to the household of the priest of Midian. (Ex 2)

Moses had sought to deliver his Jewish brethren by his own violent actions and had failed miserably, and was driven from the very ones he wished to free. His failure was complete.

Moses remained in the house of Reuel (the priest of Midian) and married one of his daughters, Zipporah, and prospered in the land of Midian for the next forty years; thoughts of being a deliverer had long been forgotten and he most likely remembered with regret and pain his first failed attempt. And even if he were disposed to deliver his people, he was no longer young. Deliverance of this kind needs a young and vigorous man. In so many ways Moses saw himself as completely inadequate for the task, and so he was.

God, however, saw things very differently and had chosen Moses to be the man he would use to deliver his people. God uses an extraordinary sight to bring Moses to a divine meeting. While tending the flocks Moses looked off into the distance and saw a burning bush; most unusually the bush was not consumed. This had to be investigated.

Moses, approaching the bush, hears the voice of God. In fear, he removes his sandals and God commands him to bring Israel out of Egypt. "Therefore, come now, and I will send you to Pharaoh, so that you may bring My people, the sons of Israel, out of Egypt." (Exod 3:10)

Moses was dumbfounded and wanted nothing to do with this task. He tried three times to avoid it. (Exod 3:11, 4:10, 4:13) Moses was so intransigent that "the anger of the LORD burned against Moses." (Exod 4:14) God's response to the first two requests to be excused are dealt with gently, but the third response, even though he gives Aaron as a spokesman to Moses, is simply a demand that he do as God has commanded. There is no more discussion; Moses must go.

We are not informed of the reasons why Moses did not want to go, but it is safe to assume that he did not believe he could do what was asked. He had tried once and failed; he was weak and he knew it. He was comfortable and old. This was really

10.2 God's Predisposition to Use the Weak

inconvenient. But it was most likely the overwhelming sense of weakness. In this he was correct; he was not, even in the remotest sense, up to the task.

However, God was not asking Moses to deliver the people by his own power but by Divine Power. Moses was to be the vessel through which God would work this miracle, not only the deliverance of his people from Egypt but in the creation of a new holy nation.

Moses was as weak as they come, and a failure and murderer at that, but God has always had a habit of using the weak. Thank God, there is hope for us.

Christ and the Cross

The greatest things accomplished on earth were accomplished by Christ in his life, death and resurrection. His life revealed the character of God and showed us how to live in the Kingdom that he was bringing into the world. His death revealed God's love for us and his resurrection revealed that God had accepted his sacrifice and brought in the New Covenant. Christ, in his death and resurrection broke the power of sin, destroyed the power of death and the grave, defeated the evil heavenly powers, and transferred us from the kingdom of darkness to the kingdom of light and gave us a future and a hope.

All this was accomplished by a landless carpenter, born in a stable, a man with no earthly possessions, a friend of sinners and outcasts, constantly at odds with the religious and governmental powers, using no violence and exercising no earthly power; he became the Lamb that was slain.

In Christ was the earthshaking, covenant-changing, delivering power of God. It was power displayed like never before, completely nonviolent, and it changed the world forever. Viewed by the world it was contemptible weakness, complete foolishness, but it was really the very power of God.

Our Weakness

Despite thoughts to the contrary, weakness is not a state into which we must place ourselves, it is the condition in which we actually find ourselves. We trust in an illusion when we trust in our own power, even the strongest among us. We may possess physical strength, a superb intellect or excel in making money; the fact remains, we do not possess anything that was not already given to us, even those abilities that we count as strength. But more than that, our displays of power are not significant; they are merely the exercise of power in unimportant and peripheral matters.

Our weakness is all encompassing and arises from two important conditions. First, we are creatures, not the creator. We cannot call a star or living being into existence (or even lesser creatures). Storms and the convulsions of the earth terrify us and remain beyond our control. We cannot extend our days indefinitely; the grave is always present, mocking us, patiently waiting for us. We are not the masters of creation. Second, we have rebelled against God and suffer a complete loss of power. Due to our rebellion, the entire creation groans; death and decay are the norm, and violence is pervasive in the animal kingdom as well as among men. In our unsaved condition we are slaves to sin, find ourselves under God's condemnation and wrath, are unable to bring acceptable works to God, and are unable to mend our relationship with him. Our situation is hopeless. Weakness is not something we must in some sense put on, for we are perpetually in a state of weakness.

10.3 The Spirit of God, Weakness and Power

In John 15 we find Christ discussing our relationship to himself as it relates to bearing fruit to God's glory. What is made crystal clear is the nature of our weakness and the necessity of Christ's power.

> Abide in Me, and I in you. As the branch cannot bear fruit of itself unless it abides in the vine, so neither can you unless you abide in Me. I am the vine, you are the branches; he who abides in Me and I in him, he bears much fruit, for apart from Me you can do nothing.
>
> John 15:4,5

Christ is emphatic, "apart from Me you can do nothing." What we cannot do apart from Christ is bear fruit; the power to bear fruit only comes from abiding in Christ. We are completely weak in this regard. But neither can we restore our relationship with God, the most fundamental thing that must be done. The word abide is quite important indicating a cooperative relationship which is partly explained several verses later.

> Just as the Father has loved Me, I have also loved you; abide in My love. If you keep My commandments, you will abide in My love; just as I have kept My Father's commandments and abide in His love.
>
> John 15:9,10

Abiding is partly accomplished by keeping Christ's commandments, that is, obedience. But abiding comes with the notion of living with a conscious awareness of our weakness and dependence on Christ, having an attentive ear to God's promptings and doing his will, imitating Christ's life, and having a consistent faith in Christ's ability to strengthen us. We are responsible to obey, but Christ is faithful to provide power. This can be captured in the idea of being led, that is, controlled, by the Spirit. In the next section we will explore this further.

10.3.1 The Spirit of God

In John 15 we see that divine power for godly living is obtained by abiding in Christ. By looking at several other verses in the gospels and the epistles we can develop this further. In Luke 24, during a post-resurrection appearance, we find Christ giving instructions regarding the future activity of the early Church.

> And behold, I am sending forth the promise of My Father upon you; but you are to stay in the city until you are clothed with power from on high.
>
> Luke 24:49

It is clear from earlier teachings that the promise of the Father is the Spirit of God. This is made explicit again in Acts chapter one.

> ... but you will receive power when the Holy Spirit has come upon you; and you shall be My witnesses both in Jerusalem, and in all Judea and Samaria, and even to the remotest part of the earth.
>
> Acts 1:8

We see that power comes to us through the Spirit of God and the Spirit plays an intimate role in the notion of abiding in Christ. The power of the Spirit[7] was, and is, absolutely essential to carrying out God's will. They were to wait for God's power before moving out. It is utter foolishness to think that we can proceed without God's power. Should we proceed without it,

---

[7] A full Trinitarian view is held herein. God is one essence, but three in person, each person having a relationship with the other, but with different responsibilities within the Godhead. Each are fully God.

10.3 The Spirit of God, Weakness and Power

either by not being one of his children or as his child proceeding in our own power, we will fail in a most important sense; even if we should succeed in some measure it will not be God who gets the glory, but ourselves. We steal from God the glory due him.

Although true, it is insufficient to say that the Spirit of God provides the power we need to bear fruit, do his works, and glorify God, for much more can be said about the nature of our relationship with the Spirit of God and how his power comes to us. To do this properly we must examine the Old Testament.

10.3.2 The Divine Presence and Fire

The first time we encounter the presence of God, signified by fire and smoke, is with Abraham in Genesis 15:9–21. The Divine Presence of God is always accompanied by fire or smoke in the Old Testament. This is a most amazing passage, recorded as a literal conversation between two persons, God and Abraham. The conversation centers on God's promise to Abraham.

> And He took him outside and said, "Now look toward the heavens, and count the stars, if you are able to count them." And He said to him, "So shall your descendants be." Then he believed in the LORD; and He reckoned it to him as righteousness. And He said to him, "I am the LORD who brought you out of Ur of the Chaldeans, to give you this land to possess it."
>
> Gen 15:5–7

Clearly, Abraham believed God, but wanted something to seal the covenant (Gen 15:8). This was not an unusual or unreasonable request and God graciously complied. The ceremony God and Abraham engaged in was solemn and reserved only for the most serious covenant making. The ceremony consisted of taking a heifer, a female goat and a ram, all of which are cut in two, in addition to a turtledove and a pigeon which were not divided. The three divided animals were laid on the ground, each half opposite the other, permitting a person to pass between them. The two parties in the covenant then walked between the pieces sealing the covenant. The implication was that if the covenant was broken, the covenant breaker should suffer the same fate as the animals.

After preparing the animals, sometime around sunset,

> ... a deep sleep fell upon Abram; and behold, terror and great darkness fell upon him.
>
> Gen 15:12

And God spoke once again the promise he was making to Abraham,[8] and God's Divine Presence, signified by the smoking oven and the flaming torch, passed between the animals.

> It came about when the sun had set, that it was very dark, and behold, there appeared a smoking oven and a flaming torch which passed between these pieces.
>
> Gen 15:17

In Moses' life we find several occurrences of fire accompanying the Divine Presence. The first time is when Moses encountered God in the desert. While out with the flock, Moses observed a bush in the distance that appeared on fire yet was not consumed, a truly amazing sight. Desert bushes that catch fire go up like a match. Upon approaching the bush he heard the voice of God;

> When the LORD saw that he turned aside to look, God called to him from the midst of the bush and said, "Moses, Moses!" And he said, "Here I am." Then He said, "Do not come near here; remove your sandals from your feet, for the place on which you are standing is holy ground." He said

---

[8] It is likely that the sleep that Abraham fell into was such that he could hear God's words and was aware of God passing between the animals.

10.3 The Spirit of God, Weakness and Power

> also, "I am the God of your father, the God of Abraham, the God of Isaac, and the God of Jacob." Then Moses hid his face, for he was afraid to look at God.
>
> Exod 3:4–6

God was not present in the common sense that God is present; the ground was holy on which Moses stood. God's Divine Presence was there, once again accompanied by fire. Notice that both Abraham and Moses were frightened at being in the company of the Divine Presence.

The second occasion is the appearance of a pillar of smoke during the day and a pillar of fire by night (Ex 13:21) as God leads the Israelites during the Exodus. This phenomenon signified God's presence among the people and was used to determine when the people broke and made camp. After the Tabernacle was constructed, a pillar of smoke by day and a pillar of fire by night resided over the Tabernacle (Num 9:15,16). When the pillar remained in a fixed location the people set up camp; when it moved, the people broke camp and followed.

It is at Mount Sinai that we have another appearance of the Divine Presence occasioned by the giving of the Ten Commandments. God's Divine Presence had made the whole mountain holy and God gave a startling command.

> "You shall set bounds for the people all around, saying, 'Beware that you do not go up on the mountain or touch the border of it; whoever touches the mountain shall surely be put to death. 'No hand shall touch him, but he shall surely be stoned or shot through; whether beast or man, he shall not live.' ... "
>
> Exod 19:12,13

This was not simply uncommon, it was extraordinary.

> So it came about on the third day, when it was morning, that there were thunder and lightning flashes and a thick cloud upon the mountain and a very loud trumpet sound, so that all the people who were in the camp trembled. ... Now Mount Sinai was all in smoke because the LORD descended upon it in fire; and its smoke ascended like the smoke of a furnace, and the whole mountain quaked violently.
>
> Exod 19:16,18

God was present on the mountain in a way that he is not normally present. This was a special manifestation of God and his glory and was accompanied by fire and smoke.

10.3.3 Pentecost, Fire and The Spirit

It was on the day of Pentecost that God fulfilled his promise and gave the Spirit of God to his people as Jeremiah prophesied. (Jer 31:31–34) The imagery is important.

> And suddenly there came from heaven a noise like a violent rushing wind, and it filled the whole house where they were sitting. And there appeared to them tongues as of fire distributing themselves, and they rested on each one of them. And they were all filled with the Holy Spirit ...
>
> Acts 2:2–4

This is the fulfillment of what Christ spoke of earlier.

> In that day you will know that I am in My Father, and you in Me, and I in you. He who has My commandments and keeps them is the one who loves Me; and he who loves Me will be loved by My Father, and I will love him and will disclose Myself to him. ... If anyone loves Me, he will keep My word; and My Father will love him, and We will come to him and make Our abode with him.
>
> John 14:20, 21, 23

10.3 The Spirit of God, Weakness and Power 213

This is, once again, a unique and singular coming of God in the person of God the Spirit. His coming was accompanied by a noise from heaven like a violent rushing wind, something we find in other Old Testament accounts of God's manifestations. And we see fire, fire dividing and coming to rest on, and then disappearing into each of those present in the upper room. The imagery is unmistakable; the Divine Presence now makes his abode in man. This is beyond words; how can we even begin to express its full meaning and import? Mighty God, whose throne is the heavens, the creator of the cosmos, the one before whom men have fallen as if dead at his presence, now dwells in man. This gives new meaning to how we approach God.

> Therefore let us draw near with confidence to the throne of grace, so that we may receive mercy and find grace to help in time of need.
>
> Heb 4:16

> Therefore, brethren, since we have confidence to enter the holy place by the blood of Jesus, by a new and living way which He inaugurated for us through the veil, that is, His flesh, and since we have a great priest over the house of God, let us draw near with a sincere heart in full assurance of faith, having our hearts sprinkled clean from an evil conscience and our bodies washed with pure water.
>
> Heb 10:19–22

How could we not have confidence to come before him? God has not just come near, he is now in us. What words could we use to express our gratitude? How does one fathom such a gift? Is there a gift that even remotely approaches this in value? I believe that if we understood what a magnificent thing God has done for us — redeemed us, moved us into his Kingdom, given us a future hope, lives in us — we would be embarrassed to ask him for anything else. We can now know God and he lives in us. What more do we really need than this? But so often we live in a murky twilight, possessors of the greatest riches in the world, and yet we remain discontented, completely unaware of this priceless gift, looking for some material blessing from God. The tragedy is overwhelming.

The impact of God being in us and being able to confidently enter the holy place is largely lost on modern day Christians. The Jewish Christian had a far deeper understanding given his knowledge of Jewish history and temple worship. The Jewish Christian could recall that when God, in his Divine Presence, came to Mount Sinai, the command was given that any human or animal that touched the mountain should be slain. In the temple, it was only once a year and only by one man, the high priest, that the Holy of Holies could be entered and atonement made for the sins of the nation. Should the priest fail in some way he could be struck dead. To emphasize the separation between man and God, a thick curtain separated the Holy of Holies from the rest of the temple. But when Christ had offered up his sacrifice for sins on the cross the curtain was torn in two.

> And Jesus cried out again with a loud voice, and yielded up His spirit. And behold, the veil of the temple was torn in two from top to bottom; and the earth shook and the rocks were split.
>
> Matt 27:50,51

Even more amazing is that God dwells in us; we are God's temple.[9]

> Do you not know that you are a temple of God and that the Spirit of God dwells in you? If any man destroys the temple of God, God will destroy him, for the temple of God

---

[9] See also 1 Cor 6:19; Eph 2:21,22

10.3 The Spirit of God, Weakness and Power

> is holy, and that is what you are.
>
> 1 Cor 3:16,17
>
> Or what agreement has the temple of God with idols? For we are the temple of the living God; just as God said, I will dwell in them and walk among them; And I will be their God, and they shall be My people.
>
> 2 Cor 6:16

Let us not forget that it was by weakness, death by the way of the cross, that this was accomplished. It was not by powerful kings, armies and weapons; it was by a lowly born carpenter who for three short years preached the Kingdom of God, had no possessions, no political power, was outside the religious establishment and died the death of a common Roman criminal and was buried in a borrowed tomb. Although it appeared to be the depths of weakness and foolishness by powerful Rome and blasphemous by Jewish authorities, it was the very power of God whereby he freed man from the bondage of sin, broke the powers of evil and placed man into his Kingdom.

We are now in a better position to more fully appreciate the Spirit of God and the power he provides. God is not simply near, he dwells in us. God's power does not come to us by some heavenly conduit; God's power comes to us by virtue of God dwelling in us. God and his power are nearer than we can understand. We do not have to engage in some activity or external practice to obtain God's power. God himself abides with us and we with him. What we must do is be controlled by the Spirit of God, be led by him. Only then will we be able to bear fruit to God's glory.

> But I say, walk by the Spirit, and you will not carry out the desire of the flesh. ... But if you are led by the Spirit, you are not under the Law. ... But the fruit of the Spirit is love, joy, peace, patience, kindness, goodness, faithfulness,

> gentleness, self-control; against such things there is no law. Now those who belong to Christ Jesus have crucified the flesh with its passions and desires.
>
> Gal 5:16, 18, 22–24

Here in Galatians we now see a direct link with John 15; by walking by the Spirit, by being led by the Spirit who now lives in us, we bear the fruit of the Spirit whereby God is glorified.

> And do not get drunk with wine, for that is dissipation, but be filled with the Spirit,
>
> Eph 5:18

The Spirit of God will lead us into obedience to God to do the plain things that God has commanded in his Word. God will prompt, remind and lead, but we are responsible to obey. And as we obey we will appropriate his power for his glory. We have been given all the power we will ever need, we need nothing more; however, we can refuse to accept it and thereby quench the Spirit, tragically shutting off his power.

10.4   Weakness and Trials

As was mentioned above, the essential characteristic of a trial is weakness. In every trial we find ourselves in a position of weakness, often accompanied by loss. For those who are aware of their weakness, trials provide an opportunity to see it more clearly and in different ways. For those usually unaware of their weakness, trials provide an opportunity to be powerfully confronted by it. Trials put an exclamation point on our weakness. If we are unaware of our weakness, it is difficult to see that we need the power of God, and it remains difficult or impossible to appropriate God's power. If we have no occasions to trust and to build endurance and patience, we are not likely to develop spiritually. It is through

10.4 Weakness and Trials

the weakness of trials that God's strength is perfected; we learn to exercise God's power rather than our own. Second Corinthians 12 teaches this principle.

> Because of the surpassing greatness of the revelations, for this reason, to keep me from exalting myself, there was given me a thorn in the flesh, a messenger of Satan to torment meto keep me from exalting myself! Concerning this I implored the Lord three times that it might leave me. And He has said to me, "My grace is sufficient for you, for power is perfected in weakness." Most gladly, therefore, I will rather boast about my weaknesses, so that the power of Christ may dwell in me. Therefore I am well content with weaknesses, with insults, with distresses, with persecutions, with difficulties, for Christ's sake; for when I am weak, then I am strong.
>
> 2 Cor 12:7–10

The trial referred to here is very difficult and painful, and is one that will not be lifted; God's intention is that it remain.[10] It has, however, been given for protection; "Faithful are the wounds of a friend." (Prov 27:6); Paul had been given the privilege of seeing Paradise and hearing "inexpressible words," things which cannot be put into words, and God knew that without this chronic trial Paul would exalt himself, perhaps even shipwreck his faith. The apostle repeatedly petitioned God to take it from him, but God's reply was final, "My grace is sufficient for you." In this chronic difficulty Christ will support him; Paul will not fail, he will not be left without comfort, and the help that will be provided will be adequate to the need. God is faithful to strengthen and comfort us to accomplish what he has called us to do and bear. After all, God is not far, he dwells in us, he will never leave us

---

[10] Barnes, *Barnes' Notes on the New Testament*, Discussion on 2 Cor 12:8,9

nor forsake us, and he has given us everything pertaining to life and godliness. And further, it is God's intention to conform us to the image of his Son, not to be destroyed by trials.

Christ's grace will be sufficient for "power is perfected in weakness."[11] The grace needed to endure the trial will come from God's power as Paul understands and further embraces his weakness. When we are confronted by our weakness we begin to see the need for God's power in our lives. Those who desire to appropriate God's power find in trials an opportunity to grow and, therefore, embrace them.

Given that it is through our weakness that God's power comes, it seems that trials are not optional, but absolutely necessary for our spiritual growth.

Paul's response to Christ's message is consistent with his other discussions on trials as well as James'. God's power comes through our weakness,[12] therefore weakness is something of which to boast. However, we do not simply make our boast of our weaknesses, but we take *great pleasure* boasting of them. What is accomplished through our weakness is truly something wonderful; the power of Christ rests upon us. Unlike the world that boasts of power and scorns weakness, we boast of our weakness. Why? Because we desire what God wants to accomplish, and know that it can only be accomplished by his power being released in our lives as we are weak.

The knowledge and desire of what God accomplishes in our trials affects the way we look at trials. Unlike those who have no

---

[11] Exactly how is power perfected in weakness? It is perfected in the sense that as we understand our own weakness and acknowledge our need of God's power we find God's power. It is not just power to endure the trial. This power reaches to all areas of our life.

[12] It is a change of mind that permits God's power to flow. If we see no weakness we receive no strength from God. Notice also that we can pick up power both in our heart (mind) and in our hands (actions).

10.4 Weakness and Trials

such understanding, we are well content, take pleasure in, think well of, approve of,

- weaknesses – those things in which our weakness is clearly seen – feebleness of body or mind, disease: infirmity, sickness

- insults – insolence as overbearing; that is, insult, injury: harm, hurt, reproach

- distresses – in want of necessities

- persecutions – suffering occasioned by persecution for the sake of Christ.

- difficulties – calamity, anguish

for Christ's; for when we are weak, then we are strong.

The Biblical view of trials is completely radical; nothing like it is seen anywhere else in the world. Christians gladly accept trials for they emphasize our weakness. This must sound like insanity, utter nonsense. Commit to an asylum the one who believes such drivel. But no, we are not fools who believe this. It is foolish in much the same way as the Cross of Christ is foolish; it is the very power of God. It makes perfect sense, and believing it is prudent when we understand reality and what is truly valuable. We may be fools in the eyes of the world, but to God we are faithful servants.

Chapter 11

The Role of Loss

Weakness and loss are the two things that most make a trial, a trial. And weakness is most often occasioned on loss, for as we are unable to prevent the loss of whatever is being lost, we are confronted by our weakness. Loss then, in our trials, is a means of bringing weakness. But loss does something else for us, namely it helps us to redirect our desires and values and keeps us from trusting in ourselves.

11.1 Philippians 3

Philippians 3 will be the primary text for this discussion. In it, Paul speaks to loss more clearly and directly than any other passage in the Bible. At the end of chapter two Paul gives the church an update regarding his intentions, who he is sending to them and expresses his thanks to them for sending one from their church, Epaphroditus, to assist him in his need. Now in chapter three he begins to give them particular warnings, especially about those who would come and deceive them.

> Finally, my brethren, rejoice in the Lord. To write the same things again is no trouble to me, and it is a safeguard for you. Beware of the dogs, beware of the evil workers, beware of the false circumcision; for we are the true circumcision, who worship in the Spirit of God and glory in Christ Jesus and put no confidence in the flesh, although I myself might have confidence even in the flesh. ...
>
> Phil 3:1–4a

Beware of the dogs, evil workers, the false circumcision.[1] This is a reference to the Judaists, those who would bring all under the Law and scorn the grace of God. Those who would so confuse and lead astray the Christians are no minor irritant, for Paul calls them workers of evil and dogs. To be called a dog in the ancient world was a profound insult; Paul is furious with these people and demonstrates his anger and contempt for them with this epithet. This is a proper and righteous anger for these would undo the work of Christ if they could. But not only does he call them dogs, but evildoers. This is quite a contrast to how they came to the early Christians; they came declaring that they had true religious knowledge that would complete the work of Christ. They were bringing truth, providing a service to both the hearers and God. They were doing no such thing; they were engaged in cold bare evil.

Paul is not yet done describing these Judaists; they are of the false circumcision. The word used here is not the normal word for circumcision but a contemptuous parody implying amputation or 'cutting in the flesh'.[2] These Judaists had no real understanding of circumcision nor did they understand what Christ had come to do and had accomplished.

---

[1] Much of what follows in the next three paragraphs is from *The Life and Letters of ST. Paul* by David Smith

[2] Smith, *The Life and Letters of St. Paul*, 517

11.1 Philippians 3

Those of the true circumcision, however, are those who worship in the Spirit and glory in Christ and put no confidence in the flesh. True circumcision is not of the flesh but of the heart. We of the true circumcision glory in the work of Christ, not in anything we have done or in any outward physical sign or mark on our body, or in the works of the Law. Abraham was not justified by circumcision, but prior to his circumcision and that by faith for "he believed the Lord; and it was reckoned to him as righteousness." (Gen 15:6) And we also know that "by the works of the Law no flesh will be justified in His sight..." (Rom 3:20) For this reason we put no confidence in the flesh, our only hope is in the work of Christ, and in this we glory.

At the end of all this Paul makes an interesting statement; "although I myself might have confidence even in the flesh."

> If anyone else has a mind to put confidence in the flesh, I far more: circumcised the eighth day, of the nation of Israel, of the tribe of Benjamin, a Hebrew of Hebrews; as to the Law, a Pharisee; as to zeal, a persecutor of the church; as to the righteousness which is in the Law, found blameless.
>
> Phil 3:4b–6

Recall that Paul is speaking to Judaists, those who would have us put our trust in the works of the Law and have confidence in the flesh. To these he says, "You think you are good Jews and believe that you have reason to trust in the works of the Law? Let me tell you what it is to be a good Jew and what it is to have reason to trust in the flesh." Paul's Jewish credentials are impeccable; he lacks nothing. Certainly he is a Jew but he is a Hebrew of Hebrews. He is a Pharisee; there were none who took the Law more seriously and sought to obey it more fully. Not only this, he put his money where his mouth was, as it were; he persecuted the enemies of God, or so he thought, with vigor and determination. It wasn't enough to obey; his belief moved him to action. And as to the legal righteousness of the Law, he was blameless. Yet despite all this he placed no confidence in the flesh. He found no occasion to trust in any of these things that benefited him.

> But whatever things were gain to me, those things I have counted as loss for the sake of Christ.
>
> Phil 3:7

Those things that the Judaists would have us trust in, those things that they considered a positive, a personal gain, those which Paul had in spades, Paul counts as loss. They are not the way to Christ and his salvation; they lead in the opposite direction and are in fact a loss. But why consider them a loss? Why not simply consider them unhelpful? Do we really need to be this extreme? We must, for all these things and things similar to them, given the disposition of our fallen nature, our unredeemed flesh, provide us with an opportunity to trust in the flesh. So great is our propensity to trust in ourselves we should consider anything that is a gain to us as loss. They not only have no value, they are a loss. We hold them in contempt, so intent are we in only trusting in the work of Christ.

> More than that, I count all things to be loss in view of the surpassing value of knowing Christ Jesus my Lord, for whom I have suffered the loss of all things, and count them but rubbish so that I may gain Christ, and may be found in Him, not having a righteousness of my own derived from the Law, but that which is through faith in Christ, the righteousness which comes from God on the basis of faith, that I may know Him and the power of His resurrection and the fellowship of His sufferings, being conformed to His death; in order that I may attain to the resurrection from

the dead.

Phil 3:8–11

Not only does Paul count the things he has mentioned as loss, he counts *all* things as loss. Nothing is to be valued; all that is gain to him is loss, loss in comparison to the surpassing value of knowing Christ Jesus his Lord. If trusting in the flesh (those things that are a gain to me) prevents me from knowing Christ and his salvation, then I have no use for them. Send them out with the rest of the garbage. Our passion, after all, is to gain Christ, to be found in his righteousness, for we have nothing to commend ourselves to God, not even the works of the Law. We desire the righteousness that comes from God on the basis of faith. We want to know Christ, he is what fulfills and satisfies, knowing him is the very essence of eternal life. (John 17:3) We want to know the power of his resurrection.

> Not that I have already obtained it or have already become perfect, but I press on so that I may lay hold of that for which also I was laid hold of by Christ Jesus. Brethren, I do not regard myself as having laid hold of it yet; but one thing I do: forgetting what lies behind and reaching forward to what lies ahead, I press on toward the goal for the prize of the upward call of God in Christ Jesus. Let us therefore, as many as are perfect, have this attitude; and if in anything you have a different attitude, God will reveal that also to you; however, let us keep living by that same standard to which we have attained.
>
> Phil 3:12–16

What Paul has told us is not something that he, or we in our life, have yet obtained. He is still in the race and has and will face defeats as the flesh reasserts itself over the Spirit. So therefore, let us press on to lay hold of the prize. Forget the failures and difficulties of the past, let them not deter us.

11.2 Loss in the Life of the Christian

If I may, I would like to widen the discussion beyond the primary thrust found in Philippians three, that is, what we trust in for salvation, and extend it in another direction.

It is interesting how attached we become to things, things material and immaterial. Although we value material things — houses, land, money, cars, the list goes on — it is often the immaterial that we value most; reputation and recognition by others, heritage and pedigree, education, mental and physical ability, personal power and authority, exemplary behavior. In any case, we improperly value both the material and immaterial. We value them because, in the ledger sheet of life, we place them in the asset column. They make us feel safe; I have enough money for a long time. I have a secure job; the people I work with appreciate and need me. I have a great reputation; no one would seek to harm me. My health is great; I can handle what lies ahead. And so it goes. What is going on is that in our hearts we feel powerful and we find comfort in this personal power. So often we have no idea that all this power and safety are illusions. And yet, we add it all up and these things end up in the asset column in our ledger sheet. What a tragedy. In reality all these things ought to be listed in the loss column. These things are not a gain, but neither are they neutral. Even as Christians we have a tremendous tendency to trust in ourselves, to take up power for ourselves, so that anything we consider as a gain to us we take as an occasion to trust in ourselves rather than in God, even if not for our salvation, then for our own provision.[3]

---

[3]This is not to say that we do not appreciate God's gifts to us. However,

11.2 Loss in the Life of the Christian

But not only is it wrong to pick up power in this way by trusting in things, it is also idolatry. An idol is anything that takes the place of God. Often our idolatry is very refined, we say we trust Christ for our salvation, but we will not trust him for our provision, trusting rather in our strength. Just look at our attitude when we lose our jobs; we become panicked, acting as if we have only ourselves to rely on; God really isn't in the picture, he is there just to save our souls, not to rely on in everyday life. (Or, we simply don't like how he is handling things.) Not only do we trust in things for our provision, but we look to them to fulfill us, to bring joy to us. It never occurs to us that loss is an integral part of God's plan for his glory and our growth. Let us lose them and see how empty we feel. We act as if we have lost everything, and we find little or no comfort in knowing God. And if we do have some meager measure of trust in God, we focus on the restoration of what we have lost, acting as if that were the greatest thing God could do. What bankruptcy. What utter poverty of the soul. We are pitiful creatures, in some ways more contemptible than the pagan, for we should know better. Yet we worship the created things rather than the creator. I marvel at God's patience with us.

How then should we view things in light of the Scripture? Surely one would think that things that provide us with a sense of security and power are not harmful. This is not what Paul held; "But whatever things were gain to me, those things I have counted as loss for the sake of Christ." We plead "Certainly, some things are of value." Paul replies that all things are loss; "More than that, I count all things to be loss in view of the surpassing value of knowing Christ Jesus my Lord, ..." But isn't there some

---

God's gifts are to be enjoyed, used for others and given thanks for, never used as an occasion to trust in ourselves. But this is exactly what we do with them if we consider them gain to ourselves.

residual value in them? To this we have, "... I have suffered the loss of all things, and count them but rubbish so that I may gain Christ." No, they are of no value; they are no more than rubbish.

Things that are gain to us are of no value to us. God may use them in the furtherance of His Kingdom, but we must not value them for ourselves, for even in this redeemed state our flesh is not yet transformed, and these things, more likely than not, will be an occasion to trust in our flesh. When we improperly embrace things they are not precious, but hindrances, obstacles to what is truly valuable: the knowledge of Christ and the righteousness of Christ.

In Philippians three we see Paul acknowledging his weakness and embracing it. Paul has no interest in developing his own strength, but to rely only on Christ. But not only did he want Christ's righteousness, he wanted Christ himself, personal knowledge of his savior, more precious than anything else he might possess. Anything that got in the way was not to be valued, it was rather to be held in contempt.

I believe that the way God would have us to view loss is this: as God brings trials to us and loss upon loss comes to us we should respond in thanks that God has removed one more thing we might have trusted in. We feel no sense of loss since we did not value it to begin with. What is it to us that we have lost it? God himself, rather than what he gives, is what we value.

With this truth so clearly laid out before us, how is it that we continue to value the things that are gain to us? The only answer is that we are unwilling to give up on our own power, it is precious to us, we do not value knowing Christ above all else and perhaps we do not trust Him fully and want to retain some power, just in case. How pathetic we are, holding onto power we do not even possess.

11.3 The Discipline of Trials

I thank God that he loves us so much that he is willing to cause us to lose those things that are gain to us in order to show us the excellence of knowing Christ, having His righteousness, the power of His resurrection and the fellowship of his sufferings, being conformed to His death, in order to attain to the resurrection from the dead. God's love for us is so great that he will, through our trials, figuratively break every finger in our hands to help us let go of those things that stand in the way of knowing him and glorifying him. This is the discipline of a loving Father.

Loss is the companion of trials and it is through loss that God redirects our desires and values. How easy it is to deceive ourselves into thinking that we do not really value things. If you don't think you are attached to things, just lose them. You'll see. Are your hands wrapped around them so tight that your knuckles are white? Lose them and you will find out. Lose every significant material asset you have, your health, job, career, reputation and recognition — everything you have worked for — and you will find out what you are attached to. What you value will be revealed in the clearest detail. Your attachments will be laid bare. The depth of your commitment to Christ and your love for him will be revealed. While things are going well it is easy to deceive ourselves and think that we do not value things, but the lie is revealed when we lose them. If we have not lost them, I fear that we really don't know if we have truly let them go.

But not only is what we value revealed in the trial, for if we are attentive, the Spirit of God will be telling us what is to be properly desired and valued, what really satisfies. As things slip through our fingers, one after the other, we either become angry with God or begin to realize that perhaps we have had it wrong all along and begin to look for things that are of real value, the things that cannot be lost. As Christians, the Spirit draws us to Christ and what he values. Christ himself is found to be the thing we desire most. With the Psalmist we say

> Whom have I in heaven but You? And besides You, I desire nothing on earth. My flesh and my heart may fail, but God is the strength of my heart and my portion forever. For, behold, those who are far from You will perish; You have destroyed all those who are unfaithful to You. But as for me, the nearness of God is my good; I have made the Lord GOD my refuge, That I may tell of all Your works.
> Ps 73:25–28

> As the deer pants for the water brooks, so my soul pants for You, O God. My soul thirsts for God, for the living God; when shall I come and appear before God?
> Ps 42:1,2

And why should we not? Christ is the most desirable of all things. He is God, the creator of the cosmos who took on human form and became a man and endured the hatred and scorn of men, so that he might die at the hands of men on a cursed cross to free us from the bondage to sin. I was utterly wretched, under his condemnation, a rebel against him, unable to save myself, dead in my sins, having nothing of value to present to him. And now I am, by his might, delivered into his Kingdom of light, he has taken away my sin and the decrees that once were used against me and is an advocate before the Father on my behalf. Is there anything sweeter than Christ? Is anything more valuable than knowing him? Would I let anything come between Christ and myself? Would I want anything but his power? Would I not want what he wants, desire what he desires? Oh, to live and die for him and share everything I may with him, this lover of my soul. More precious than words can describe is Christ and the knowledge of him. More valuable than all the riches of the world, even my own life, is Christ.

Chapter 12

Our Hope in Christ

Christians are not without hope in the world, nor are we without very real comfort in the present. These two, a future hope and real comfort in the present, are profoundly helpful. With this future hope and present comfort it becomes possible to patiently endure suffering, even when the world seems to fall apart around us. Christ himself is our example "who for the joy set before him endured the cross, ..." (Heb 11:3). A knowledge and understanding of our future inheritance in Christ can have a profound effect on our ability to endure in much the same way as it did for Christ.

Trials do something very helpful in this regard; they cause us to seriously reflect on our hope in Christ, and as we reflect, our understanding deepens and the comfort we derive from our hope increases.

As Peter puts it, (1 Pet 1:3–9) the Father, according to his great mercy, has caused us to be born again to a living hope through Christ's resurrection to obtain an inheritance which is imperishable and undefiled and will not fade away. It is reserved in heaven for us who are protected by God's power for a salvation to be revealed in the last time. That we have this hope is cause for great joy even though we are distressed by trials. Further, we also have the comfort of knowing that our trials will prove our faith, making it more precious than gold, resulting in praise and honor at the coming of Christ.

Peter is striving to help us understand how excellent is our hope (our inheritance); it is imperishable, undefiled and will not fade away. This describes nothing on earth. Notice also that the heirs are protected by none other than God himself. This is indeed cause for great joy. But here, Peter only just scratches the surface of what our inheritance entails. As we carefully consider of what our hope in Christ consists we will find ourselves overwhelmed by God's lavish care and love, finding more precious than ever Christ who bought us and made us sons and daughters of God and say with all the saints, "Worthy is the Lamb."

But before we begin this study, let's take a moment and see what we have been saved from and then what we as children of God have already inherited, what we already enjoy. What we currently enjoy is beyond any human expectation or agency and when combined with our future hope in Christ is doubly comforting, giving us further cause to glorify God.

In the sections that follow the reader will find considerable repetition. I have deliberately done this in an effort to drive home what it is that God has done for us.

12.1 Our Previous Condition

In order to place our inheritance into a proper context it is helpful to consider what was our condition apart from Christ, for we have been saved *from the kingdom of darkness to true life in the Kingdom of God.*

Previously we were children of wrath (Eph 2:3), we were under condemnation and wrath (John 3:18 (KJV), John 3:36), we were under the law of sin and of death (Rom 8:2), we lived futile lives

(Eph 2:1). We were subject to slavery all our lives through the fear of death (Heb 2:15). We lived in a domain of darkness (Col 1:13) and we were dead in our transgression (Col 2:13).

Our lives were characterized by rebellion, self-will (1 Pet 2:) immorality, impurity, sensuality, idolatry, sorcery, enmities, strife, jealousy, outbursts of anger, disputes, dissensions, factions, envying, drunkenness, and carousing (Gal 5:19–21).

So wrath, condemnation, rebellion, futility, bondage and the fear of death defined our lives. We were without hope in the world, utterly lost, destined to an eternity apart from God. And then, in the fullness of time, Christ came (Gal 4:4–7) and freed the prisoners long held in sin, healed the sick and made a people for himself, on whose hearts, the very law of God is written. (Jer 31:31–35)

12.2 Our Present Inheritance

As to the present experience of our inheritance, there is a vast amount of Scripture and it is difficult to know which passages to focus on. Each one has that which commends it. Several passage, however, stand out: Romans chapters six and eight, Ephesians chapters one and two and Colossians 1:13 and 2:1–22.

In the discussion below it will be helpful to look at our present hope from three separate perspectives; 1) our standing with God, 2) God's provision, and 3) the restoration of community and the restoration of individual human relationships.

12.2.1 Our Standing With God

Rather than condemnation and wrath we now have peace with God. We have eternal life and the forgiveness of sins. We stand in the grace of God and we have been reconciled to God. We have been called into fellowship with God and been redeemed from the curse of the law. We are now the children of God, no longer slaves, and fellow heirs with Christ. We have been called to freedom, not bondage to sin. Christ is our advocate and hight priest. We may now come before the throne of God with confidence; no veil separates us from the Holy of Holies. We are lacking in no gift. God has lavished his love upon us. He has granted to us his precious and magnificent promises, so that by them we become partakers of the divine nature, having escaped the corruption that is in the world by lust. (2 Pet 1:4)

All this and more has God already done for us. In light of our previous condition it is even more incredible. Wonderfully, we have been transfered from the kingdom of darkness to the Kingdom of God's Son, or as Peter puts it, he "has called you out of darkness into his marvelous light;" (1 Pet 2:9). In a very real sense we now have eternal life for "This is eternal life, that they may know you, the only true God, and Jesus Christ whom you have sent." (John 17:3)

Romans 6

The main theme in this passage is that we have been baptized into Christ's death and raised in the likeness of his resurrection. The meaning of this and its implications are staggering.

In Christ's death our old self was crucified. We were crucified with him "in order that our body of sin might be done away with, so that we would no longer be slaves to sin; for he who has died is freed from sin." (Rom 6:6,7)

The obvious question becomes, "How shall we who died to sin still live in it?" (Rom 6:2) We who were slaves to sin, held in bondage, are now free. We no longer need to live lives characterized by sin. We are not figuratively free, but free indeed. "Even so consider yourselves to be dead to sin, but alive to God in Christ Jesus." (Rom 6:11)

12.2 Our Present Inheritance

Because we have died with Christ we believe that we will also live with him. (Rom. 6:8-11) Christ having been raised form the dead, is never to die again. He died to sin once for all and the life that he lives, He lives to God. We are, therefore, to consider ourselves dead to sin, but alive to God in Christ Jesus.

We are not to let sin reign in our mortal bodies so that we obey its lusts, for sin will not be a master over us, for we are not under law but grace. (Rom 6:12,14)

What Christ has done is extraordinary, not only have we been reconciled to God, but he has set us free from the bondage of sin. Previously we were unable to do that which is good, living in shame, apart from God and the people of God. But now, in the freedom purchased by Christ, we may choose to live lives no longer defined by sin, but lives characterized by righteousness, doing good works pleasing to God and bringing glory to him. We are able to live lives *unto* God.

Romans 8

Romans chapter eight is very comforting and an amazing presentation of what God has done for us. It is a particularly important passage for those in trials.

The chapter beings with the declaration that there is now no condemnation for those who are in Christ Jesus. (Rom 8:1) This is wonderful enough, for we who were under condemnation no longer live in fear of judgment, but God has only just begun; much more is yet to come.

We may now live lives dominated by righteousness rather than sin. We have been set free from the law of sin and of death. Christ has condemned sin in the flesh so that the requirement of the Law might be fulfilled in us. We may now walk according to the Spirit resulting in life and peace. Life under condemnation, separated from God and his people, is not life at all and is dominated by conflict. Peace was not our lot. (Rom 8:2-11)

We are now God's children, but not only this, we are heirs of God. Nor have we received from God a spirit of slavery leading to fear again, but a spirit of adoption as sons. The Spirit of God testifies with our spirit that we are the children of God. We are not left to wonder if we are right with God. We are now heirs of God and fellow heirs of Christ if we suffer with him. Think of it, God considers us fellow heirs with Christ, we share in the inheritance of God the Son. It staggers the mind. We who were condemned and without hope now share in the inheritance of God the Son; his righteousness has been imputed to us, God's love is freely given to us, we have access to the Father, and we will share in his bodily resurrection. What joy this should bring to our hearts, what thankfulness this should bring to our lives, and finally, how would we live? Naturally, we would live lives worthy of our calling (Rom 8:12-17) and engage in the good works to which we have been called, and in so doing bring glory to God. (Eph 2:10)

But in addition to all this, far more is to come, for the sufferings of this present time are not worthy to be compared with the glory that is to be revealed to us. The creation itself eagerly awaits the revealing of the sons of God, for in that moment it will be released from its slavery to corruption into the freedom of the glory of the children of God. (Rom. 8:18-25)

In verses 26 and 27 we find that the Spirit of God helps us in our weakness by interceding for us with groanings too deep for words. We are unable to pray as we should, but God comes and does what we cannot. His care is total.[1]

God himself also watches over and directs our lives, for he causes all things to work together for good to those who love

---

[1] Notice that God's care and love are not given haphazardly but deliberately. We ought to do the same as we love and care others.

12.2 Our Present Inheritance

God. Not only this, he knew us from eternity past, predestined us to be conformed to the image of his Son, called us, justified us, and has glorified us. (Rom 8:28–31)

In verses 31–39 Paul enters a crescendo. If God is for us who can possibly be against us? No one! So great is God's love that he did not spare is own Son, but delivered him over for us all. How then could God do anything other than freely give us all things?[2] Who can bring a charge against God's children so that God would withdraw his love? No one! Should a charge be brought against us, Christ himself intercedes. Nothing can separate us from the love of God.

> Who will separate us from the love of Christ? Will tribulation, or distress, or persecution, or famine, or nakedness, or peril, or sword? Just as it is written, "For Your sake we are being put to death all day long; We were considered as sheep to be slaughtered." But in all these things we overwhelmingly conquer through Him who loved us. For I am convinced that neither death, nor life, nor angels, nor principalities, nor things present, nor things to come, nor powers, nor height, nor depth, nor any other created thing, will be able to separate us from the love of God, which is in Christ Jesus our Lord.
>
> Rom 35–39

The life we now live is like nothing we could have anticipated, so magnificent is Gods love for us.

---

[2] All things that glorify God are good for us. This is not to be read in the way the health, wealth and prosperity crowd read it. We must use God's definition of "the good."

Ephesians

We have been blessed with every spiritual blessing. He chose us before the foundation of the world to be holy and blameless before him. In love, he predestined[3] us to become children of God. (Eph. 1:3-5)

In Christ we have redemption through his blood, the forgiveness of our sins according to the riches of his grace which he lavished on us.(Eph 1:7,8) And God has given us the Spirit as a pledge of our inheritance. (Eph 1:13,14)

We who were dead in our trespasses and sins — living in the lusts of our flesh, indulging the desires of the flesh and of the mind, and were by nature children of wrath — God has made alive because of his great love and has raised us up with Christ and seated us with him in the heavenly places *so that in the ages to come he might show the surpassing riches of his grace in kindness toward us in Christ Jesus* (Eph 2:1-8).

Previously we (the Gentiles) were excluded from the commonwealth of Israel, and strangers to the covenants of promise, having no hope and without God in the world. But now, we who were far off have been brought near, both groups — Jew and Gentile — having been made one. (Eph 2:11-13)

Colossians

God has rescued us from the domain of darkness, and transferred us to the kingdom of his beloved Son, in whom we have redemption, the forgiveness of sins. (Col 1:13,14)

---

[3] Rather than individual predestination, which amounts to determinism, it is more correct to understand this as predestining the corporate body. Individuals are predestined as they are part of the body. Those in the body will be saved. This does not teach that there is an unconditional elections as Reformed theology teaches. Robert Shank gives a very helpful exposition of corporate election in his book *Elect in the Son.*

12.2 Our Present Inheritance

Although we were formerly alienated and hostile in mind, engaged in evil deeds, he has now reconciled us in his fleshly body through death, in order to present us before him holy and blameless and beyond reproach. (Col 1:21–22)

In Christ, all the fullness of Deity dwells in bodily form, and in him we have been made complete. We have been buried with him and raised up with him. (Col 2:9–12)

When we were dead in our transgressions and the uncircumcision of our flesh, he made us alive together with him,

> having forgiven us all our transgressions, having canceled out the certificate of debt consisting of decrees against us, which was hostile to us; and He has taken it out of the way, having nailed it to the cross. When He had disarmed the rulers and authorities, He made a public display of them, having triumphed over them through Him.
>
> Col 2:13b–15

A People of God

It was to Israel that the covenants were given. It was through the Jewish people that salvation was to come. We, the Gentiles, did not share in their blessings. We were not the people of God, we were not recipients of God's special love and care. Neither did we have the Law and the prophets to instruct us and lead us into truth. We Gentiles lived in darkness with no such blessing.

But now the barrier between the Jew and the Gentile has been removed and we are one people and both recipients of God's salvation. The ancient prophecy is fulfilled: those who were not a people have become the people of God.

> Therefore remember that formerly you, the Gentiles in the flesh, who are called "Uncircumcision" by the so-called "Circumcision," which is performed in the flesh by human hands

remember that you were at that time separate from Christ, excluded from the commonwealth of Israel, and strangers to the covenants of promise, having no hope and without God in the world. But now in Christ Jesus you who formerly were far off have been brought near by the blood of Christ. For He Himself is our peace, who made both groups into one and broke down the barrier of the dividing wall, by abolishing in His flesh the enmity, which is the Law of commandments contained in ordinances, so that in Himself He might make the two into one new man, thus establishing peace, and might reconcile them both in one body to God through the cross, by it having put to death the enmity. And He came and preached peace to you who were far away, and peace to those who were near; for through Him we both have our access in one Spirit to the Father. So then you are no longer strangers and aliens, but you are fellow citizens with the saints, and are of Gods household, having been built on the foundation of the apostles and prophets, Christ Jesus Himself being the corner stone, ...

Eph 2:11–20

Peter puts it so wonderfully in his epistle.

But you are a chosen race, A royal priesthood,[4] a holy nation, a people for Gods own possession, so that you may proclaim the excellencies of Him who has called you out of darkness into His marvelous light; for you once were not a people, but now you are the people of God; you had not

---

[4] When Israel is first numbered for the purposes of war the Levites were not numbered among the warriors. The Hebrew priesthood, the Levites, were not to be warriors. Interestingly, Christians are considered a royal priesthood. This is consistent and lends support to what Christ, Paul, Peter, and the early church fathers taught; Christian nonviolence is normative Christian behavior.

received mercy, but now you have received mercy.

1 Pet 2:9,10

Temples of God

We have already spoken on this topic but it bears repeating. We are now temples of God, places where God himself dwells. We are temples of God both corporately and individually.

> And coming to Him as to a living stone which has been rejected by men, but is choice and precious in the sight of God, you also, as living stones, are being built up as a spiritual house for a holy priesthood, to offer up spiritual sacrifices acceptable to God through Jesus Christ.
>
> 1 Pet 2:4–5

> Do you not know that you are a temple of God and that the Spirit of God dwells in you? If any man destroys the temple of God, God will destroy him, for the temple of God is holy, and that is what you are.
>
> 1 Cor 3:16,17

As we have previously seen, the imagery is such that the very Presence of God dwells in man as it did in the Holy of Holies. God is no longer far but near, intimately so.

12.2.2 God's Provision

As to life and godliness, we lack nothing. (1 Cor 1:7; 2 Pet 1:2,3) God has fully prepared us to live lives honoring to him and free from the bondage to sin; having been crucified with Christ we died to sin and in his resurrection we have been made alive and sin is no longer master over us.

God, however, has not only given us our freedom, but given us his Spirit, providing power to live a life pleasing to him.

And finally, we may rely on God to supply all our needs.

> And my God will supply all your needs according to His riches in glory in Christ Jesus.
>
> Phil 4:19

> For this reason I say to you, do not be worried about your life, as to what you will eat or what you will drink; nor for your body, as to what you will put on. Is not life more than food, and the body more than clothing? Look at the birds of the air, that they do not sow, nor reap nor gather into barns, and yet your heavenly Father feeds them. Are you not worth much more than they? And who of you by being worried can add a single hour to his life? And why are you worried about clothing? Observe how the lilies of the field grow; they do not toil nor do they spin, yet I say to you that not even Solomon in all his glory clothed himself like one of these. But if God so clothes the grass of the field, which is alive today and tomorrow is thrown into the furnace, will He not much more clothe you? You of little faith! Do not worry then, saying, 'What will we eat?' or 'What will we drink?' or 'What will we wear for clothing?' For the Gentiles eagerly seek all these things; for your heavenly Father knows that you need all these things. But seek first His kingdom and His righteousness, and all these things will be added to you.
>
> So do not worry about tomorrow; for tomorrow will care for itself. Each day has enough trouble of its own.
>
> Matt 6:25–34

12.2.3 The Restoration of Relationships

God has made possible the complete restoration of human relationships. However, we must not think only in terms of individual relationships, but also of human relationships in a community. God is not simply collecting individuals, but is rather calling a

12.2 Our Present Inheritance

people for himself. Christ came to bring in the Kingdom of God, not sell individuals fire insurance. Salvation occurs in the broader context of the Kingdom of God. For many, personal salvation is central while the Kingdom of God is peripheral. This thinking represents a distinctly non-Biblical position.

Unfortunately, the Kingdom is poorly understood with most Christians seeing the Body of Christ only as a collection of individuals rather than a functioning community of brothers and sisters. In actuality the Kingdom of God, as we have already seen in the chapters above, is a unique social, economic, political and religious structure bringing glory to God and presenting the message of the Gospel to the unsaved world, in no small way, by the way those in it live in love and care for one another, in addition to their words. The Kingdom stands over and against the world, it is contrary to the world, and it is a foretaste of life in heaven under the rule of God among the people of God.

In the world outside the Kingdom of God relationships find their foundation in power and authority. It is the same for a king and his subjects, employers and employees, wifes and husbands, men and women. We find hierarchical power structures and their accompanying authority everywhere. These power and authority structures are not in themselves evil, but given the fallen condition of man, they most often are used to dominate and oppress others. Suffering, alienation and isolation result.

But if power and authority are the basis of relationships outside the Kingdom of God, we may well ask if there is a different basis for relationships for citizens of the Kingdom of God? To this we have clear teachings in the Scripture. In it we find that the basis of relationships for Kingdom citizens is nothing like that in the rest of the world. The word radical doesn't even begin to describe it. It is what God's salvation looks like as he restores what we have broken.

In Matthew, chapter twenty-three, we find Christ condemning the Pharisees for their hypocrisy, love of attention, honor seeking and their love of titles. In the middle of this message Christ pauses and instructions his disciples.

> But do not be called Rabbi; for One is your Teacher, and you are all brothers. Do not call anyone on earth your father; for One is your Father, He who is in heaven. Do not be called leaders; for One is your Leader, that is, Christ. But the greatest among you shall be your servant. Whoever exalts himself shall be humbled; and whoever humbles himself shall be exalted.
>
> Matt 23:8–12

Servants are the greatest among the citizens of the kingdom of God. Humility is valued, not prideful seeking of honor. And servanthood is not only for the "really spiritual," but expected of all who name Christ as LORD and God. When God looks for the great among us he looks for servants.

Some will object that there must be leaders and teachers. Someone must take charge. These functions are indeed employed in the Kingdom of God, but the teacher only teaches what the Teacher has taught and the leader only leads where the Leader has already lead. We really have only One Father, One Teacher and One Leader and we are all brethren. None are elevated above others in power or authority. Elevation comes only in humility as God elevates those who are servants, those who are slaves to all.

In Mark chapter ten we find another lesson presenting the basis of relationships among God's people. It is occasioned upon a request made by two of the twelve. After Christ has just told them he is to suffer and die at the hands of the Jewish and Roman leaders, the brothers, James and John come to Christ and ask permission to sit in the seats of honor and power, on Christ's left and right, when Christ comes into his glory. It is an obscene

12.2 Our Present Inheritance

request given the present context, but Christ is amazingly gentle in his response. The rest of the twelve are not so inclined and, as one would expect, become indignant.

Knowing what is happening, Christ calls the twelve to himself and gives a most extraordinary lesson on greatness and relationships in the Kingdom.

> Hearing this, the ten began to feel indignant with James and John. Calling them to Himself, Jesus said to them, "You know that those who are recognized as rulers of the Gentiles lord it over them; and their great men exercise authority over them. But it is not this way among you, but whoever wishes to become great among you shall be your servant; and whoever wishes to be first among you shall be slave of all. For even the Son of Man did not come to be served, but to serve, and to give His life a ransom for many."
>
> Mark 10:41–45

In these four verses Christ shatters the conventional basis of relationships.[5] Gentile rulers lord it over their subjects and exercise authority over them. It not this way among citizens of the Kingdom of God. There is no lording it over or exercising authority. But some will protest that there must be some leadership and authority. Indeed, One is our Father, One is our Leader, One is

---

[5] I am not arguing that we no longer have distinct functions within the Body of Christ or in our homes. God appoints pastors and elders for our instruction and protection, parents are also given for instruction and protection, and in the case of young children, discipline. God has also made husbands the head over their wives as Christ is head over the Church. We ought to listen to those that are responsible for us, but the basis of even these relationships is submission, not power and authority. We must also not forget that God has given authority to the secular government for our protection. This authority must also be obeyed, but only as it does not demand that we violate God's law.

our Teacher and we are all brothers and sisters. And the great among us are servants and the first among us are slaves of all, for we have God the Son, the first among us, coming to serve and giving his life as a ransom. We lead and teach only what God has already taught and where he has lead.

Among the citizens of the Kingdom there are no structures of power and domination and we exercise authority over no one for we are all brothers and sisters.

When men look for the great among them they look for the powerful. When God looks for the great, the powerful among men are not noticed, for God is looking for servants, those who have made themselves slaves to all.

But we may ask, "What sort of servant are we to be?" Surely there is some glamor to it? We have our answer, in part, from the passages above, for Christ is describing serving from the bottom. The servant exercises no authority or power over others. This is made perfectly clear as Christ teaches the twelve at the last supper.

Christ has one final lesson on servanthood before his ultimate act of service. In the upper room the supper is ready, but one last thing must be done before they eat.

> Then He poured water into the basin, and began to wash the disciples' feet and to wipe them with the towel with which He was girded. ... So when He had washed their feet, and taken His garments and reclined at the table again, He said to them, "Do you know what I have done to you? "You call Me Teacher and Lord; and you are right, for so I am. If I then, the Lord and the Teacher, washed your feet, you also ought to wash one another's feet. For I gave you an example that you also should do as I did to you. Truly, truly, I say to you, a slave is not greater than his master, nor is one who is sent greater than the one who sent him.

12.2 Our Present Inheritance

> If you know these things, you are blessed if you do them."
>
> John 13:5, 12–17

We find Christ, our Teacher and Leader performing what is, perhaps, the lowest task that could be performed, and in so doing he tells us that we are to serve one another in the same manner. It must be remembered that a Jewish slave could not be commanded to wash his master's feet. It was too much to ask even of a slave. But here we see God the Son do just this, showing us the very nature and heart of servanthood.

At that moment there was probably nothing Christ could do that was more lowly, more degrading, so looked down upon, so beneath him. Christ's point is not that we wash each other's feet every opportunity we get. Christ is teaching something far more demanding: no act of service is beneath us. Nothing is too low. It is never "someone else's job," but ours. This lesson is made all the more striking for it is God incarnate washing their feet. For any of us to think that servanthood, even the lowest, is beneath us is rebellion of the worst kind against God's clear teaching. Servanthood of this sort is normal and expected, there is nothing especially praiseworthy, for we are only doing what God has commanded.

> He does not thank the slave because he did the things which were commanded, does he? So you too, when you do all the things which are commanded you, say, 'We are unworthy slaves; we have done only that which we ought to have done.'
>
> Luke 17:9,10

We are all to be servants and the greatest among us are servants to all. We serve from the bottom. In a way, there are no servant-leaders, just servants. Those who lead, lead only as they are found to be servants, as they are shown to be bond-slaves of God. From this we understand that God rules over their lives and in their obedience to God we are willing to heed their counsel. And even then, these "leaders" only lead where God has already lead and teach only what God has already taught and their tools do not include authority and power, but prayerful persuasion and gentleness.

In the demand of servanthood upon our lives we see our complete dependence on God to accomplish his will and move people. As God's people, we are not responsible for results and outcomes. We do not "do whatever it takes" to get the job done. We must not exercise authority, but what we must do is be faithful to all God commands; to love all, forgive all, care for the needy and oppressed and spread the gospel. In these acts of service there is power, God's power, and in these there is glory, glory for God, and in these there is praise from God which we will hear if we remain faithful. "Well done thou good and faithful servant."

We have left unanswered an important question; "How is it possible for people to function in a community and personal relationships that are not based, at least in part, on power and authority?" Some will say that this simply cannot be done. God, however, has accomplished this by freeing us from the bondage of sin for we died with Christ and were raised with him in newness of life. We are being conformed to the image of his Son, the very image of a servant. Love, forgiveness and *mutual submission* form the basis of relationships. What need is there for power and authority for those with one Father, one Leader and one Teacher and whose law of life is love, forgiveness and mutual submission? This is life in God's Kingdom.

The passages describing this way of life are many[6] and I present only a few, but the theme is the same throughout the

---

[6]Rom 12:9–21; 1 Cor 8—9; 1 Cor 12:12–27; Phil 2:1–11; Col 3:18–25; 1 Pet 2:13—3:12

12.2 Our Present Inheritance

whole New Testament.

> Be devoted to one another in brotherly love; give preference to one another in honor; not lagging behind in diligence, fervent in spirit, serving the Lord; rejoicing in hope, persevering in tribulation, devoted to prayer, contributing to the needs of the saints, practicing hospitality.
>
> Rom 12:10–13

> Therefore if there is any encouragement in Christ, if there is any consolation of love, if there is any fellowship of the Spirit, if any affection and compassion, make my joy complete by being of the same mind, maintaining the same love, united in spirit, intent on one purpose. Do nothing from selfishness or empty conceit, but with humility of mind regard one another as more important than yourselves; do not merely look out for your own personal interests, but also for the interests of others.
>
> Phil 2:1–4

Somewhat different, but no less important is the destruction of barriers and distinctions among people. Apart from Christ it is perfectly natural, even if sinful, for men to recognize, even insist, that there be distinctions and divisions among us. These distinctions bring strife, hatred, exploitation and warfare. In Christ, distinctions and group identification have no place. There are no relevant political, national, social, racial, economic, gender, etc. distinctions.[7] Nothing separates the children of God and others. There is no longer an "us and them." My neighbor is all men,

---

[7] Nationalism and patriotism are particularly vexing sins for Christians living in the Western industrialized nations. We insist on keeping these distinctions. We do not live as if there are no longer any relevant distinctions among us.

even my enemy, and I am to love and do good to them all. (Eph 3:1–13)

But beyond this is even a greater gift; God has not only torn down the barriers separating us and made a new basis on which to build human relationships, but he has, and is still, calling a people for himself, a community, but even more, a Kingdom. As individuals we can live well, but together in community we can really begin to experience life in ways that begin to resemble what we will experience in heaven.

As I have reflected on God's restoration of human relationships I have experienced the greatest freedom and comfort. Freedom, for I am not responsible for results and outcomes, I don't "make things happen." I must become wholly dependent upon God — my only tasks are to be faithful, serve and spread the gospel. Comfort, for I know I can trust God to do what he has promised. And great joy comes from knowing that God has called a people, of which I am part, to live in love, mutual submission, exercising no authority over one another, serving one another, preferring to care for others before ourselves, and caring to such an extent that there are no needy among them. We are people with no distinctions among us. We are all equal brethren. What a gift! We have one Father, one Leader and one Teacher. We are truly free.

12.3 Our Future Hope

> "Things which eye has not seen and ear has not heard, And which have not entered the heart of man, All that God has prepared for those who love Him."
>
> 1 Cor 2:9

Despite all that has been revealed to us of our inheritance to come, we have only just seen the smallest bit. So much more

12.3 Our Future Hope

awaits us. We have yet to see the depths of God's love to be showered upon us. But what know now is glorious.

Our present sufferings are not worthy to be compared to the glory that is to be revealed to us. So much has already been given, but so much is yet to come. We are now the "children of God, and it has not appeared as yet what we will be. We know that when He appears, we will be like Him, because we will see Him just as He is. And everyone who has this hope fixed on Him purifies himself, just as He is pure." (1 John 3:2,3) We are "fellow heirs with Christ, if indeed we suffer with him so that we may also be glorified with him." (Rom 8:17)

In Romans 8:17 we see an important connection between our inheritance and suffering; to enjoy our inheritance we must suffer with Christ. The meaning here is not really all that mysterious. Has not Christ said

> For whoever is ashamed of Me and My words, the Son of Man will be ashamed of him when He comes in His glory, and the glory of the Father and of the holy angels.
>
> Luke 9:26

By refusing to identify with Christ we will avoid suffering with him and fail to obtain our inheritance. If we should fully identify with him we will be hated by the world (John 15:18–25) and some of those who kill us will believe they are doing the work of God. Suffering with Christ comes directly from identifying with Christ. So we see that if we have not suffered with Christ we have not identified with him; we are friends with the world, not a child of God and certainly not a fellow heir with Christ.

But if we are a true child of God we share in the greatest liberation and restoration of all time. That which is broken will not simply be mended, but made anew, for we await a new heaven and a new earth (2 Pet 3:10–13) and our mortal bodies will shed their mortality and put on immortality in the resurrection.

> For this perishable must put on the imperishable, and this mortal must put on immortality. But when this perishable will have put on the imperishable, and this mortal will have put on immortality, then will come about the saying that is written, "Death is swallowed up in victory. O death, where is your victory? O death, where is your sting?" The sting of death is sin, and the power of sin is the law; but thanks be to God, who gives us the victory through our Lord Jesus Christ.
>
> 1 Cor 15:53–57

We also know that our Savior *"will transform the body of our humble state into conformity with the body of his glory, by the exertion of the power that he has even to subject all things to himself."* (Phil 3:21)

The whole of creation will be set free and we will be free as never before. We will in truth be pure and holy before God. All pain and tears will be wiped away. God will have completed the work which he began in us. (Phil 1:6) And we shall be in the place that Christ had prepared for us and we will be in his presence evermore, singing praise to the Lamb that was slain, for worthy is the Lamb. (John 14:1–3) We shall be home, living with God's people, under God's rule.

> Behold, I am coming quickly, and My reward is with Me, to render to every man according to what he has done. I am the Alpha and the Omega, the first and the last, the beginning and the end.
>
> Blessed are those who wash their robes, so that they may have the right to the tree of life, and may enter by the gates into the city.
>
> I, Jesus, have sent My angel to testify to you these things for the churches. I am the root and the descendant of David, the bright morning star.

12.3 Our Future Hope

He who testifies to these things says, "Yes, I am coming quickly". Amen. Come, Lord Jesus.

Rev 22:12–14, 16, 20

Even so, come quickly Lord Jesus.

Chapter 13

Our Response

The only reasonable response, the prudent response, to trials is to "count it all joy." Four little words, and yet they fall with such weight, crashing against human wisdom, breaking it to pieces. How could it be otherwise? The preaching of the cross is foolishness and unable to be understood by the world. (1 Cor 1:18; 2:14)

For God's children, the truth of James' words should be patently obvious. Their truth was obvious to James and it should be for us given the witness of the Scriptures, the Prophets, Christ, Apostles, and all the saints that have preceded us. The weight of evidence supporting the response "count it all joy" is simply overwhelming, admitting no other.

And yet we still find it difficult to embrace trials. Why should this be, and how do we change? And if our heart is turned in the proper direction, how do we stay so directed?

To redirect our heart and mind to embrace trials we must be transformed by the power of God. But we must also be informed; we must be redirected to something concrete. To this end, this book has been written. We must first start with God, for the fear of God is the beginning of wisdom. Beginning anywhere else leads to error or at least a misapplied emphasis. God is sovereign over the affairs of men, and in particular, our lives. We submit and surrender to his rule.[1] We agree with God that all must be directed to his glory and give our lives in its pursuit.

Unlike all other Sovereigns, ours, while directing the end of all things to his glory, lavishes upon us all good things; love, a full relationship with the Sovereign, resurrection and an eternal home; and in such extravagant demonstrations, glorifies himself further. (Eph 1)

The second thing we must understand is the Kingdom of God, for it is in the context of the Kingdom of God that God is glorified in the largest sense and it is in this same context that trials occur and find their greatest redemption.

We have seen that the Kingdom of God is unlike the kingdoms of this earth, founded on indiscriminate love and forgiveness, non-violence, care for all, mutual submission, removal of all barriers between people and finally, social and economic justice. And it is by the demonstration of our love for one another within the Kingdom that the world knows that we are Christ's disciples and the message of the Gospel enters the world with power. In Acts we see that the witness of the apostles was powerful because there were no needy among them.

Love is most powerfully and visibly demonstrated when we care for those in need. But notice, those in need are those in trials. We see then that trials form a foundation of much of the most important activity within the Kingdom. Trials are indispensable. In them, along with the Kingdom, we see God redeeming the evil men have brought.

Third, we must see that God uses trials to bring about matu-

---

[1] We do this knowing that His rule is not only what glorifies himself, but is most beneficial for us.

rity, thereby, making us fit citizens for his Kingdom, able to know him more fully, find joy in our lives, and better able to glorify him. It is to the image of Christ that this process of maturity is directed.

But knowledge alone is insufficient to redirect our heart and mind to embrace trials. We well know Satan and his angels know much and are no better off. What is essential, even for the child of God, is the power of God to fundamentally remake our minds and affections. It is by the Spirit of God, as we obey, that our hearts and minds are remade and our focus is placed on things that glorify God.

We now ask: How do we consistently patiently endure?

13.1 Patiently Enduring

What can we do in cooperation with God that will develop faithfulness so that we are found, at all times, patiently enduring? There is much; Paul tells us to work out our salvation with fear and trembling. We must labor at it. It must not be a pastime, something that is hit and miss, something that we hope gets done.

It is an unusual labor, however. Even as we labor in this work we are fully aware that without the power of God all of our labor is in vain. At all times there is a tension between labor and trust in God to bring obedience and good works. As we obey and labor, we must make sure that we never listen to the Siren's song of self-sufficiency or personal strength. Instead, we boast in our weakness for in weakness God's strength is perfected. We trade weakness for strength. We always realize that personal strength is an illusion.

At all times we must place God at the center of our lives, bow down to him as our King and unconditionally obey him. We desire what he desires and obey his commands. We commit ourselves to being like Christ. We study his life and become real disciples.

We commit to loving and forgiving indiscriminately, we refuse retaliation and violence in all our relationships, we place ourselves and our interests last, we commit to caring for our brothers and sisters and we refuse to acknowledge any barriers between us. In other words, we live as Christ lived, living out Kingdom principles. Notice how concrete this is. No fuzzy hand-waving. We know exactly what is demanded of us.

We must also hold all things, even our own lives, in contempt. We must never embrace a thing or a person in such a manner that they replace God or interfere in our relationship with him or in doing his will. All things and relationships must be subordinate to God. The proper response to things is to consider them as loss, nothing more than rubbish,[2] for, more often than not, we cling to them and they get in the way of knowing Christ and the power of his resurrection. We guard our affections carefully. We refuse to lay up treasure on earth and we value things invisible.

Being conformed to the image of Christ must become a central preoccupation of our life. We must study Christ's life and teachings, meditate on them, let them permeate our thinking, and then live as he did and obey what he commanded. We must consider Christ's life to be normative; at the end of each day we want to have a character that is more like his.

We must be committed to life in the Kingdom of God. We cannot live a victorious life outside of the Kingdom. Each of us have functions to fulfill within the Kingdom and we must have the love and support of our brothers and sisters. And we must be about the building of the Kingdom. For the child of God, life — as it is properly understood — outside the Kingdom is simply not possible.

---

[2] We value what God gives. We do not disdain his gifts, but we refuse to become attached to them and let them supplant God.

13.1 Patiently Enduring 261

13.1.1 Advice from James

We began this chapter with a reference to James' command to count it all joy when we enter trials.

> Consider it all joy, my brethren, when you encounter various trials, knowing that the testing of your faith produces endurance. And let endurance have its perfect result, so that you may be perfect and complete, lacking in nothing.
>
> Jas 1:2–4

After presenting the command, James proceeds to give advice on how to embrace our trials. He begins with our need for wisdom.

Embracing trials, even when we know they benefit us, is contrary to human wisdom. We desperately need God's wisdom. We need God to help us understand his economics of trials. To this end James tells us to pray for God's wisdom (Jas 1:5–8).

> But if any of you lacks wisdom, let him ask of God, who gives to all generously and without reproach, and it will be given to him.
>
> Jas 1:5

We must have God's wisdom if we are to understand God's sovereignty over our lives, the singular value of knowing God, living in his power and sharing in the sufferings of Christ. We must learn to desire what accomplishes God's will and conforms us to the image of Christ and we must desire and build God's Kingdom. These things are contrary to man's wisdom, but we must exchange the wisdom of man for the wisdom of God.

It is God's will that we embrace trials, and we know that if we ask anything according to his will we will receive it. Therefore, we know that God will give us the required wisdom if we ask. But James warns us to ask in faith, not doubting. *Doubt and unbelief are profound denials of God's character, revealing that we consider him untrustworthy.* It is a terrible affront to the character of God and a denial of all he has done in the past. If we do not ask in faith, let us not expect to receive what was asked. No only this, if we continue in our unbelief, we will develop a life characterized by instability.

James follows this advice with instruction for two distinct groups.

> But the brother of humble circumstances is to glory in his high position; and the rich man is to glory in his humiliation, because like flowering grass he will pass away.
>
> Jas 1:9,10

The person in humble circumstances is to glory in their high position. Extraordinary. How is it that humble circumstances are a high position? In all likelihood, this condition was brought on by trials and, as such, is to be embraced and counted all joy. In what way, however, are we to understand it to be a high position? It is the condition in which God is building endurance so that we may be complete and lacking in nothing. We are in a condition of weakness, a condition in which God's power can come into the world through us. It is from a humble position that God can exalt us. God resists the proud, but gives grace to the humble. It is a high position indeed.

In a similar manner, the rich are to glory in their humiliation. The rich are to embrace the trials that God brings to their life. The rich must also find their faith brought to maturity through trials. Negatively, the rich, by virtue of their wealth, have a greater occasion to trust in themselves and be chained more tightly to the world and its riches. It is extremely difficult for the rich to enter the Kingdom of God and it is a great blessing for God to bring trials and humiliation to the rich.

After these admonitions James reminds us of our hope in Christ.

13.1 Patiently Enduring

> Blessed is a man who perseveres under trial; for once he has been approved, he will receive the crown of life which the Lord has promised to those who love Him.
>
> Jas 1:12

If we persevere we will receive the crown of life: life with the eternal Triune God, enjoying him forever, free from death, the grave and sin, all sorrows and tears forgotten. We must ever have our destiny before us, for it will help us focus our efforts and restore our strength. This life can be horribly difficult, even to the point where it defies description, but God, through Christ, God the Son, has defeated the powers, death and sin and one day will fully restore his creation and consign the evil ones to everlasting punishment and those bearing his mark, those who have endured, to everlasting life.

> This is eternal life, that they may know You, the only true God, and Jesus Christ whom You have sent.
>
> John 17:3

James now addresses a very real possibility that exists in the midst of trials — temptation to turn away from God, becoming one of those who do not endure. Some may even be inclined to say that it is God's doing that they are so tempted.

> Let no one say when he is tempted, "I am being tempted by God"; for God cannot be tempted by evil, and He Himself does not tempt anyone.
>
> Jas 1:13–18

This course is particularly attractive in the case of persecution. Perhaps, by our identification with Christ, we are facing loss, imprisonment or death. Or perhaps our loved ones are so threatened. We might reason: "Surely God does not want the death or imprisonment of my loved ones. If I renounce my faith all this will end." Not only is this course of action sinful, but the temptation to do so is not from God; it comes from our own lust and personal self-interest.

The temptation to abandon our trials, and hence God, comes from a belief that they are not good or that they cannot be from God. James makes it very clear that such thinking is terribly wrong.

> Do not be deceived, my beloved brethren. Every good thing given and every perfect gift is from above, coming down from the Father of lights, with whom there is no variation or shifting shadow. In the exercise of His will He brought us forth by the word of truth, so that we would be a kind of first fruits among His creatures.
>
> Jas 1:16–18

Our trials are good and perfect gifts coming from God himself who brought us forth by the word of truth so that we would be a kind of first fruits among his creatures. God is using trials as a means to make us into creatures that did not exist in the past; God is making us into the image of God the Son, the God/Man, who in his humanity, is the most lovely human to grace God's creation.

13.1.2 The Armor of God

Trials are times of great conflict and can be described in terms of warfare. They are times of great opportunity, for we may advance quickly and far in our faith. But tremendous opportunity for evil is possible if we abandon our faith and turn our back on God. It is this last possibility on which the powers of evil are focused. For the evil powers, our victory in trials is a double loss; not only are we not defeated, but God's cause is greatly advanced. Much is at stake, and they often mount a vicious and powerful

13.1 Patiently Enduring

offense. Should we attempt to withstand this onslaught in our own strength we are doomed to failure. We must rather be strong in God and the power of his might.

> Finally, be strong in the Lord and in the strength of His might. Put on the full armor of God, so that you will be able to stand firm against the schemes of the devil. For our struggle is not against flesh and blood, but against the rulers, against the powers, against the world forces of this darkness, against the spiritual forces of wickedness in the heavenly places. Therefore, take up the full armor of God, so that you will be able to resist in the evil day, and having done everything, to stand firm.
>
> Eph 6:10–13

Our warfare is not against flesh and blood. Great powers, powers that exercise control over the world, war against us. Ancient powers trained in the art of evil for millennia are arrayed against us. Despite all this, means to resist, even to stand firm in their violent attacks, are available to us. The means are nothing less that the armor and power of God.

The powers arrayed against us have been defeated: "When He had disarmed the rulers and authorities, He made a public display of them, having triumphed over them through Him." (Col 2:15) And in the day of judgment they, and death, will be consigned to the pit. However, till that time they continue to rage against God and his people, and in this battle we must employ God's armor.

God's armor consists of a powerful offensive weapon and secure defensive protections: truth which makes us free; righteousness, the imputed righteousness of Christ; the gospel of peace; the shield of faith to protect against the evil one's flaming arrows; the sword of the Spirit, God's Word, which is able to pierce "as far as the division of soul and spirit ... and able to judge the thoughts and intentions of the heart." (Heb 4:12)

In addition to this armor we are to pray at all times in the Spirit. We are to be alert and persevere and bring petitions for all the saints. We are in a war, our flesh continues to tempt us, and Satan and his servants seek to destroy God's plans and us. We really must be alert and persevere, for our enemies, internal and external (the flesh), know no rest. But we must understand that the powers can be defeated and God, through Christ, has provided the means.

Before leaving this section I want to emphasize a triad; prayer, God's Word and God's Kingdom. In one way or another, these have all been mentioned in the last two sections, but a few more words will not hurt. If we are to be found faithful we must rely on God's power. To do this we must be devoted to prayer as we just mentioned. By prayer God's will is realized and our dependence on his power affirmed. In God's Word we find strength and God teaching us about himself and his Kingdom and showing us his will. In God's Kingdom we find the fellowship, encouragement and assistance from the brethren to faithfully endure. And in the Kingdom we can, likewise, encourage and assist others in need.

13.2 Building the Kingdom of God

The preoccupation of this book has been the theological context of suffering and difficulty from a Christian perspective. We have found that Christian communities built on Kingdom principles play an essential role in the theological and practical contexts of suffering and difficulty. We have also seen that the importance of these communities far exceeds their importance for just suffering and difficulty; these communities are the very basis of a powerful witness of the Church to the world. Without them we do not present real Christianity to the world; they only see a poor facsimile.

As we look about, however, we see little evidence of such com-

13.2 Building the Kingdom of God

munities. Some exist, but they are very few in number. In response, we must set about building God's Kingdom, by building communities and engaging in evangelism.

The order, building communities followed by evangelism, is important. The reason I emphasize the order, community followed by evangelism, is that a community of believers living in love, sacrificially committed to each others' interests and needs regardless of race, social or economic status, exercising indiscriminate forgiveness, refusing violence and living in peace is the most powerful evangelical witness we can possibly present to the world. The impact of a community like this far exceeds that which any one person can achieve, no matter how committed, in demonstrating God's love and presenting a foretaste of life in heaven.

Do not think that personal evangelism is unimportant, it is important, but personal evangelism is not done as effectively as it might if the community absent. The community of believers provides the foundation of a powerful personal witness.[3]

In our cultural environment it will be difficult to build such communities; many obstacles exist and there are few who will share this vision. The task looks almost impossible. Where can an isolated individual begin? At the very start we must rely on the power of God, and in our lives implement practices based on Kingdom principles, love others, sacrificially commit ourselves to others' interests and needs regardless of race, social or economic status, exercise indiscriminate forgiveness, refuse violence and live in peace. The most telling practices will be the help and assistance we give to our needy brothers and sisters. We must also preach and teach the Kingdom, helping others see what Christ and the

---

[3] Neither am I saying that we must postpone personal evangelism until we have functioning communities. These must happen simultaneously, but we must not think that personal evangelism can proceed effectively apart from a community. It can be done, but it labors under a terrible handicap and is far less effective that it might otherwise be.

Apostles taught and what it would mean if we really obeyed God in these matters. Lastly, we must seek out and find others of like mind and build our communities one person at a time.

Building the Kingdom of God, in our day, as it is presented in the New Testament, is a daunting task, but build this Kingdom we must if we want to see God glorified with men coming to a saving knowledge of Christ, being transferred from the kingdom of darkness to the Kingdom of Light.

13.3 A Final Thought

Years ago, during a difficult trial, a friend gave me a poem.[4]

Flying

When we walk to the edge of all the knowledge we have

And take that step of faith into the unknown

We must believe that one of two things will happen.

There will be something solid for us to walk on or

God will teach us how to fly.

I have always been comforted and challenged by this poem. It captures so well the life of faith. But the last line always seemed mysterious, not quite understandable. I think that it will always, in some sense, remain a mystery, but I believe that I know something of what it means to fly. Flying is counting it all joy. Living joyfully in the midst of trials with the God of love.

---

[4]I have searched for the author of this poem, but have been unable to identify them.

Bibliography

Trocme, Andre *Jesus and the Nonviolent Revolution*, Translated by Charles E. Moore Maryknoll, NY: Orbis Books, 2003

Barnes, Albert *Barnes' Notes on the New Testament*, Grand Rapids, Mich.:Kregel Classics, 1962

Camp, Lee C., *Mere Discipleship*, Grand Rapids: Michigan, 2003

Hart, David Bentley *The Doors of the Sea*, Grand Rapids, Michigan: Erdmans, 2005

Henry, Matthew *Matthew Henry's Commentary on the Whole Bible* Modern Edition, Peabody, Massachusetts: Hendrickson Pub., 2003

Kraybill, Donald B. *The Upside-Down Kingdom*, Scottdale PA: Herald Press, 2003

Lohfink, Gerhard *Jesus and Community*, Philadelphia, PA: Fortress Press, 1984

Lohfink, Gerhard *Does God Need the Church*, Collegeville, Minnesota: The Liturgical Press, 1999

MacDonald, William, *True Discipleship*, Kansas City, Kansas: Walterick Publishers, 1975

McClain, Alva J. *The Greatness of the Kingdom*, Winona Lake, Indiana: BMH Books, 1974

Shank, Robert *Life in The Son*, Bloomington, Minnesota: Bethany House Publishers, 1989

Shank, Robert *Elect in the Son*, Minneapolis, Minnesota: Bethany House Publishers, 1989

Smith, David, *The Life and Letters of St. Paul*, New York, London: Harper & Brothers

Thiessen, Henry C. *Introductory Lectures in Systematic Theology*, Grand Rapids, Michigan: Erdmans, 1974

Verduin, Leonard *The Anatomy of a Hybrid*, Grand Rapids, Michigan: Erdmans, 1976

Yoder, John Howard, *When War is Unjust*, Eugene, Oregon: Wipf & Stock, 1996

Yoder, John Howard *The Politics of Jesus*, Grand Rapids, Michigan: Erdmans, 1972

Yoder, John Howard *Nevertheless*, Scottdale, PA: Herald Press, 1992

Yoder, John Howard *What Would You Do?*, Scottdale, PA: Herald Press, 1992

www.ingramcontent.com/pod-product-compliance
Lightning Source LLC
Chambersburg PA
CBHW051631230426
43669CB00013B/2260